Islamophobia

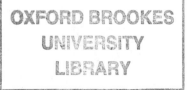

Islamophobia

*The Challenge of Pluralism in the
21st Century*

Edited by
JOHN L. ESPOSITO AND
IBRAHIM KALIN

OXFORD
UNIVERSITY PRESS

2011

OXFORD
UNIVERSITY PRESS

Oxford University Press, Inc., publishes works that further
Oxford University's objective of excellence
in research, scholarship, and education.

Oxford   New York
Auckland   Cape Town   Dar es Salaam   Hong Kong   Karachi
Kuala Lumpur   Madrid   Melbourne   Mexico City   Nairobi
New Delhi   Shanghai   Taipei   Toronto

With offices in
Argentina   Austria   Brazil   Chile   Czech Republic   France   Greece
Guatemala   Hungary   Italy   Japan   Poland   Portugal   Singapore
South Korea   Switzerland   Thailand   Turkey   Ukraine   Vietnam

Published by Oxford University Press, Inc.
198 Madison Avenue, New York, New York 10016

www.oup.com

Library of Congress Cataloging-in-Publication Data
Islamophobia: the challenge of pluralism in the 21st century / edited
by John L. Esposito and Ibrahim Kalin.
    p.   cm.
Includes bibliographical references and index.
ISBN 978-0-19-975364-2; 978-0-19-975365-9 (pbk.)
1. Islam—Public opinion. 2. Muslims—Public opinion. 3. Islam and politics.
4. Muslims—Non-Muslim countries. 5. Islam—21st century.
I. Esposito, John L. II. Kalin, Ibrahim.
BP52.I854   2011
297.09′049—dc22   2010013086

9 8 7 6 5 4 3 2 1

Printed in the United States of America
on acid-free paper

Foreword

"Islamophobia and the Challenges of Pluralism in the 21st Century" is a timely topic in a world in which the relationship between Islam and the West matters more than ever before. The increasing interdependence and coexistence among dissimilar peoples makes mutual acceptance and respect requisites for social harmony in our interconnected world; thus, the need for the Muslim and the Western worlds to accommodate each other is especially important given the central role these two large communities have been playing in global relations for the last fourteen centuries.

Religion is an indispensable component of human life. From time immemorial, religion has shaped the cultural identity of individuals and communities as well as the building of civilizations. In addition to the importance religion carries for all peoples of the world, Islam has been a central factor in the lives of its adherents. Its system of faith has guided them not only in spiritual and moral matters but also in their total world outlook. Islam has a distinctive place in Muslim life; as a sociological reality it influences and guides attitudes and behavior. It is therefore natural that Muslims cannot dismiss attacks directed against their religion as mere opinions but feel deeply offended and sometimes react strongly.

The weight of Islam in social life differs from one country to another. State systems and intellectuals' attitudes vary significantly, ranging from the Islamic to the secular-oriented, creating a diversity of opinions about the place of Islam in the public sphere, as to where the line between religion and politics should be drawn. Such diversity certainly depends in part on the existence and sustainability of democracy in Muslim countries. Democracy, engaging civil society and public opinion, together with socioeconomic development, can lead to the modernization of societies and help them fight marginalization and radicalization.

Notwithstanding the diverse orientations of governments, the teachings of Islam generally constitute the basic code of ethics that guides Muslims in their daily lives, as witnessed throughout the history of Islamic civilization. These teachings include moral excellence, honor, virtue, justice, piety, equity, compassion, and human dignity. Christianity and Islam share a common monotheistic vision, as well as these basic teachings. However, despite this closeness and the fact that our histories are tightly linked—offering compelling reasons to live together and cooperate—much of the history of the Muslim world and the West has too often been marked by mutual hostility, giving rise to an enduring tradition of distrust and animosity.

We have always looked at our past and our present from different and, more often, contradictory angles, trying to disavow or ignore each other. I do not think that theology and religion have been a major factor in this antagonism. To find the root causes one has to look elsewhere. Islam, since its inception, has recognized Judaism and Christianity, biblical prophets, and the Torah and the Gospels as revealed religions and their adherents as "the people of the Book." Islam sees both Judaism and Christianity not as "others" to tolerate but as standing *de jure*, as revealed religions from God. Moreover, their legitimate status is not sociopolitical, cultural, or civilizational *but religious. Islam does* not see itself as coming to the religious scene *ex nihilo* but as reaffirming the same truth presented by all of the prophets of Judaism and Christianity.

Muslims have always been committed to pluralism and tolerance. Historically, Muslims played a pioneering role in acquiring knowledge and disseminating expertise in various fields and sharing it with other civilizations. Under the centuries-long rule of Islam, non-Muslims could practice their faiths: Their religious institutions and places of worship were repaired and maintained with public funding, and their respective personal laws remained in effect. Islam adopts religious and cultural pluralism as a guiding principle in social administration. As Karen Armstrong points out, "in the Islamic empire, Jews, Christians and Zoroastrians enjoyed religious freedom. This reflected the teaching of the Koran, which is a pluralistic scripture, affirmative of other traditions. Muslims are commanded by God to respect the 'people of the book,' and reminded that they share the same belief and the same God."[1] Muslims, Christians, and Jews lived together under Islamic rule in Jerusalem, Andalusia, Cairo,

Istanbul, and many cities and towns throughout the Ottoman Empire, and communities flourished throughout the Muslim world.

Today, Islam is increasingly regarded by some in the West as a source of intolerance, extremism, and terrorism, one whose adherents are out to destroy Western values. By contrast, the Muslim world is increasingly regarding the West as an arrogant, imperialistic colonizer prone to propagate Western materialism and mass culture, to destabilize and destroy Islam, and to exploit the Muslim world's potential while imposing Western values and way of life on the rest of the world. In recent years, some newspapers in Europe, under the guise of opening debate on taboo issues, have proclaimed that the West has been silenced by Islam and found it fit to publish the infamous Danish cartoons of the Prophet Mohamed. However, their attempts have proved to obscure rather than enlighten and have also needlessly offended and thus been condemned by many Muslims. Such an approach adds fuel to the fire and merely reinforces prejudices on both sides.

This controversy was also an occasion for some in the Western media to invoke the fundamental right of freedom of expression. Nobody can contest this right, which is at the heart of every enlightened society. However, while we consider this a clear indication of growing Islamophobia and discrimination toward Islam and Muslims, we also see behind this imposed polarity between freedom of expression and respect for religious beliefs an attempt to test the people's will and a lack of understanding of their sensitivities to the sacred constants of their faith. I firmly believe that one should recognize the inalienable right to freedom of expression; however, this right should be exercised responsibly and judiciously.

One of the principal causes of the rising intolerance of Islam in many parts of the world is ignorance or, if I may say so, lack of proper understanding of Islam, often rooted in a failure to distinguish between mainstream Islam and Muslims and the words and actions of extremists. In my own life as a scholar and now as the head of a center for Muslim-Christian understanding, I have had a chance to devote time to commonalities and differences between religion, culture, and history of science. I have come to the conclusion that every culture and religion has goodness embedded in it and that all of these together have enriched human civilization. The pioneering works of Muslim, as well as Western, philosophers, scientists, and scholars in the fields of mathematics, astronomy, medicine, geography, jurisprudence, the arts, and architecture, to name a just few, have contributed enormously to the shape of modern civilization.

Islamophobia has two basic causes: One is related to political attitude, and the other to the interpretation of history. The former stems from the reaction that has been directed toward Islam in the face of terrorist attacks, in particular 9/11 and the post-9/11 attacks in Europe, whose culprits' religious affiliation happens to be Islam. Attributing the acts of these terrorists to their faith suggests a prejudice against Islam and Muslims since no similar association is attributed to terrorist attacks by criminals of any other faith. To equate these acts of terrorism, which are prohibited by Islam and which violate its essential principles and rules, with mainstream Islam empowers and encourages these extremists. Accepting the claims contributes to legitimizing both the claims and their goals.

Unfortunately, today some political commentators and "experts" promote Islamophobia. Their basic premise is that Muslims, from the rise of Islam to the present, have sought to annihilate Christianity and Islamize Europe. This unfounded and reductionist historiography denies or deliberately overlooks Islam's fourteen-century-old history of religious, political, demographic, and intellectual interactions with other cultures and its share in the development of the world's common heritage and its humanistic outlook. While this antagonistic view has not enjoyed support in most scholarly circles, it negatively affects public opinion.

The dangerous mindset of centuries-old prejudices must be addressed, and work toward harmony and understanding must become a priority in both the West and the Muslim world. Sadly, in recent years the reports of the Organization of the Islamic Conference and other international organizations, including Western institutions monitoring Islamophobia in Europe, have warned the world of the emergence and continued growth of Islamophobia, a new form of racism in Europe and the United States based on discrimination and intolerance of Islam and Muslims.

Based on this concern and threat to our relations, I have called for a genuine "historical reconciliation between Islam and Christianity" that will mark a new era in the history of humankind and human civilization. Similar initiatives were taken between Judaism and Christianity in the face of anti-Semitism a few decades ago and have proven successful and productive. This would further develop the initiative taken by the Eucharistic Congress of the Vatican in 1965. This body issued a document titled "The World of Light Encyclical: Dialogue between Christians and Muslims," which called for an Islamo-Christian dialogue and acknowledged the value of the Islamic faith, Islam's favorable attitude toward Christianity, and Islam's contribution to the advancement of human civilization.

Neither Christianity nor Islam is monolithic; therefore, reconciliation efforts should involve representatives from all sects of both religions along with all stakeholders such as scholars, thinkers, policymakers, and the media. These efforts should promote a mindset anchored in the moral imperative of respecting each and every human being and unstintingly foster the concept of pluralism. This task must be supported and nurtured by international leaders and organizations. Both education and a fair and objective media have prominent roles to play in this endeavor.

Islam and the West could and should co-exist in peace and harmony, as the common denominators that link them outweigh their differences and facilitate this reconciliation between them:

- *Geographical proximity*: The present reality is that Muslims and Westerners are living together under the same rule in almost all Western societies.
- *Similar spiritual reference*: As part of the entire history of monotheistic religions, Islam is a continuity of Abrahamic tradition and culture.
- *Shared values*: There is no inherent conflict between Islam and modernity, and Muslims are committed to pluralism and the right of people to cherish their diversity.

Certain common strategic interests for the West and Islam need to be developed and nurtured in the coming decades. Our world is going through a rapid development, and new realities and new centers of power may emerge. This makes it all the more imperative for the West and the Muslim world to reconcile their differences, dispel their misunderstandings, and look to the future with a new spirit.

Ekmeleddin Ihsanoğlu
Secretary General of the Organization of the Islamic Conference

NOTE

1. Karen Armstrong, "The Curse of the Infidel," *Guardian*, June 20, 2002, http://www.guardian.co.uk/world/2002/jun/20/religion.september11.

Contents

Contributors

Anas Al-Shaikh-Ali (Commander of the Order of the British Empire) has a PhD in American Studies and has taught literature and translation at universities in the Middle East. He is a founding member and current chair of the Association of Muslim Social Scientists (AMSS) (UK) and current academic advisor to the International Institute of Islamic Thought (IIIT) and director of its London office and translation department. He is a founding trustee of the Foundation for Education and Development (FED) 2000 UK, a founding trustee and former chair of the Forum Against Islamophobia and Racism (FAIR), former chair of the board of governors of the Avenue School, and founding executive director of Legacy Publishing, Ltd. He is also joint editor with Shiraz Khan of the IIIT Occasional Papers Series and the AMSS UK Zaki Badawi Memorial Lecture Series. His research interests include Islam in Western popular culture, Islam and the media, Muslim education in Europe, and Muslim discourse in Europe. He has lectured and published in both Arabic and English on these topics. Among his recent published papers is "Public Opinion and Political Influence: Issues in Contemporary Popular Fiction" (in *Citizenship, Security, and Democracy: Muslim Engagement with the West*, 2009). His expert advice was instrumental in the production of the joint British Council/AMSS UK publication *British Muslims: Media Guide*. He was awarded a CBE in June 2009 for services to community relations. He is currently a research fellow at the Department of History, Royal

Holloway, University of London, and member of the management board of the Prince Alwaleed Bin Talal Centre of Islamic Studies, University of Cambridge. He is also a fellow of the Royal Society of Arts and is listed in *The 500 Most Influential Muslims*, 2009.

Ekmeleddin Ýhsanoðlu is secretary general of the Organization of the Islamic Conference. He was founder and then chairman (1984–2000) of the Department of History of Science, Istanbul University. His particular interests are Islamic culture and scholarship. He has been a lecturer and visiting professor at several universities, including the University of Exeter; Ankara University; Inönü University, Turkey; and Ludwig Maximilian University in Munich.

Gabriel Greenberg, originally from Boston, attended Wesleyan University in Connecticut, where he graduated with honors in history. While working on *Islamophobia*, he moved to Israel, where he has been studying Judaism and working for an organization that promotes coexistence in the Middle East. Greenberg is beginning rabbinical school in the fall of '08.

Ibrahim Kalin received his PhD from George Washington University, Washington, D.C. His field of concentration is post-Avicennan Islamic philosophy with research interests in Ottoman intellectual history, interfaith dialogue, mysticism, and comparative philosophy. He has contributed to several encyclopedias, including the *MacMillan Encyclopedia of Philosophy*, 2d ed., and the *Encyclopedia of Religion*, 2d ed. He has published widely on Islamic philosophy and the relations between Islam and the West, including a book titled *Knowledge in Later Islamic Philosophy: Mulla Sadra on Existence, Intellect, and Intuition* (Oxford University Press, 2010). He was a faculty member at the College of the Holy Cross, Worcester, Massachusetts (2002–2005), and has served as the founding director of the SETA Foundation for Political, Economic, and Social Research based in Ankara, Turkey. He joined the faculty of the Prince Alwaleed Bin Talal Center for Muslim-Christian Understanding at Georgetown University in the fall of 2008.

Jocelyne Cesari is principal research fellow at the French National Center for Scientific Research (CNRS). Her training, professional experience, and academic expertise are in political science, the Middle East, and Islamic studies. She has written numerous books and articles on Muslim minorities in France and elsewhere in Europe and their transnational links with the Muslim world at large. Her continuous investigation into Islam as a minority religion in secular and democratic contexts took her to the United States. Since 1998, she has held several fellowships and professorships at Harvard and Columbia universities. She is currently research associate at the Center for Middle Eastern Studies at Harvard University, where she is in charge of a research seminar on Islam in Europe and in the United States in the aftermath of September 11. She also teaches a class titled Muslims in Multicultural America and one on transnational Islam in the Anthropology Department.

John L. Esposito is university professor, professor of religion and international affairs and of Islamic studies, and founding director of the Prince Alwaleed bin Talal Center for Muslim-Christian Understanding at the Walsh School of Foreign Service, Georgetown University. Esposito specializes in Islam, political Islam from North Africa to Southeast Asia, and religion and international affairs. He is editor in chief of the four-volume *Oxford Encyclopedia of the Modern Islamic World, The Oxford History of Islam, The Oxford Dictionary of Islam, The Islamic World: Past and Present*, the six-volume *Oxford Encyclopedia of the Islamic World*, and Oxford Islamic Studies Online. His more than thirty-five books include *Who Speaks for Islam? What a Billion Muslims Really Think* (with Dalia Mogahed), *Unholy War: Terror in the Name of Islam, The Islamic Threat: Myth or Reality? Islam and Politics, Political Islam: Radicalism, Revolution, or Reform?* and *Islam and Democracy* (with J. Voll). His writings have been translated into more than twenty-eight languages, including Arabic, Turkish, Persian, Bahasa Indonesia, Urdu, several European languages, Japanese, and Chinese.

Juan R. I. Cole is Richard P. Mitchell Distinguished University Professor of History at the University of Michigan. He has written extensively about Egypt, Iran, Iraq, and South Asia. He has given numerous media interviews on the war on terrorism since September 11, 2001, as well as on the Iraq War and the building conflict with Iran since 2003. He writes a regular column for Salon.com. He continues to study and write about contemporary Islamic movements, whether mainstream or radical, whether Sunni and Salafi or Shi'ite. Cole has a command of Arabic, Persian, and Urdu and reads some Turkish, knows both Middle Eastern and South Asian Islam, and has lived in a number of places in the Muslim world for extended periods of time. For three decades, he has sought to put the relationship of the West and the Muslim world in historical context, and his most recent book is *Napoleon's Egypt: Invading the Middle East* (2007). He is also the author of *Sacred Space and Holy War: The Politics, Culture, and History of Shi'ite Islam* (2002).

Kate Zebiri is senior lecturer in Arabic and Islamic studies at the School of Oriental and African studies, London. She has written books on conversion to

Islam, Muslim-Christian relations, and modern Islamic scholarship and is currently doing research on contemporary Western Sufism.

Mohamed Nimer works as a research director at the Council on American-Islamic Relations (CAIR), Washington, D.C. His research has focused on Muslim politics and development and the American Muslim experience. His work culminated in the publication of his book *The North American Muslim Resource Guide: Muslim Community Life in the United States and Canada* in 2002. His other publications include "Muslims in American Public Life," in Yvonne Haddad's *Muslims in the West: From Sojourners to Citizens*. He has also written reports and other educational material on the issues of discrimination and religious accommodation. Nimer is a U.S. citizen who was born in the Middle East, attended college in the United States, and has lived in this country since 1983. He earned his doctoral degree at the University of Utah with a specialization in political science in 1995.

Peter Gottschalk (BA in history, College of the Holy Cross; MA in South Asian studies, University of Wisconsin–Madison; PhD in the history of religions, University of Chicago) is associate professor of religion at Wesleyan University. His research and teaching concentrate on the confluence of religious cultures in South Asia, with a particular focus on Muslims and Hindus in contemporary rural India. His work investigates issues of identity, social memory, modernity, and epistemology. Among other works, he has written *Beyond Hindu and Muslim: Multiple Identity in Narratives from Village India* (2000), *Islamophobia: Muslims and Islam in American Political Cartoons*, coauthored with Gabriel Greenberg (2007), *Islamophobia: Making Muslims the Enemy* (2007), also cowritten with Gabriel Greenberg, and codesigned the interactive website "A Virtual Village" (2001).

Sam Cherribi (PhD, University of Amsterdam) is senior lecturer in sociology and directs the Emory Development Initiative (EDI). A former member of the Dutch parliament and the Council of Europe, at Emory he has also served as assistant to the provost and liaison to the Carter Center. He also represented the Netherlands in the Assembly of the Council of Europe (1994–September 2002), where he served on the board of directors of the council's North-South Institute, which promotes democracy in Africa. In the Assembly of the West European Union, he also served on the influential political committee on strategic European defense issues.

Sherman A. Jackson is an Arthur F. Thurnau Professor of Near Eastern Studies, visiting professor of law and professor of Afro-American studies at the

University of Michigan–Ann Arbor. He received his PhD from the University of Pennsylvania in 1991. He has taught at the University of Texas at Austin, Indiana University, and Wayne State University and was recently offered a full professorship at Stanford University. From 1987 to 1989 he served as executive director of the Center of Arabic Study Abroad in Cairo, Egypt. In addition to numerous articles, he is the author of *Islamic Law and the State: The Constitutional Jurisprudence of Shihâb al-Dîn al-Qarâfî* (Brill, 1996), *On the Boundaries of Theological Tolerance in Islam: Abû Hâmid al-Ghazâlî's Faysal al-Tafriqa* (Oxford, 2002) and, most recently, *Islam and the Blackamerican: Looking toward the Third Resurrection* (Oxford, 2005). He is cofounder of the American Learning Institute for Muslims (ALIM), a former member of the Fiqh Council of North America, past president of the Sharî'ah Scholars' Association of North America (SSANA), and a past trustee of the North American Islamic Trust (NAIT). He is featured on the *Washington Post Newsweek* blog, "On Faith," and is listed by Religion Newswriters Foundation's ReligionLink as among the top ten experts on Islam in the United States.

Sunaina Maira is associate professor of Asian American studies at the University of California–Davis. She is the author of *Desis in the House: Indian American Youth Culture in New York City* and coeditor of *Youthscapes: The Popular, the National, the Global* and *Contours of the Heart: South Asians Map North America*, which won the American Book Award in 1997. Her most recent book, *Missing: Youth, Citizenship, and Empire after 9/11*, is on South Asian Muslim immigrant youth and issues of citizenship and empire after 9/11.

Tahir Abbas, BSc (Econ), MSocSc, PhD, FRSA, is reader in sociology and founding director of the Birmingham University Centre for the Study of Ethnicity and Culture, United Kingdom. His research expertise is in the sociology of race, ethnicity, and multiculturalism; Islam and Muslims in Britain and the West; South Asians in education; and ethnic entrepreneurialism. He was previously senior research officer at the Home Office and the Department of Justice in London. A recognized author of more than one hundred books, papers, articles, reviews, and opinion columns in national and international publications, he is a fellow of the Royal Society of Arts and a member of the Lunar Society. He has held numerous research grants and worked with government departments and civil society organizations throughout Asia, Europe, and North America. His most recent book is *British Islam: The Road to Radicalism* (2009), and he is also the editor of *Islamic Political Radicalism: A European Perspective* (2007) and *Muslim Britain: Communities under Pressure* (2005).

Acknowledgments

There are many people who helped make this volume possible. First and foremost are our contributors who provided excellent manuscripts and were extraordinarily responsive to editorial comments regarding revisions. We thank the Organization of Islamic Conference and its Secretary General, Prof. Ekmeleddin Ihsanoglu, who provided financial support for a conference at Georgetown and the development of a manuscript.

Oxford University Press and Cynthia Read, executive editor, have been critical in support for the production of this volume. Liz Smith has done an invaluable job in shepherding the manuscript through the production process. I have been fortunate to have several of Georgetown's best graduate students as research assistants: Abdullah al-Arian and Hadia Mubarak provided invaluable research assistance; Melanie Trexler combined research with meticulous and thorough proofreading.

We are especially grateful to an extraordinary administrative team at the Prince Alwaleed bin Talal Center for Muslim-Christian Understanding Center: Alexa Poletto, associate director, Denisse Bonilla-Chaoui, executive assistant, and Adam Holmes, program coordinator, outstanding professionals who were critical to the conference that initiated the Islamophobia project. Alexa Poletto in particular shepherded the volume through extensive contacts with authors, reading and initial editing of the text, and oversight of its final production.

John L. Esposito and Ibrahim Kalin
Washington, D.C.
December 2009

Introduction

We should invade their countries, kill their leaders, and convert them
to Christianity. We weren't punctilious about locating and punishing
only Hitler and his top officers. We carpet-bombed German cities; we
killed civilians. That's war. And this is war.

—Ann Coulter, *National Review*

Islam is something we can't afford any more in the Netherlands. I
want the fascist Qur'an banned. We need to stop the Islamisation of
the Netherlands. That means no more mosques, no more Islamic
schools, no more imams.

—Geert Wilders, Dutch politician and
leader of the Party of Freedom

These people [Arabs and Muslims] need to be forcibly converted to
Christianity. . . . It's the only thing that can probably turn them into
human beings.

—Michael Savage, syndicated
talk-radio host

Western European societies are unprepared for the massive
immigration of brown-skinned peoples cooking strange foods and

maintaining different standards of hygiene. . . . All immigrants bring exotic customs and attitudes, but Muslim customs are more troublesome than
most.

—Daniel Pipes, columnist and political
commentator

Muslims everywhere behave with equal savagery. They behead criminals, stone
to death female—only female—adulteresses, throw acid in the faces of women
who refuse to wear the chador, mutilate the genitals of young girls, and ritually
abuse animals.

—Robert Kilroy-Silk, British politician and
well-known talk-show host

Islam has attacked us. . . . The God of Islam is not the same God. . . . Islam
is a very evil religion. . . . All the values that we as a nation hold dear, they
don't share those same values at all, these countries that have the majority of
Muslims.

—Franklin Graham, Christian evangelist and
missionary

Islamophobia did not suddenly come into being after the events of 9/11.
Like anti-Semitism and xenophobia, it has long and deep historical roots. Its
contemporary resurgence has been triggered by the significant influx of
Muslims in the West in the late 20ᵗʰ century, the Iranian revolution, hijack-
ings, hostage-taking and acts of terrorism in the 1980s and 1990s, attacks
against the World Trade Center and Pentagon on 9/11 and subsequent terrorist attacks in Europe. *Islamophobia and the Challenge of Pluralism in the 21ˢᵗ
Century* addresses the dangerous growth of Islamophobia in Europe and
America. The volume brings together new research and fresh perspective on
Islamophobia as a religious, cultural and political phenomenon. Experts from
Europe and America analyze and discuss the status of Islam and Muslims in
the West, the causes of the alarming increase and impact of Islamophobia in
domestic and foreign policies, and the role of the American and European
media.

Statistics and attitudes documented by a number of research institutions all
point towards an alarming increase in Islamophobia in the West. In November
1997, the Britain's Runneymede Report, *Islamophobia: A Challenge for Us All*,
launched in the U.K. defined Islamophobia as "the dread, hatred and hostility
towards Islam and Muslims perpetrated by a series of closed views that imply

and attribute negative and derogatory stereotypes and beliefs to Muslims." It results in exclusion, discrimination, and false presumptions/stereotypes –

- exclusion from economic, social, and public life;
- discrimination in the blatant form of hate crimes and subtler forms of disparagement;
- the perception that the religion of Islam has no common values with the West, is inferior to the West [or to Judaism and Christianity], and that it really is a violent political ideology rather than a source of faith and spirituality, unlike the other Abrahamic religions, Judaism and Christianity.

Conditions were ripe for discriminatory behavior towards Muslims before 9/11. The British Crime Survey 2000 estimated that in 1999 the number of racially motivated offences in England and Wales was 280,000. The risk of being a victim of a racially motivated crime was 4.2% for Pakistanis and Bengalis (who are primarily Muslim), compared to 0.3% for whites.

9/11 exacerbated and fed the growth of both Islamophobia in the West and anti-Americanism in the Muslim world. In 2002, The European Monitoring Center on Racism and Xenophobia (EUMC) published *The Summary Report on Islamophobia in the EU after 11 September 2001*, which documented increased and widespread acts of discrimination and racism against Muslims in fifteen EU member countries and warned of Islamophobia and anti-Semitism becoming acceptable in European society.[1] In a follow-up report in 2004, the Runnymede Trust concluded that Islamophobia was a pervasive feature of British society and characterized media reporting on Muslims and Islam as biased and unfair.[2] Indeed in recent years, far right anti-immigrant political parties and political commentators in Europe have demonized Islam and Muslims and the net result has been a virulent form of cultural racism.[3] Similarly, in the U.S., the Council on American Islamic Relations (CAIR) documented an increase of reported hate crimes between 2004 and 2005. Further, in 2005, the organization processed a total of 1,972 civil rights complaints, which was a 29.6 percent increase in the total number of complaints of anti-Muslim harassment, violence and discriminatory treatment from 2004.[4]

The international scope of Islamophobia was recognized and addressed by the United Nations, when Kofi Annan, then Secretary General of the United Nations, called a 2004 UN conference, "Confronting Islamophobia: Education for Tolerance and Understanding." Annan underscored the global need to acknowledge and address this new form of increasing bigotry "[when] the world is compelled to coin a new term to take account of increasingly widespread bigotry — that it is a sad and troubling development. Such is the case with 'Islamophobia'. . . . Since the September 11 attacks on the United States, many Muslims, particularly in the West, have found themselves the objects of suspicion, harassment and discrimination. . . . Too many people see Islam as a monolith and as intrinsically opposed to the West . . .

A 2006 USA Today-Gallup Poll found that substantial minorities of Americans admit to having negative feelings or prejudices against people of the Muslim faith, and favor using heightened security measures with Muslims as a way to help prevent terrorism. Fewer than half the respondents believed U.S. Muslims are loyal to the United States. Nearly one quarter of Americans, 22%, said they would not like to have a Muslim as a neighbor; 31% said they would feel nervous if they noticed a Muslim man on their flight and 18% said they would feel nervous if they noticed a Muslim woman on the flight. About 4 in 10 Americans favored more rigorous security measures for Muslims than those used for other U.S. citizens: requiring Muslims who are U.S. citizens to carry a special ID and undergo special, more intensive, security checks before boarding airplanes in the United States.

Four years later, we see no improvement in such attitudes. A 2010 Gallup Center for Muslim Studies report found that more than 4 in 10 Americans (43%) admit to feeling at least "a little" prejudice toward Muslims — more than twice the number who say the same about Christians (18%), Jews (15%) and Buddhists (14%). Nine percent of Americans admitted feeling "a great deal" of prejudice towards Muslims, while 20% admitted feeling "some" prejudice. The findings are based on "Religious Perceptions in America: With an In-Depth Analysis of U.S. Attitudes Toward Muslims and Islam," released in January 2010.[5]

Mosque construction has become a catalyst for increased anti-Muslim sentiment in the last few years. The Muslim American community's efforts to construct new mosques to accommodate their growing population has sparked intense opposition and Islamophobic comments by politicians, media, right-wing bloggers and political pundits. On June 22, 2010, a *New York Post* editorial attacked plans to construct new mosques in the state of NY, claiming,

There's no denying the elephant in the room. Neither is there any rejoicing over the mosques proposed for Sheepshead Bay, Staten Island and Ground Zero because where there are mosques, there are Muslims, and where there are Muslims, there are problems.

Before New York becomes New Yorkistan, it is worth noting that
the capital of Great Britain was London until it became known as
"Londonstan," degenerated by a Muslim community predominantly
from South Asia and Africa, whose first generation of "British Asians"
has made the United Kingdom into a launching pad for terrorists.[6]

In some states, opposition to mosque construction has been led by politicians.
For example, in June 2010, a Republican candidate of the 6th district of Tennessee opposed the Murfreesboro's Muslim community's proposal to build a new
mosque. In a public statement, candidate Lou Ann Zelenik said the Muslim
center is not part of a religious movement, but a political one "designed to
fracture the moral and political foundation of Middle Tennessee."[7] She wrote,
"Until the American Muslim community find it in their hearts to separate
themselves from their evil, radical counterparts, to condemn those who want to
destroy our civilization and will fight against them, we are not obligated to open
our society to any of them."[8] This charge that Muslims do not condemn terrorism is made repeatedly in the media despite the fact that post 9/11 many,
many statements have been issued by Muslim leaders and organizations from
all over the world, including a major joint statement by global religious and
intellectual leaders (the Amman Message). Unfortunately major media outlets,
who do not seem to find them "newsworthy," and thus they may be found on
the internet. See for example, http://www.ammanmessage.com/; http://www.
cair-net.org/html/911statements.html; http://www.beliefnet.com/story/111/
story_11121_1.html

In the aftermath of the attacks in America and in Europe, the relevance
and viability of multiculturalism as a policy in the U.S. and Great Britain was
challenged by those who charged that such an approach contributed to domestic terrorism. They charged that it retarded Muslim assimilation and civic engagement, perpetuating foreign loyalties, and providing a space for militant
radicals. The process of integration, in which immigrant citizens and residents
could retain their religious and ethnic differences, was rejected by many, in
particular the far right in Europe, who demand total assimilation.

Modern-day prophets of doom predict that Europe will be overrun by Islam,
transformed by the end of the century into "Eurabia." The media, political
leaders, and commentators on the right warn of a "soft terrorism" plot to take
over America and Europe. Bernard Lewis, a Middle East historian and adviser
to the Bush administration on its failed Iraq policy, received widespread coverage when he chided Europeans for losing their loyalties, self-confidence, and
respect for their own culture, charging that they have "surrendered" to Islam in
a mood of "self-abasement," "political correctness," and "multi-culturalism."

The anti-immigrant drumbeat about the impending demise of Europe's religious and cultural identity in the face of an Islamic threat has been aided by media coverage that lumps diverse identity, demographic, economic, and social conflict issues together under the umbrella of religion. Rioting in French ghetto areas inhabited by North African Arabs is portrayed as "Muslim" rather than as protests against poverty and hopelessness. Muslim boycotts in London protesting Danish cartoons that depicted Muhammad as a terrorist with a bomb in his turban and conflicts over the hijab in France, Turkey, and Denmark are seen exclusively as "religious issues" rather than also as issues of civil rights and freedoms such as women's right to dress as they choose. Because European Muslims are defined simply in terms of their faith, these problems and issues are incorrectly seen as "Muslim issues" when in fact, given their nature and primary causes, they require social, not religious, solutions or policies.

A common charge both with regard to Muslim-West relations and the integration of Muslims in America and Europe is that Islam is incompatible with the realities of modernity and Western culture and values. Some, from prominent politicians, academics, and political commentators to anti-immigrant, xenophobic European nationalist party leaders, speak of an historical clash of civilizations.

Ibrahim Kalin in "Islamophobia and the Limits of Multiculturalism" argues that the debate over Islam and Muslims in the West has been shaped and largely determined by the secular-liberal ideals of the European Enlightenment which cannot accommodate a non-Western religion such as Islam. Kalin discusses how the narrow scope of a liberal political system, which defines secularization as the only and normative "emancipatory power" in the modern world, marginalizes 'Islam' and Muslims in a world of Western modernity. With the privatization of religion under the secular framework of Western modernity, there is little or no accommodation for Islam – which is then subjected to the historical specificities of each respective nation's Christian, secular experience.

Kalin also argues that the current attitudes towards Islam and Muslims determine the limits of multiculturalism in Europe and the US and that a proper understanding of such phenomena as Islamophobia, xenophobia and discrimination against Muslim is related in an essential way to the debate over pluralism and multiculturalism in the West.

The nexus of Islamophobia, multiculturalism, and Muslim-West relations goes far beyond both 9/11 and the United States.[9] Needless to say, attitudes towards Muslim communities in Europe and the United States are part of a complex set of issues. There is no easy way to discuss pluralism, multiculturalism and the future of Western societies without discussing the precarious place of Islam and Muslims in the debate over civic engagement and integration.

Jocelyne Cesari's "'Islamophobia' in the West: A Comparison between Europe and America" explores the factors that influence the status of Muslims living in Europe and America, in particular the structural causes for discrimination. "Islamophobia," she contends, "overlaps with other forms of discrimination like xenophobia, anti-immigration sentiments, and the rejection of the validity of cultural differences."

Cesari maintains that in contrast to America, Islamophobia is often difficult to identify in Europe where Muslims, who are mostly immigrant laborers, are socially marginalized in contrast to American Muslims who are more socially and economically integrated. The connection in Europe of "Muslim" immigrants with Islam and terrorism is unique in contrast to America where the negative connotation of "immigrant" is typically associated with low-skilled Mexicans. Immigration is discussed in the U.S. in terms of socioeconomic factors and issues; but in Europe conversations on immigration center on radicalization, terrorism and Islam.

The ability of European Muslims to integrate has been exacerbated by international constraints – in particular the fight against "Islamic terrorism" with the significant changes in immigration regulations and tightening of security legislation, influenced by the US Patriot Act and Secret Evidence and their equivalents in Britain and many other European countries. While anti-terrorism legislation has been important in the arrests of extremists, the misuse and abuse of anti-terrorism measures coupled with immigration restrictions have resulted in discrimination towards religious and ethnic minorities and fed anti-immigrant and anti-Muslim sentiments in their societies. If one aspect of integration is a sense of psychological belonging, then policies that single-out and alienate members of a society based on their ethnicity or religion do very little to promote integration; in fact, they do the opposite.

Though Cesari does not believe that the media is overtly Islamophobic, sensationalist news stories conflate foreign and domestic Islam and imply that all immigrant populations are radicals.[10] This is compounded by certain public intellectuals whose hard-line critiques of Islam itself conflate the religion of Islam with the actions of a small minority of Muslim extremists and terrorists and thus contribute to Islamophobia.[11] Cesari concludes that current European multicultural policies are in fact not promoting pluralism and equality and should be re-worked to include minority (Islamic) cultural values.

Sam Cherribi extends Cesari's study in "An Obsession Renewed: Islamophobia in the Netherlands, Austria, and Germany." In this work, he demonstrates how the Dutch media affected the growth of Islamophobia in Germany and Austria since 2000. Cherribi maintains that politicians, taking their cues from media reports across Europe about immigration and a lack of Muslim integration, have supported far-right, populist parties. Overtime, the media and far-right parties have institutionalized distrust of Muslims.

To demonstrate the interconnectedness of xenophobia and Islamophobia in Dutch and Danish media, Cherribi compares and contrasts the Dutch movie *Fitna* produced by Geert Wilder, which caused an uproar among Muslim populations, with the controversial Danish cartoons' portrayal of the Prophet Muhammad. The result of these negative depictions was documented in a 2007 ERCI (Commission Europeénne Contre Le Racisme et L'Intolérance) study of media coverage which revealed an increase of Islamophobic incidents in the work place and in education in the Netherlands.

While the cartoons tested what Muslims would and would not accept in the media about their religion, *Fitna* sought to provoke and solicit a negative response towards Muslims. In January 2009, the Amsterdam Court of Appeal ordered Geert Wilders' prosecution for "the incitement to hatred and discrimination."[12] Wilders was banned from entering the United Kingdom in February 2009 as a "threat to one of the fundamental interests of society."[13]

A ripple effect could be seen in other European countries like Austria and Germany. The Freedom Party of Austria's of Jorg Haider, a voice of anti-Islamic sentiment, cast Muslim migrants in Europe as a central political issue. Studies demonstrated that his rhetoric resulted in an increase in the number of Austrians who rejected their Muslims neighbors. Roland Koch, governor of Hesse and member of Angela Merkel's Christian Democratic Party, was praised for his anti-immigrant comments, which were directed primarily at Turkish Muslim immigrants. Blaming immigrants for crime in Germany, Koch stated that there were too many "criminal young foreigners" in Germany and that immigrants must abide by Germany's Christian rules.[14]

Despite Great Britain's early and seemingly successful espousal of multiculturalism, in recent years the fabric of its society has been tested. Tahir Abbas' "Islamophobia in the UK" notes that in contrast to much of Europe, which has legislated politics to protect people based on "race" rather than "religious" markers, in Britain, such legal protection is only given to ethnically defined religious communities, Jews and Sikhs. Although they are a very significant presence in Britain, Muslims do not have similar laws to protect them from Islamophobia: "Despite Muslims being targeted by right-wing groups, with more subtle forms of racist prejudice and hatred after 9/11 and 7/7, Muslims, nevertheless, remain outside the domain of anti-racist legislation." Thus, in contrast to the Jewish and Sikh communities, Muslims do not have similar laws to protect them from Islamophobia, to require respect for Islamic beliefs or to prohibit publication of religiously offensive materials. Abbas' research highlights three case studies that have affected British Muslims and contributed to Islamophobia: Salman Rushdie's *Satanic Verses*, the

Danish cartoons, and controversial comments by former Foreign Minister and then current Home Secretary Jack Straw regarding Muslim women's dress.

In "Islamophobia and Anti-Americanism: Measurements, Dynamics, and Consequences." Mohammad Nimer observes that Islamophobia and anti-Americanism are linked and reinforce each other. Nimer sees a circular cause-and-effect relationship between Islamophobia and anti-Americanism globally: when Muslim terrorists attack the US, America engages in anti-Muslim rhetoric and policies. This reinforces anti-American sentiment among Muslims in the international arena and promotes more terrorist attacks. As Islamophobia increases, so does anti-Americanism. Feeding this relationship are mutual misconceptions that Muslims and Americans have of each other, incorrect notions that result in harsh rhetoric and violent behaviors.[15] The fallout can be seen in America where Islamophobia can be measured in polls on American views of Muslims and Islam, anti-Muslim incidents reported by the FBI and CAIR which continue to rise,[16] and the impact of a politics of prejudice evident in Barack Obama's distancing himself from his Muslim roots.

Sherman Jackson's "Muslims, Islam(s), Race, and American Islamophobia" analyzes the extent to which Islamophobia is a form of racism, with a specific spin that is rooted in the American experience. Jackson maintains that the failure of immigrant Muslims to come to grips with their racial identity within the American landscape, their "racial agnosticism," reinforces whiteness and white supremacy in America, resulting in their being regarded as "un-American" and thus increases Islamophobia in the US.

Jackson attributes many second generation Muslims' not feeling "American" to this failure to deal with racial issues. Jackson believes that blackness is critical to American identity. Without belonging to America "through the prism of blackness," whiteness is the exclusive authenticator of what is American. Jackson warns that if Muslim immigrants do not carve out their own racial category in America, others will do it for them. He cites, as an example, Rush Limbaugh's calling Obama an Arab, not an African-American. By doing this, Limbaugh was putting Obama in a category of people to whom Americans feel no debt. This rhetoric placed Obama completely outside the category of "American."[17] Thus, Jackson concludes: if Muslim immigrants continue to choose to a "racial agnosticism," America will assign them a race and this will only increase anti-immigrant Islamophobia in the future.

Sunaina Maira in "Islamophobia and the War on Terror: Youth, Citizenship, and Dissent" extends the discussion of the impact of Islamophobia and racism to Muslim youth. Understanding Islamophobia within the larger historical and political contexts in which it emerged – colonialism, modernity, racism and imperialism - enables us to better understand the responses of Muslim

American youth, a dissent often peppered with discussions of multiculturalism, Orientalism, racism, and feminism.

Although the 9/11 attacks intensified the discourse about Islam and Islamophobia, Maira believes that the state of emergency in which Muslim communities find themselves is not exceptional. Rather, Sunaian believes, it is typical of an American experience that historically has marginalized and excluded certain groups from citizenships at particular historical moments. Muslims and Middle Easterners are the current subordinated group.

Maira focuses on Muslim immigrant youth, and how they have constructed their "Muslim identity" in response to the impact of 9/11 and Islamophobia. Maira writes in a previous work, "After the terrorist attacks, popular feeling was that 'somebody had to pay' domestically, as well as internationally, to restore the illusion of national security for Americans. The groups whose civil rights were considered expendable were two populations who historically have had little power to combat infringement on their civil rights: immigrants and Arab Americans."[18] Citing Stephen Schulhofer, she describes how at least 1200 and up to 3000 Muslim immigrant men were rounded up and detained in the aftermath of 9/11, without any criminal charges, some in high security prisons. Virtually none of the detainees has been identified publicly and the locations where many have been held remain secret.[19] As a result, many young Muslims have come to identify more closely with other youth of color, perceiving themselves as also victims of racial discrimination.

At first blush, the notion of the "good Muslim" citizen might suggest that Islamophobia can be countered by religious multiculturalism and tolerance. However, Maira maintains that Islamophobia and racism cannot be eradicated simply by greater religious tolerance, since Islamophobia is linked to U.S. foreign policy and its global involvement.

Juan Cole in "Islamophobia and American Foreign Policy Rhetoric: The Bush Years and After" looks at the interconnectedness of Islamophobic rhetoric during the administration of George W. Bush on American foreign policy, its influence on America's image in the Middle East and its impact on foreign policies as well as the 2008 elections.

Though Bush spoke of Muslims as a peaceful people and distinguished Islam from the acts of terrorists immediately after 9/11, he simultaneously linked the Muslim world to terrorism. By 2006, Bush's speeches bordered on "fear-mongering," shifting his rhetoric from the "global war on terror" to the struggle with "Islamofascism" which in turn set the tone for the Republican campaign and the 2008 presidential elections.

In 2006, around the midterm of the electoral process, Islamofascism became part of American political discourse, adopted by George Bush and members of Congress. Cole argues that this phrase is problematic for two reasons. First, to say that "Islam" is fascist implies that an entire religion and all civilizations whose citizens practice Islam are fascist. Bush could have said that a "Muslim" was a terrorist without implying that all Muslims are terrorists; calling this terrorism "Islamic," however, he marked all Muslims as terrorists. Second, the term "Islamofascism" links European authoritarianism to Islam as a religion. "Even if one could establish that their ideas had any similarity to European fascism, they should be called Muslim fascists and not Islamic ones, since Islam as a religion is universalist in character and therefore anti-fascist."[20]

Examining speeches given by George Bush and VP Dick Cheney, Cole demonstrates how both depicted an imagined Islamic enemy that warranted US aggression. While the President and Vice President claimed to differentiate between proponents of "Islamic fascism" and "normative" Muslims, people in the Middle East were not convinced. US attempts at replacing the threat of the Soviet Union with Muslims did not align with reality. Many countries in the Muslim world are major non-NATO allies (i.e. Pakistan, Morocco, Egypt, etc.) and other states have strong economic ties. Thus, the Republican Party turned the Muslim world into the new "enemy" of the West while simultaneously maintaining close economic and diplomatic ties with these countries. Bush's aggressiveness damaged the image of the US for Muslims.

Republican presidential candidates (McCain, Romney, Tom Tancredo (R-CO), Giuliani, and Huckabee) embraced Islamphobic rhetoric during the 2007-2008 presidential primaries by portraying Muslims as the "enemy" seeking to establish an Islamic state. Though the Democrats did not embrace the same Islamophobic rhetoric with the same vigor, the party was affected by it. Obama attempted to distance himself from his Muslim heritage and at a rally, low-level Obama employees removed two Muslim women wearing headscarves from the bleachers where they would be visible on TV. Further, the Obama campaign fired Mazen Asbahi, the national coordinator for Muslim and Arab American outreach, after the Bush administration charged him with associating with "shadowy" people and organizations. These charges were insubstantial.

Literature and art have been a powerful vehicle for the dissemination of Islamophobic discourse and images historically. Anas Al-Shaikh-Ali's "Islamophobic Discourse Masquerading as Art and Literature," Kate Zebiri's "Orientalist Themes in Contemporary British Islamophobia," and Peter Gottschalk and Gabriel Greenberg's in "From Muhammad to Obama: Caricatures, Cartoons, and Stereotypes of Muslims" demonstrate the extent to which Islamophobia has been conveyed in popular culture, in literature, the arts, and media both in the past and today.

In "Islamophobic Discourse Masquerading as Art and Literature" Al-Shaikh-Ali discusses the extent to which classics that entertained Western audiences for generations like "The White Man's Burden" by Kipling, *Camp of Saints* by Raspail, *The True Travels and Adventures of Captain John Smith*, and *Don Quixote* conveyed an Islamophobic message and legacy whose xenophobic content remains influential globally. Today, this xenophobic ideology is continued in popular fiction, films, pictures, and music. Fictitious thrillers and other contemporary literature like the religiously based and enormously popular *Left Behind* are key vehicles whose Islamophobic messages have reached millions of readers. Anas highlights the prevailing double standard. If the best selling *Left Behind* series about Armageddon, the return of Jesus and the mass religious cleansing of the world had been written by a Muslim suggesting a global religious cleansing would occur with the return of Muhammad, it would have been widely denounced. In contrast, this Christian series, received widespread coverage in Europe and America and was even distributed by the British army to its soldiers.

Kate Zebiri, in "Orientalist Themes in Contemporary British Islamophobia" examines the relationship between contemporary British Islamophobia and Orientalist (academic scholarship, art and literature) themes of the past. She demonstrates that while contemporary British popular culture, still reflects age-old hostilities to Islam, it has nonetheless changed and evolved according to the nature of society today. Her analysis focuses on the three main themes – gender, violence and foreignness – that emerged from her field research (interviews with British Muslim converts) and study of the media. In contrast to newspaper coverage, which places more emphasis on politics and, correspondingly, violence, interviews with the general public reveals the extent to which non-Muslim Brits view "Muslim Otherness" through the prism of the hijab (headscarf). Issues related to gender and sexuality, symbolized by the hijab, rather than religious concerns, epitomized Islam's Otherness when set against the norms of contemporary mainstream Western society.

While violence has been no less persistent a theme than gender in anti-Muslim discourse, the reasons for its prominence today are different from the past when Muslim-Christian relations in Europe were affected by the threat of Muslim military expansion. In recent decades, Zebiri maintains, the alleged violence of Islam is related more to the rise of political Islam, jihadist activism and so-called 'Islamic terrorism'. So too, foreignness, the Otherness of Islam and Muslims – the perception of an alien culture, values, and way of life—have been constructed differently in a world of nation-states. In contrast to early centuries of Muslim-Christian/European encounter, when foreignness/Otherness were seen in primarily religious terms, with Islam being viewed as heretical, in the twenty-first-century Western nations like Britain are more concerned with issues of national identity, immigration and social cohesion. Thus, critics charge that Muslims have failed to integrate, that they have unreasonable demands, they have mixed loyalties, they support extremism, and that their values and interests are incompatible with those of mainstream society.

Zebiri concludes that a significant factor in understanding contemporary Islamophobia is a belief in the seemingly unusual capacity of Muslims/Islam to resist – in terms of culture, moral values, and religiosity - Western universalistic aspirations and appear to challenge prevailing trends of relativism and pluralism. The representation of Muslims as barbaric, irrational, backward, repressive of women, irredeemably alien and Other, goes hand in hand with the alternative view of the Self – whether it be the West, Europe, or Britain – which is modern, progressive, rational, civilized, humane and liberal.

But, is there a significant difference between Europe and an historically multicultural America? In "From Muhammad to Obama: Caricatures, Cartoons, and Stereotypes of Muslims," Peter Gottschalk and Gabriel Greenberg's find evidence of Islamophobia in their review of the past fifty years of American political cartoons, concluding that Muslims have been a foil for an assumed set of American norms and thus are not depicted as part of the "normal" American landscape. While some editorial cartoons do not reinforce an Islamophobic stereotype, Gottschalk and Greenberg maintain that the vast majority of cartoons do support Islamophobia and that editorials tend to emphasize the "normalcy" of an America in which Muslims are absent.

Islamophobia, like anti-Semitism, will not be eradicated easily or soon. Islamophobia is not simply a problem for Muslims; it is "our" problem. Governments, policymakers, the media, educational institutions, religious and corporate leaders have a critical role to play in transforming our societies and influencing our citizens and policies to contain the voices of hate and the exclusivist theologies (of militant religious and secular fundamentalists alike) if we are to promote global understanding and peace.

Anti-Muslim rhetoric and hate crimes proliferate. Legitimate concerns in America and Europe for domestic security have been offset by the abuse of anti-terrorism legislation, indiscriminate arrests and imprisonments that compromise the civil liberties of Muslims. The net result is a growing climate of suspicion, deterioration of relations between Muslims and non-Muslims, and the growth of Islamophobia. Muslim leaders have been hard pressed to assert their faith and rights as citizens in the West, affirming freedom of expression while rejecting its abuse as a cover for prejudice. They have been challenged to draw a sharp line between legitimate and illegitimate uses of force and violence, between acts of resistance and acts of terror, and legitimate forms of dissent and violent demonstrations or attacks that inflame the situation, reinforcing Western stereotypes.

Globalization and an increasingly multicultural and multireligious West test the mettle of cherished democratic principles and values. Islamophobia, which is becoming a social cancer, must be recognized and be as unacceptable as anti-Semitism, a threat to the very fabric of our democratic pluralistic way of life. The continued threat and response to global terrorism coupled with the resurgence of xenophobia and cultural racism threaten the fabric of liberal democracies in the West and their Muslim citizens in particular. A fine line must be drawn to distinguish between the faith of Islam and those who commit violence and terror in the name of Islam, between the majority of mainstream Muslims and the acts of a minority of Muslim extremists and terrorists. Blurring these distinctions risks the adoption of foreign and domestic policies that promote a clash rather than a co-existence of cultures. They play into the hands of preachers of hate (Muslim and non-Muslim, religious and political leaders, and political commentators) whose rhetoric incites and demonizes, alienates and marginalizes.

NOTES

Epigraph sources: http://www.nationalreview.com/coulter/coulter091301.shtml; Ian Traynor, "Profile: Geert Wilders," http://www.guardian.co.uk/world/2009/feb/12/profile-geert-wilders; "Savage: Arabs Are 'Non-humans' and 'Racist, Fascist Bigots,'" *Mediamatters.org*, May 14, 2004, http://mediamatters.org/items/200405140003; "Robert Kilroy-Silk," *Wikipedia*, Sept. 4, 2006, Sept. 8, 2006, http://en.wikipedia.org/wiki/Robert_Kilroy-Silk; http://www.beliefnet.com/News/2001/11/Preachers-Anti-Islam-Remarks-Mobilize-White-House.aspx.

1. Muhammad Anwar, "Muslims in Britain: Issues, Policy, and Practice," in *Muslim Britain: Communities under Pressure*, ed. Tahir Abbas, 31 (London: Zed, 2005).

2. The follow-up report in 2004, *Islamophobia: Issues, Challenges, and Action* (London: Runnymede Trust), 73, found that while there had been some improvements, levels of anti-Muslim prejudice had increased in certain quarters.

3. Chris Allen, "From Race to Religion: The New Face of Discrimination," in *Muslim Britain*, ed. Abbas, 54. There have also been some positive developments in the wake of 9/11, such as a new openness in certain sections of the media (and generally responsible reporting in the immediate aftermath of 9/11), new opportunities for dialogue between Muslims and government, and new Muslim initiatives to combat extremism. See Dilwar Hussain, "The Impact of 9/11 on British Muslim Identity," in *Islam and the West Post 9/11*, ed. Ron Geaves, Theodore Gabriel, Yvonne Haddad, and Jane Idleman Smith (Aldershot, UK: Ashgate, 2005), 125–26.

4. http://www.cair.com/Issues/Islamophobia/Islamophobia.aspx (accessed June 26, 2010)

5. Shavana Abruzzo, "New Yorkistan? Don't rule it out!" *New York Post* (June 22, 2010), http://www.nypost.com/p/news/local/brooklyn/ new_yorkistan_don_rule_it_out_bc 8AbFztnOFKtaFWMTyohL?CMP=OTC-rss&FEEDNAME=#ixzz0rsvvD6q8g (accessed June 26, 2010).

6. Travis Loller, "Candidate denounces Murfreesboro mosque proposal," *Associated Press* (June 24, 2010), http://news.yahoo.com/s/ap/20100625/ ap_on_el_ho/us_candidate_mosque_tenn_2 (accessed June 24, 2010).

7. Ibid.

8. http://www.muslimwestfacts.com/mwf/125387/Religious-Prejudice-Stronger-Against-Muslims.aspx

9. For a background analysis, see my "Roots of Misconception: Euro-American Perceptions of Islam before and after September 11th," in *Islam, Fundamentalism, and the Betrayal of Tradition*, ed. Joseph Lumbard, 143–87 (Bloomington: World Wisdom, 2004).

10. Jocelyne Cesari, "Islamophobia in the West: A Comparison between Europe and the United States," 9.

11. Ibid. 10.

12. LJ Nummer, "Amsterdam Court of Appeal Orders the Criminal Prosecution of the Member of Parliament of the Dutch Second Chamber Geert Wilders," *Rechtspraak* (Jan. 21, 2009), http://www.rechtspraak.nl/Actualiteiten/ Amsterdam+Court+of+Appeal+ orders+the+criminal+prosecution ı of ı the ı Member+ of+Parliament+of+the+Dutch+S.htm (accessed June 26, 2010).

13. "Home Office Letter to Geert Wilders," February 10, 2009, http://www. geertwilders.nl/images/images/letter-denying-geert-wilders-entry-into-uk.pdf (accessed June 26, 2010).

14. David Crossland, "Far-Right NPD Praises Koch's Tough Talk on Immigration," *Spiegel Online* (Jan. 4, 2008), http://www.spiegel.de/international/germany/ 0,1518,526724,00.html (accessed June 26, 2010).

15. Mohamed Nimer, "Islamophobia and Anti-Americanism: Measurements, Dynamics, and Consequences," 8.

16. Ibid, 3.

17. Sherman A. Jackson, "Muslims, Islam(s), Race, and American Islamophobia," 16-18.

18. Sunaina Maira, "Youth Culture, Citizenship and Globalization: South Asian Muslim Youth in the United States after September 11th," *Comparative Studies of South Asia, Africa and the Middle East* 24.1 (2004): 219-231.

19. Maira, "Youth Culture," citing Stephen J. Schulhofer, *The Enemy Within: Intelligence Gathering, Law Enforcement, and Civil Liberties in the Wake of September 11* (New York: Century Foundation Press, 2002), 11.

20. Juan Cole, "Islamophobia and American Foreign Policy Rhetoric: The Bush Years and After," 7.

Islamophobia

I

The Context of
Islamophobia

I

Islamophobia and the Limits of Multiculturalism

Ibrahim Kalin

A few months before his death in October 2004, Jacques Derrida called for "the need to deconstruct the European intellectual construct of Islam."[1] Having been born in Algeria, which was then under French occupation, and having thus seen both sides of the river, Derrida was referring to the suppression of the Islamic element in the history of the Mediterranean and, by extension, of Europe. While the Greek, the Jew, and the Arab are considered the three prototypes that have shaped the history of the Mediterranean, only a Euro-Christian memory, Derrida argued, has reached the modern period. Given the complexities of this history, even the much-quoted phrase "Judeo-Christian" is a misnomer as it refers more to the Jewish origins of Christianity than to the role of Jews in European and Mediterranean history. Not surprisingly, Islam plays virtually no role in this particular construction of history.

As if echoing Derrida's concerns on a different level, Charles Taylor has argued that the current debate about multiculturalism in Western countries has become a debate about Islam and Muslims. Taylor claims that multiculturalism has become suspect and in extricably linked up with Islam because "almost every reason for toleration's apparent fall into disrepute concerns Islam."[2] Taylor's remark that the debate about Islam and Muslims in Western societies is turning into a crisis of multiculturalism is alarming to say the least. By and large, Islam has become part of a public debate to determine how far multiculturalism will go. A good example of how an Islam-related issue in Europe opens up larger debates is the French government's 2004 decision to ban the wearing of the headscarf in public schools. At the time, the media campaign in support of the ban went way beyond girls' covering their heads in public schools. The debate covered almost everything—from the "true spirit" of France and Europe to violence against women, integration, assimilation, and pluralism.[3] Throughout the headscarf controversy, which continues to this day in France, Germany, Turkey, and beyond, the outer limits of pluralist and multiculturalist policies in Europe have been debated and negotiated in opposition to or in support of the "civic integration" of Muslim communities.[4] Attacks on multiculturalism have become indirect attacks on Islam and Muslims.

The interlinking of Islam and multiculturalism is confirmed by the rising tide of *Islamophobia*, a term that has come to denote acts of intolerance, discrimination, unfounded fear, and racism against Islam and Muslims. In 2007, United Nations High Commissioner for Human Rights Louise Arbour said that "bigotry and prejudice, especially in regard to Muslims, were common in Europe," and she "called on governments to tackle the issue." Basing her remarks on a report by Doudou Diène of Senegal regarding intolerance toward Muslims in Europe, she added that Europeans "are shocked at times when it is pointed out that bigotry, prejudice and stereotyping [are] still sometimes very present in their attitude toward others."[5]

The 2008 World Economic Forum's *Islam and the West: Annual Report on the State of Dialogue* points to the growing tension between Islamic and Western societies. Based on a major survey conducted in twenty-one countries in 2007, the report shows that the majority of those polled believe that relations between Islam and the West are getting worse.[6] It is striking that the vast majority of Muslims believe that the West does not respect Islam, whereas many Westerners hold just the opposite view and believe that Westerners do respect Muslims.[7] This is more than a breakdown of communication. The existing conceptual frameworks at work in Muslim-West relations, however one may define them, have so far failed to establish a common ground and inspire a shared horizon.

Needless to say, the current attitudes toward Muslim communities in Europe and the United States are part of a complex set of issues. There is no easy way to discuss pluralism, multiculturalism, and the future of Western societies without discussing the precarious place of Islam and Muslims in the debate. The same is equally true for the Muslim world. In an increasingly interconnected world, Islamophobia, just like any other form of intolerance and discrimination, cannot be seen in isolation from what is happening around us. Islamophobia did not suddenly come into being after the events of 9/11. In many ways, the trauma caused by 9/11 merely helped bring the problem to the surface. Clearly the problematic nexus of Islamophobia, multiculturalism, and Muslim-West relations goes far beyond both 9/11 and the United States.[8]

Islam, Multiculturalism, and Its Discontents

The main argument of this chapter is simple, yet saddled with implications for the future of multiculturalism on the one hand and Muslim-West relations on the other. Given the growing complexity of cultural and religious identities in late modernity, multiculturalism has deepened in Western societies and produced new modes of identity and social agency. Yet, multiculturalism, I argue, has also reached its limits in the current debate over Islam and Muslims. The debate is shaped and largely determined by the secular-liberal ideals of the European Enlightenment, which cannot accommodate a non-Western religion such as Islam. What turns Islam into a distant and marginal member of the multiculturalist world of Western modernity is the narrow scope of the liberal political system, which defines secularization as the only emancipatory power in the modern world. Within the secular framework of Western modernity, religion has been privatized, and individual choice has become the sole basis of establishing meaning and legitimacy for one's actions. In Peter Berger's words, "the conception of the naked self, beyond institutions and roles, as the *ens realissimum* of human being, is the very heart of modernity."[9] In the current context of late modernity, the privatization and secularization of religion permeate the European and American religious landscapes. Contrary to what many think, this does not prove that the West has become a godless civilization. Rather, it confirms, as Cox argues, the changing nature of being religious in a posttraditional world.[10] This is certainly different from the experience of Muslim societies, where, in most cases, modernization has not necessitated a comprehensive secularization.[11]

The different modalities of relation between religion and modernity are a point of contention not only between the larger Muslim world and the West but also between Western societies and Muslim communities living in the West. Different frameworks of meaning and legitimacy shape individual agency and social behavior. Yet a major problem arises when it comes to understanding the Muslim moral framework and Islamic cultural behavior within an exclusively secular and political context. While a delicate balance has been maintained between a reified notion of culture and human agency within the intellectual circles of Europe and the United States, "Muslim culture" has mostly been defined as an oppressive force that not only influences but also determines the individual and collective thinking and behavior of Muslims. In such cases, *culture* as a master term is employed in a way "that denies human agency, defining individuals through their culture, and treating culture as the explanation for virtually everything they say or do."[12] Cultural racism arises out of monolithic notions of religious, ethnic, and cultural groups that are seen as united by a central value system with virtually no room for diversity or human agency. It is also generated and sustained by a set of implicit and explicit hierarchies of culture whereby certain types of cultural behavior are identified as "modern, civic, civilized, liberating and rational" while others are depicted as "retro, violent, bigoted, irrational and obscurantist."

One of the underlying tensions of multiculturalism, which concerns Muslim communities as well, can be described as one between cultural parochialism and normative critique. Critics charge that multiculturalism gives up on all universal standards and values and runs the risk of creating or encouraging parallel societies without a common ground. This is more than a rhetorical issue, for it determines perceptions, attitudes, and policy. For instance, should the forced marriages observed in some non-Western communities be allowed as part of a policy of multiculturalism, or should they be regulated by an agency (e.g., the nation-state or an international body) to encourage and facilitate "civic integration"? In recent years, European governments have adopted different policies, leading to integration and acceptance, as well as rejection and alienation. The reason is a critical one: The notion of "culture" employed in both theory and policy has not kept up with the realities on the ground and often reflects the secular liberal presumptions and attitudes of Western societies. Clearly, the inclusion and integration of Muslim societies in the West require a radical revisiting of some fundamental assumptions of Western liberalism and secular multiculturalism.[13] In order for multiculturalism to work for everyone, celebration of difference cannot stop short of Islam and Muslims.

Any discussion of social diversity and multiculturalism should attend to changing notions of integration, assimilation, and social cohesion. The models of "melting pot" versus "salad bar" and other forms of managing ethnic and religious diversity have changed over the years, reflecting the deep conceptual and political changes in Europe, the United States, and the Muslim world. In a famous speech delivered in 1966, Roy Jenkins, then British home secretary, rejected the "melting pot" model, which would "turn everybody out in a common mould, as one of a series of carbon copies of someone's misplaced vision of the stereotyped Englishman." Instead, Jenkins proposed a definition of integration "not as a flattening process of assimilation but as equal opportunity, coupled with cultural diversity, in an atmosphere of mutual tolerance."[14]

What is striking is that while Jenkins's condemnation of forced assimilation and praise of "equal opportunity, cultural diversity and mutual tolerance" are shared by many European governments, these governments' actual policies of diversity have reflected different realities, often leading to tacit cultural confrontations and tensions. Moreover, in the aftermath of the attacks of September 11 and other attacks in Europe, both rhetoric and policy in Europe and the United States have begun to change and narrow the scope of multiculturalism. Thus, Labor home secretary David Blunkett said in 2001 that "we have norms of acceptability and those who come into our home—for that is what it is—should accept those norms."[15]

It is clear that pluralism, multiculturalism, and cosmopolitanism, along with all the nuances among them, cannot be construed as giving up on any universal standard and value; issues of justice and equality have a degree of universality regardless of cultural uniqueness. A "politics of recognition," to use Charles Taylor's phrase, should allow a middle ground for cultural specificity on the one hand and a set of universal normative principles on the other.[16] Whatever its use for civic integration or social cohesion, such a middle ground is required to uphold certain moral principles that are universal and cross-cultural. And this is where another false assumption is often presented: The assumption that because different minority groups have distinct religious, ethnic, and cultural traditions, their central value system is largely incompatible with that of their host societies. Exaggerating cultural differences to the point of moral incompatibility is a tactic often employed by cultural conservatives to maintain a certain imagery of European or Western civilization. The same mistake is also committed by Muslim groups in the name of political opposition and resistance. Just as human agency flows through cultural collectivities and shapes them in various ways, shared moral values move across diverse ethnic and religious communities.

There is a long history of debate over moral particularism versus moral universalism.[17] Those who deride multiculturalism and define Islamic values as incompatible with those of the West claim that Muslims are unable to integrate into host societies where they are minorities. While the terms "integration," "host society," and "minority" need to be critically defined, the majority of Muslims see little conflict in the essential and universal moral values they consider to be shared by Muslim and Western societies. Abdullah bin Bayyah, one of the foremost authorities of Sunni Islam, rejects moral relativism and affirms the existence of universal values that transcend cultural specificities. Basing his reasoning on a broad notion of "common sense," bin Bayyah believes that "shared values do exist. The best proofs for this are the human faculties of reason . . . and of language. Every rational mind recognizes justice and every language has a word for it . . . the same can be said for 'truth,' 'liberty,' 'tolerance,' 'integrity' and many other concepts. These are praised by all cultures and expressed positively in all languages."[18]

The Scope of Islamophobia

The word *Islamophobia* came into use in the 1990s. The 1997 Runneymede Report, *Islamophobia: A Challenge for Us All*, was launched in November 1997 by then British home secretary Jack Straw. The report defined Islamophobia as "the dread, hatred and hostility towards Islam and Muslims perpetrated by a series of closed views that imply and attribute negative and derogatory stereotypes and beliefs to Muslims." The report added that Islamophobia is based on "an outlook or world-view involving an unfounded dread and dislike of Muslims, which results in practices of exclusion and discrimination." Defined in these broad terms, Islamophobia factors into a range of contentious issues, from politics and immigration to schools and the workplace.

While the term *Islamophobia* continued to be used in various ways, the first major report after 9/11 was published by the European Monitoring Center on Racism and Xenophobia (EUMC). Titled *Summary Report on Islamophobia in the EU after 11 September 2001*, the report documented acts of discrimination and racism against Muslims in fifteen EU member countries. The report's findings showed that "Islamic communities and other vulnerable groups have become targets of increased hostility since 11 September. A greater sense of fear among the general population has exacerbated already existing prejudices and fuelled acts of aggression and harassment in many European Member States. At the same time, attempts to allay fears sometimes led to a new interest in Islamic culture and to practical inter-faith initiatives."

When updated in 2004, the Runneymede Report documented some encouraging developments. Acts of hatred and discrimination against Islam and Muslims, however, continued to be on the rise. The Danish cartoon crisis and its aftermath are still fresh in the global memory. The speech by Pope Benedict XVI at Regensburg University in 2006 continues to be seen as a sinister attack on Islam by the most important Christian figure in the world.[19] Further, to the bewilderment of social and political scientists both in the United States and the Muslim world, former U.S. president George W. Bush used the word "Islamo-fascism," which served only to reinforce anti-American sentiments in the Muslim world. During the U.S. election campaign of 2008, Barack Husayn Obama's "Muslim past" and alleged "Muslim identity" became rallying points for misguided religious exclusivism and cultural racism.

The fear factor in the West's relation to Islam also surfaces in the opposition of some countries to Turkey's European Union membership. To cite a striking example, when the EU commission issued a positive report about Turkey's membership progress in 2004, Frits Bolkenstein, the EU's internal market commissioner, quoted Bernard Lewis and expressed concern over Europe's becoming "Eurabia." He said, "I don't know if it will take this course, but if he's [Lewis] right, the liberation of Vienna [from the Ottomans] in 1683 would have been in vain."[20] The commissioner, who was referring to the defeat of the Ottomans at the gates of Vienna, could have easily chosen from among a number of economic and political reasons to oppose Turkey's EU membership. Instead, he used a clearly culturalist-essentialist argument to push Turkey outside Europe. And this pushing out is not limited to Turkey alone.

Islamophobic acts manifest themselves in numerous ways. Some are explicit and obvious, some subtle and implicit. They take various forms and display varying degrees of aggression. Sometimes they come in the form of verbal and physical attacks on Muslim individuals. In some cases, mosques, Islamic centers, and Muslim properties are attacked and desecrated. In the workplace, health services, schools, and housing, Islamophobia takes the form of suspicion, staring, hazing, mockery, rejection, stigmatizing, and outright discrimination. In other public places, it may take the form of indirect discrimination, hate speech, or denial of access to goods and services.[21]

The 2006 EUMC report shows that "Muslims are often disproportionately represented in areas with poor housing conditions, while their educational achievement falls below average and their unemployment rates are higher than average." The same report notes the following:

> [T]here is a large body of evidence that demonstrates the persistent scale and dimension of discrimination in employment . . . derived from controlled experiments in employers' recruitment practices ("discrimination testing"), opinion surveys on discriminatory attitudes, and surveys of perceived discrimination by migrant . . . the data show that not all migrants are equally exposed to racism and discrimination in employment. Muslims appear to be particularly affected.[22]

At the societal level, the political loyalty of Muslims living in Europe and the United States is questioned, and they are accused of dual or multiple loyalties. They are presented as less committed to democracy, constitutional rights, and human rights than others because of their religious affiliation. Their religious identity is seen as an obstacle to respecting and abiding by their country's constitution and laws. The general accusation is that Muslims regard themselves as Muslim before considering themselves British, French, or Spanish. Moreover, this, some argue, jeopardizes their full citizenship in the countries in which they live. Ethnic and religious profiling thus turns into a tool of political discrimination and alienation.

A report by the International Helsinki Federation notes that in Germany "since September 11 thousands of Muslims have been subjected to screening for their personal data, house searches, interrogations, and arrests solely because their profiles have matched certain basic criteria, foremost of which is affiliation to Islam."[23] Perhaps the most dramatic case of overt discrimination based on a questioning of political loyalty came from the Baden-Wurttemberg region in Germany, where Muslim immigrants were asked questions to determine

> whether an applicant's formal "acceptance" of liberal democratic values, which is required by German nationality law, corresponds to his or her "real convictions." All questions are formulated in terms of a binary opposition between liberal democracy and a certain idea of Islam, as prescribing or condoning arranged marriage, patriarchy, homophobia, veiling and terrorism. (e.g., question 23: "You heard about the assaults on 11 September 2001 in New York and on 11 March 2004 in Madrid. Were the protagonists in your eyes terrorists or freedom fighters?")[24]

Such binary oppositions introduce a deep dichotomy between religious identity and national loyalty. While it is true that Muslims feel attached to the *ummah*, the transnational Muslim community, the religious association of a person does not function at the same level as preferring a particular country or political order over others. As Rowan Williams points out, a Muslim's attachment to the *ummah* is similar to a Christian's loyalty to the church.[25] The religious loyalty in question clearly predates the political loyalty required by the nation-states in which we live. Furthermore, it is a major challenge for all communities and nations, Muslim or non-Muslim, majority or minority, to maintain their loyalty to the society in which they live while upholding the universal principles of justice and equality, which extend beyond national boundaries.[26] To raise the issue of multiple loyalties only in relation to Muslims betrays a racist point of view. Critical Islamic thinking in Europe and the United States is thus seen as suspect and discarded for similar reasons. Unless the conditions of being European citizens are set as being white, Christian, and secular or a combination of these traits, the critical engagement of Muslims with their governments cannot be seen as misplacing one's loyalty.[27]

The one-sided and often irresponsible media coverage of events related to Muslims has become a breeding ground for Islamophobic sentiments and acts. Muslim symbols and figures are ridiculed and derided not only on marginal Internet sites but occasionally in the mainstream print media as well. Negative stereotypes of Islam and Muslims are presented as part of news reporting, TV debates, political speeches, and religious sermons. The stereotypes of Islam make up a long list of descriptors such as monolithic, sexist, oppressive, irrational, bigoted, authoritarian, and violent.[28] Such comments would be unacceptable today if they were directed at Jews, blacks, or other communities, but they are used freely for and about Muslims. As an American media expert pointed out more than twenty years ago, "you can hit an Arab free; they are free enemies, free villains—where you couldn't do it to a Jew or you can't do it to a black anymore."[29] In January 2004 a European journalist wrote that "Arabs are threatening our civilian populations with chemical and biological weapons. They are promising to let suicide bombers loose in Western and American cities. They are trying to terrorize us, disrupt our lives."[30] The irony is that the journalist who wrote these words believed that Iran was an Arab country.

Considering its current forms, Islamophobia has become a form of racism because it targets a group of people and incites hatred against them on the basis of their religious beliefs, cultural traditions, and ethics backgrounds. With the rise of hatred and discrimination against Muslims, racism has come to combine not only race but also ethnicity, language, culture, and religion all at the same time.[31] In this sense, Islamophobia is not racially blind. The old racism based on biological inferiority resurfaces as ethnic, cultural, and religious racism. In the case of Islam, words such as militant, uncivilized, oppressive, barbaric, authoritarian, promiscuous, and violent are used to depict the religious beliefs *and* the cultural practices of Muslims. "Racially inferior" has gradually been replaced by "religiously inferior."[32] In this sense, it is impossible to separate Islamophobia from the ethnic and racial hatred of Arabs, Asians, and blacks.[33]

The definition of racism given by the Council of Europe's European Commission against Racism and Intolerance (ECRI) confirms that Muslims are discriminated against on the basis of all the elements of racism combined. According to ECRI's General Policy Recommendation no. 7 of December 2002, "racism" means "the belief that a ground such as 'race,' colour, language, religion, nationality or national or ethnic origin justifies contempt for a person or group of persons, or the notion of superiority of a person or a group of persons." The same document defines "direct racial discrimination" as "any differential treatment based on a ground such as race, colour, language, religion, nationality or national or ethnic origin, which has no objective and reasonable justification."[34]

At the cultural and intellectual level, Eurocentrism continues to be a problem that hurts not only non-Western societies but also Westerners themselves. A unipolar world leads to the economic, political, intellectual, or artistic marginalization of the vast majority of world populations. It strips people of a sense of agency and empowerment. Much of the current sentiment of dispossession and frustration we see in non-Western societies is the result of the systematic disenfranchisement of Muslims and other non-Westerners.

A unipolar and Eurocentric model of cultural and civilizational order no longer provides a sense of security and participation for all citizens of the world. A multipolar and multicentered world has to arise to undo the misdeeds of both cultural isolationism and Eurocentrism. A world order that is no more than an excuse for the "white man's burden" cannot foster a culture of peace and civilized diversity. The future of the relationship between Islamic and Western societies will largely depend upon our ability to go beyond "us versus them" language. This ability will in turn shape the extent to which the large number of Muslims living in Europe and the United States will be allowed to be part of Western societies as equal citizens.

Multiple Worlds or a World without a Center?

A multipolar and pluralist world is not a world without standards or values. It is a world in which all cultures and societies are seen as equals but are urged to vie for the common good. This is not a wishy-washy multiculturalism that runs the risk of eroding common ground between cultures and creating parallel communities. Rather, it is an act of enriching oneself by recognizing others. It is through such acts that we can foster an ethics and culture of coexistence that will neither tolerate racism, xenophobia, Islamophobia, or hate crimes against Muslims nor condone the demonization of Jews, Christians, and Westerners.

Part of the problem lies in creating a conflict between an absolute self and an absolute other. Much of the language of clash today is based on an oppositional framework in which Islam is set against values such as justice, equality, human rights, and human dignity. Many Muslims make the same mistake in reverse in the name of indigenous oppositions, belated nationalism, or communal uniqueness.[35] Speaking of the self and the other as an opposition, however, does not necessarily lead to an essential conflict. The distance between self and other can be construed as a healthy tension that has utility in expanding one's self-understanding and reaching out to the world beyond the individual.

Clearly, there is a danger in dissolving all of the boundaries between the self and the other: It creates a sense of insecurity and homelessness, which we see everywhere today from the streets of Cairo to Spain. Globalization, while providing new "opportunity spaces," has also deepened this sense of insecurity. It is felt deeply especially in Muslim countries, where the eroding effects of modernization have created a profound sense of mistrust and resentment toward the modern world in general and the West in particular. In short, a radical liberal view of the self only leads to an insecure self, which, in turn, exacerbates the sense of alienation.[36]

Muslims living in the West face similar tensions. In the name of integration, they are asked to embrace assimilation and thus lose their identities. They are expected to become French, German, or Danish as if there were such neat identities that could be applied to all Europeans. Interestingly, attempts at codified definitions of "Frenchness" or "Germanness" have yielded practically no cultural identifiers. A 2002 document by the British Home Office on the "fundamental tenets of British citizenship" defined them as to "respect human rights and freedoms, uphold democratic values, observe laws faithfully and fulfill our duties and obligations." Another report seeking to identify the "common elements of nationhood" came up with the following principles: "a more visible support for anti-discrimination measures, support for women's rights, a universal acceptance of the English language . . . and respect for both religious differences and secular views."[37] A similar attempt in Germany ended up in an almost identical statement wherein "Germanness," which the immigrant communities are expected to internalize, was defined along the same lines of liberal democratic values.[38]

It should be noted that most immigrant communities, Muslim and non-Muslim alike, accept these values as ideals to which both majority and minority communities are supposedly committed. The differences arise when they are used to (re)define and (re)shape the cultural preferences of minority communities. Combined with the deep-rooted culture of mistrust and suspicion, demands for civic integration or outright assimilation result in the further alienation of European Muslims and force them to become subcultures within Europe.[39] Yet, in reality, individuals living in the modern world all have multiple identities and show a remarkable ability to dovetail their shades and layers without falling into an identity crisis. This is true both within the individual self and across different cultural groups.[40]

While the general attitude toward Islam and Muslims in the United States is not colored by long historical memories and deep cultural prejudices as is the case in most of Europe, the current trend is worrisome.[41] The hate campaigns launched in the name of combating groups such as al-Qaeda are laying the ground for policies of fear and intimidation. Terms such as *Islamic terrorism*, *Islamic extremism*, and *Islamo-fascism* are finding their way into the political vocabulary of presidents, top government officials, reporters, commentators, secular ideologues, and religious pundits.)

Perception and Reality

A good example of how perception shapes reality is the coverage of conflicts in Muslim countries. Even though many violent conflicts take place around the world, the ones that get the most media attention are those in the Muslim world. This is partly because most of them are tied to Western interests, but it can also be traced to a deep cultural bias. While millions have been brutally and tragically killed in Africa, Latin America, and Asia in conflicts that are deplorable and must be unequivocally rejected, the general impression is that the bloodiest clashes always happen in Muslim lands. A major media survey conducted in twenty-four countries in 2007 shows that the Western media coverage of political conflicts and communal violence in Muslim-majority countries is more than ten times as much as that of issues such as education, culture, economic development, citizenship, religion, and ethics. The focus on political and militant groups in the Muslim world have "depicted (Muslims) engaged in political, militant and extremist activities. In contrast, Christians and Jews were most often presented in the context of religious activities."[42]

The exclusive selection of political conflicts in the Middle East and the Muslim world leaves ordinary readers in the West with the impression that only conflict happens in Muslim countries. From the point of view of media reporting, conflict is always prioritized over peace and settlement. This choice, shared by almost all media outlets in the world, could be criticized on political and moral grounds. Yet the structural problem is the asymmetry between coverage of conflicts and coverage of "normality" in Muslim countries. The cultural and artistic life of most Muslim countries, for instance, gets very little coverage in major media outlets in Europe and the United States, whereas the same cannot be said for Britain or France. When violence is reported in Britain or France, it is weighed against the coverage of other social, religious, cultural, and artistic events (i.e., events that give a sense of normality and stability). But when the overwhelming majority of news coverage in relation to Muslim countries concentrates on conflict and violence, no sense of quotidian life and normality is detected. A further danger in this perceptual bias is what some scholars call the "securitization of Islam," whereby Islam is approached from an exclusively security point of view and presented as an existential threat to Western civilization.[43]

A study of the coverage of Islamic and Muslim themes in the German media, for instance, reveals that exclusive focus on political issues and violent conflicts in the Middle East constructs an overly political picture of the region. Often such coverage, even if it is correct in its details and shows a reasonable degree of cultural sensitivity, lacks a proper contextualization for the general consumer of news in Germany.[44] The second problem is that media coverage without proper contextualization leads to reductionist and essentialist claims about Muslim culture and religion, often masquerading as expert assessment and in-depth analysis. While other conflicts are covered and analyzed as political conflicts, those that involve Muslims are usually analyzed in connection with the Muslim tradition, beliefs, and practices. Suddenly the analysts become interested in digging deeper to understand the root causes of violent conflicts.

For instance, in the case of the Protestant-Catholic conflict in Northern Ireland, where the conflict is as much political as it is religious, religion is not brought up as an element of political analysis. It is mentioned as one fact among others, and no further meaning is attached to it. In the case of conflicts in the Muslim world, however, the whole argument takes a new turn. Religious, cultural, historical, and even eschatological explanations are put forward to explain how and why Muslim culture produces violent, irrational, backward, and suicidal acts. In Britain, for instance, the British Muslim youth who carried out the London bombing are defined as "home-grown terrorists," whereas no such appellation has been used for "Northern Irish–born individuals participating in terrorist activities both in the province and in the mainland."[45]

[And the reverse never happens. None of the so-called Middle East experts or Islam analysts mention the positive qualities of Muslim culture to explain the things that go right instead of wrong. A good example is the coverage of Iranian-born Anousheh Ansari's space travel. On September 18, 2006, Ansari's became the first Muslim woman to travel into space, an event that received modest coverage in the media. Yet there was virtually no discussion or analysis of Ansari's culture, religion, or ethnicity as factors that may have propelled her to take this extraordinary trip and make the headlines worldwide. The situation was no different when Bangladeshi banker Muhammad Yunis was awarded the Nobel Peace Prize for his ambitious and extremely successful project of giving small loans to help poor people. Like Ansari and countless other Muslim figures who have had their success stories, Yunis is from the Muslim world and must have some connection with the cultural and religious history of the society in which he grew up. Yet again, no "expert view" was directed upon his accomplishment as a Muslim banker. It seems that, when it comes to Muslims, everything bad happens for a religious reason, and everything good happens for other reasons.]

The cultural disconnect that underlies these perceptions here is clear: While the general Western audience is informed about their cultural and religious landscape, they lack a minimum of knowledge to contextualize the news about Islam and Muslims. Bombarded with negative depictions of the Muslim world on a daily basis, Westerners cannot differentiate between what is normative and mainstream Islam and what is a diversion. These same people can distinguish between abortion clinics bombers, Timothy McVeigh, and David Koresh on the one hand and what many Christians would consider to be mainstream Christianity. There is little need to explain the difference between violence committed in the name of Judaism and Christianity and the essential teachings of these religions. People do not link terrorism to these religions because, regardless of their views, they know enough about them. Obviously, this is not the case with Islam.

A troubling result of this ignorance is the treatment of Islamophobia as a nonissue by intellectuals, public figures, and policymakers. Insulting, intimidating, and threatening Muslim individuals and communities and in some cases committing violence against them is presented as a reaction to what is described as the existential threat of Islamic extremism and terrorism. Such justifications give the impression that violent acts perpetrated against Muslims have a reason and thus can be excused. Islamophobia is used to construct, justify, and sustain racist and exclusivist political discourses to the extent that the motto "Islamophobic and proud of it" becomes an ideological mark. Islam is presented as an enemy and as an "other" to construct purist and exclusivist national identities,[46] as well as to justify religious exclusivism.[47]

In conclusion, I refer to two consequences of Islamophobia that concern both Muslim-West relations and the larger debate about multiculturalism. First of all, Islamophobic acts prevent Muslims from fully participating in the political, social, cultural, and economic life of the societies in which they live. While Muslim communities themselves share the blame for failing to claim their agency, Islamophobia feeds a constant sense of victimization and marginalization among second- and third-generation Muslims. It makes them feel foreign, distant, and unwelcome. It creates parallel societies both conceptually and physically, whereby the civic cohesion of different ethnic and religious communities within the society becomes increasingly difficult to achieve.

Second, the constant presence of pressure and intimidation bars Muslims themselves from self-criticism. Confronted with frontal attacks driven by racist and Islamophobic attitudes, Muslims of various religious and political bends shy away from openly criticizing fellow Muslims and end up defending some of the most extreme and illogical ideas and actions, which would under normal circumstances be rejected as contrary to an Islamic ethos. The fear is that they will be betraying their Muslim brothers and sisters in the midst of a war launched against them. Yusuf al-Qaradawi, one of the most influential religious figures in the Muslim world, is reported to have avoided addressing the problem of Muslim extremism "for fear that what I write, especially these days, could be misinterpreted or even deliberately explained to serve purposes contrary to my intentions."[48] Confronted with guilt by association and communal stigmatization, even the most conscientious and analytical members of the Muslim community take refuge in the kind of group solidarity that makes self-criticism look like a self-defeating strategy.

I have argued that the current debate over multiculturalism is inextricably linked with a parallel debate over Islam and Muslims. The limits and nature of the multicultural space of modern societies are constantly negotiated through a vast network of social and political agencies. The physical and conceptual lines between Western societies and Muslim communities are blurred by a variety of multilayered facts and multiple interactions. This, however, does not prove that identity claims are jettisoned or abnegated. Rather, they are shaped and transformed in ways that defy claims to singularity and particularity. As the shared spaces of identity and agency between Islamic and Western societies become more and more intertwined, they give rise to what Nilufer Gole calls "interpenetrations," a process that transforms all of the actors involved.[49] A healthier debate on multiculturalism and countering Islamophobia will be possible only when we carefully understand and acknowledge the extent and consequences of this process of interpenetration.

NOTES

1. Mustapha Cherif, *Islam and the West: A Conversation with Jacques Derrida* (Chicago: University of Chicago Press, 2008), 38.

2. Charles Taylor, "The Collapse of Tolerance," *Guardian* (Sept. 17, 2007), http://www.guardian.co.uk/commentisfree/2007/sep/17/thecollapseoftolerance.

3. Cf. Bowen, *Why the French Don't Like Headscarves*.

4. Cf. Valerie Amiraux, "The Headscarf Question: What Is Really the Issue?" in *European Islam: Challenges for Society and Public Policy* (Brussels: Center for European Policy Studies, 2007), 124–43.

5. Evan Roberts, "U.N. rights chief sees bigotry in Europe on Islam," Reuters, Sept. 17, 2007, http://www.reuters.com/article/worldNews/idUSL1789786020070917.

6. *Islam and the West: Annual Report on the State of Dialogue 2008* (Geneva: World Economic Forum, 2008), 21. http://www.weforum.org/pdf/C100/Islam_West.pdf

7. According to the Gallup World Poll, "Muslims around the world say that the one thing the West can do to improve relations with their societies is to moderate their views towards Muslims and respect Islam." Quoted in John Esposito and Dalia Mogahed, *Who Speaks for Islam: What a Billion Muslims Really Think* (New York: Gallup Press, 2007), 61. A prominent Muslim scholar concurs: "One of the most important values that can solve the world's problems is that of respecting diversity,

indeed loving it—regarding it as a source of enrichment and beauty, as an essential element of the human experience." Abdallah bin Bayyah, "Shared Values" in *The State We Are In: Identity, Terror, and the Law of Jihad*, ed. Aftab Ahmad Malik (Bristol, UK: Amal, 2006).

8. For a background analysis, see my "Roots of Misconception."

9. P. Berger, B. Berger, and H. Kellner, *The Homeless Mind* (New York: Vintage, 1974), 213.

10. Harvey Cox, *Religion in the Secular City: Towards a Postmodern Theology* (New York: Simon and Schuster, 1985).

11. For more on this, see José Casanova, *Public Religions in the Modern World* (Chicago: University of Chicago Press, 1994); and Talal Asad, *Formations of the Secular: Christianity, Islam, Modernity* (Stanford: Stanford University Press, 2003).

12. Anne Philips, *Multiculturalism without Culture* (Princeton, NJ: Princeton University Press, 2007), 9.

13. For a defense of this position, see Tariq Modood, *Multiculturalism* (Cambridge, UK: Polity, 2007).

14. Roy Jenkins, *Essays and Speeches* (London: Collins, 1970), 267; quoted in Anne Philips, *Multiculturalism without Culture*, 4.

15. Quoted in Christian Joppke, "The Retreat of Multiculturalism in the Liberal State: Theory and Policy," *British Journal of Sociology* 55, no. 2 (2004): 251.

16. Charles Taylor, "The Politics of Recognition," in *Multiculturalism and the Politics of Recognition*, ed. Amy Gutmann (Princeton, NJ: Princeton University Press, 1992).

17. The contemporary Muslim world has yet to recover the universal discourse of the traditional Islamic civilization. Muslim modernists and apologetics usually define the "universal" as that which has been produced in the Western intellectual tradition since the Enlightenment. This very narrow definition of the universal clearly betrays a politics of identity rather than critical analysis. For a point of view that goes beyond European universalism, see Seyyed Hossein Nasr's two recent works, *The Heart of Islam: Enduring Values for Humanity* (New York: HarperCollins, 2002) and *The Garden of Truth: The Vision and Promise of Sufism, Islam's Mystical Tradition* (New York: HarperOne, 2007).

18. Abdallah bin Bayyah, "Shared Values," 48.

19. Even the initiative *A Common Word*, to which the pope has responded positively, and the two visits he paid to Turkey in 2006 and Jordan in 2009 have not been able to alleviate the concerns of many about the pope's attitude toward Islam and Muslims. For Pope Benedict's speech at the Common Word meeting at the Vatican in November 2008 and other texts, see http://www.acommonword.com.

20. David Gow and Ewen MacAskill, "Turkish accession could spell end of EU, says commissioner," *Guardian* (Sept. 8, 2004). http://www.guardian.co.uk/world/2004/sep/08/turkey.eu

21. For a survey of socioeconomic discrimination against Muslims in Europe, see Tufyal Choudhury, "Muslims and Discrimination," in *European Islam: Challenges for Society and Public Policy*, ed. Samir Amghar, Amel Boubekeur, and Michael Emerson, 77–106 (Brussels: Center for European Policy Studies, 2007).

22. European Union Monitoring Center on Racism and Xenophobia, *Muslims in the European Union*, 8, 46. http://fra.europa.eu/fraWebsite/attachments/Manifestations_EN.pdf

23. International Helsinki Federation, *Intolerance and Discrimination against Muslims in the EU*, 78.

24. C. Joppe, "Beyond National Models: Civic Intergation Policies for Immigratns in Western Europe," *Western European Politics* 30, no. 1 (2007):15.

25. See his *Islam, Christianity, and Pluralism*, Zaki Badawi Memorial Lecture Series, Lambeth Palace and the Association of Muslim Social Scientists (AMSS) London, UK, 2007), 7. Also available in "Islam, Christianity and Pluralism" in *Islam & Christian-Muslim Relations* 19, issue 3 (Jul 2008): 342.

26. The question of multiple loyalties has been addressed by a number of Muslim scholars. For an engaging discussion, see Tariq Ramadan, *Western Muslims and the Future of Islam* (New York: Oxford University Press, 2004). For a discussion of British Muslims, see *British Muslims: Loyalty and Belonging*, ed. Mohammad Siddique Seddon, Dilwar Hussain, and Nadeem Malik (Leicester, UK: Islamic Foundation, 2003).

27. A good example of how racial and religious considerations get mixed up is Merryl Wyn Davies, a Muslim convert in Wales, UK. Every time she is interviewed by a journalist, she is asked the following question: "How does a nice, sensible Welsh girl like you end up joining a religion of militant fundamentalists who suppress women?" Quoted in Muir and Smith, *Islamophobia*, 65.

28. Cf. Kumar, "Islam and Islamophobia."

29. Sam Keen, *Faces of the Enemy: Reflections of the Hostile Imagination* (San Francisco: Harper and Row, 1986), 29, 30; quoted in Shaheen, *Arab and Muslim Stereotyping*, 12.

30. Quoted in Muir and Smith, *Islamophobia*, 8.

31. As Tahir Abbas points out, "the British discourse on racialized minorities has been transformed from 'colour' in the 1950s and 1960s to 'race' in the 1960s, 1970s, and 1980s; to 'ethnicity' in the 1990s and to 'religion' in the present climate." Abbas, "After 9/11."

32. Cf. Grosfoguel and Mielants, "Long-Durée Entanglement."

33. For anti-Arab racism in the United States, see Salaita, *Anti-Arab Racism in the United States*.

34. *International Action against Racism, Xenophobia, Anti-Semitism and Intolerance in the OSCE Region* (OSCE and ODIHR, 2004).

35. For a survey of "anti-Westernism" as an oppositional identity in the Japanese and Ottoman cases, see Cemil Aydin, *The Politics of Anti-Westernism in Asia: Visions of World Order in Pan-Islamic and Pan-Asian Thought* (New York: Columbia University Press, 2007).

36. Rowan Williams argues against the "all is the same" kind of religious pluralism in the case of Islam and Christianity because it not only ignores the obvious theological differences between them but also underestimates "their strong sense of the historical particularity of the origins of their faith and of the universal missionary imperative which their practice embodies." For his penetrating analysis, see his *Islam, Christianity, and Pluralism*.

37. Quoted in Joppke, "Retreat of Multiculturalism," 253.

38. For the experience of Turkish Muslims in Europe, see the collection of essays in Küçükcan and Güngör, eds., *Turks in Europe*.

39. There are few comprehensive case studies of Muslim communities living in European countries and their experiences of cultural encounter. A good survey of Turkish Muslims in Holland is Talip Küçükcan and Veyis Güngör, *EuroTurks and Turkey-EU Relations: The Dutch Case* (Amsterdam: Turkevi Research Center, 2006). For Muslims in Britain, see Philip Lewis, *Islamic Britain: Religion, Politics, and Identity among British Muslims* (London: Tauris, 2002), and Tahir Abbas, ed., *Muslim Britain: Communities under Pressure* (London: Zed, 2004).

40. To quote bin Bayyah again, "a person can be of Asian origin, Muslim by faith, and British by nationality and upbringing—all at the same time." Bin Bayyah, "Shared Values," 50.

41. The Gallup survey released on May 7, 2009, shows that the United States and Canada have more religious cohesion and integration than Europe. See http://www.gallup.com/poll/118273/Canada-Show-Interfaith-Cohesion-Europe.aspx.

42. *Islam and the West: Annual Report on the State of Dialogue 2008*, 104.

43. Cf. Jocelyne Cesari, "The Securitization of Islam in Europe," *Challenge Research Paper* 15 (April 2009): 1-15. http://www.euro-islam.info/ei/wp-content/uploads/pdfs/the_securitisation_of_islam_in_europe.pdf

44. For the German case, see Hafez, "Images of Islam and the West in German Media."

45. Allen, "Islamophobia and Its Consequences," 153.

46. The British National Party (BNP) is a good example of how the fear of Islam is used to launch a racist political campaign. The BNP started its "Islam out of Britain" campaign in 2001 and widely distributed a leaflet titled "The truth about I.S.L.A.M." In the leaflet, "I.S.L.A.M." was used as an acronym for "Intolerance, Slaughter, Looting, Arson, and Molestation of Women." For an analysis of the BNP's campaign and the state of Islamophobia in 9/11 Britain, see Allen, "Justifying Islamophobia."

47. Of all the anti-Islamic Christian polemics in recent years, one of the most fascinating episodes was Orlando's "Holy Land Experience" theme park. Founded by a Protestant ministry that seeks to convert world Jewry to Christianity, the Holy Land Experience Park introduced a number of extremely anti-Islamic themes after 9/11 and espoused an open confrontation and war between American (Protestant) Christians, Jews, and Muslims. For an analysis, see Stockdale, "'Citizens of Heaven' versus 'The Islamic Peril'."

48. Quoted in Yusuf al-Qaradawi, *Islamic Awakening: Between Rejection and Extremism* (Herndon, VA: International Institute of Islamic Thought, 2006), xi.

49. Nilufer Gole, *Interpénétrations: L'Islam et l'Europe* (Paris: Galaade Éditions, 2005).

2

Islamophobia in the West: A Comparison between Europe and the United States

Jocelyne Cesari

Although the term *Islamophobia* first appeared in a 1922 essay by Orientalist Étienne Dinet,[1] it was only in the 1990s that it became common parlance in defining the discrimination Muslims faced in Western Europe. From the Crusades to colonialism, multiple confrontations between the Muslim world and Europe mark the history of negative perceptions of Islam.[2] However, Islamophobia is a modern and secular anti-Islamic discourse and practice appearing in the public sphere with the integration of Muslim immigrant communities and intensifying after 9/11. The term has been increasingly used in political circles, the media, and even Muslim organizations, especially since the 1997 Runnymede Report.[3] However, academics are still debating the legitimacy of the term[4] and questioning how it differs from other terms such as *racism, anti-Islamism, anti-Muslimness,* and *anti-Semitism.*

The term *Islamophobia* is contested because it is often imprecisely applied to very diverse phenomena, ranging from xenophobia to antiterrorism. It groups together all kinds of different forms of discourse, speech, and acts by suggesting that they all emanate from an identical ideological core, which is an irrational fear (a phobia) of Islam.

However, the term is used with increasing frequency in the media and political arenas and sometimes in academic circles. The European Monitoring Centre on Xenophobia and Racism (EUMC) report documenting the backlash against Muslims in Europe after

September 11 was titled "Summary Report on Islamophobia in the EU after 11 September 2001." In France it has been used in several important academic studies although it is still rejected by the Consultative Commission on Human Rights (France Report). In *Le Monde*, a premier news journal, the term has appeared in more than 30 articles in the past year and more than 150 in the past ten. However, a search of *Der Spiegel*, a premier news journal in Germany, shows uses in only 6 articles in the past year. Another term in more regular usage seems to be "Islamfeindlichkeit," which expresses the anti-Muslim sentiment but does not imply the same fear. The term and even the idea have only recently appeared in academic work, where previously the study had been about Muslim communities rather than German attitudes toward them (Germany Report).

The use of the word is very common in the United Kingdom (UK Report), where the aforementioned Runnymede Report of 1997 helped launch its popularity. An examination of the archives of *The Guardian* reveals that the term has been used hundreds of times within the last year, often by prominent politicians and commentators. Notable also is the existence of the Forum Against Islamophobia and Racism (FAIR), created by Muslim activists. By contrast, in the United States, the term appears only twenty-six times in the *New York Times*, and except for editorials by Muslim activists, always refers to the situation in Europe. However, it has been regularly used by the Council on American Islamic Relations (CAIR). A search through other media reveals that the term is appearing more frequently, perhaps partly because of its use by activist groups.

Several recent studies on European Muslims deal with Islamophobia. The EUMC reports on discrimination against Muslim populations in Europe have been the first to generalize the term and thus give it some credibility at the European level.[5] The EUMC reports examine the European reaction to Muslim minorities in their own countries, identifying attacks against Muslims, anti-Islamic rhetoric, and the efficacy of the government in the European countries in minimizing community tensions. Both EUMC reports note a marked rise in anti-Islamic attitudes and attacks in European countries for a short period of time after the events of 9/11 and 7/7. However, both reports state that the physical acts of aggression against Muslims were disparate and isolated incidents and that hostile attitudes expounded in certain sections of the media and the political spectrum were counterbalanced by the concerted efforts of European governments to make sharp distinctions between those who committed the acts of terrorism and the general populace. The report on the impact of the July 7, 2005, bombings lauds the UK's political and community leaders for their immediate reassurances to the Muslim community; the government's initiatives of engaging with the Muslim community by setting up Muslim consultation groups; and efforts by the police to implement reporting and communication mechanisms in order to de-escalate potential community tension. However, the EUMC uses data gathered by national agencies that have different methods of quantifying discrimination and whose home countries often have diverse policies for recognizing ethnic minorities. In addition to these methodological flaws, the EUMC reports approach the term *Islamophobia* uncritically.

In the United States, the report of the Congressional Research Service (CRS) on Muslims in Europe describes the impact of different integration policies on Muslim populations after 9/11 and assesses their influence on extremism among Muslims. The report looks at the challenges European countries face in integrating their Muslim population due to their lack of a common legal or political framework on immigration, security, and integration. The authors state that British, French, German, and Spanish integration strategies have failed to create a sense of loyalty to the national identity among their Muslim subjects and that this, coupled with the high levels of socioeconomic disadvantages faced by the Muslim communities relative to the indigenous population in most European countries, have been exploited by terrorist elements. The report notes that European countries are reassessing their relationship with the Muslim communities in light of the threat posed by "homegrown" terrorists through an intensification of dialogue with moderate elements in Muslim communities, new antidiscrimination legislation, introduction of citizenship markers, and tighter immigration and security policies.

These reports exemplify two separate trends in the field: The CRS analyzes different state policies on the integration of Muslim populations, while the EUMC records levels of discrimination encountered by European Muslims. None of the aforementioned reports combines these approaches (analysis of state policies and analysis of discrimination) to develop a comprehensive framework for understanding post-9/11 Muslim populations.

In a unique effort to understand the status of Muslims in Europe, the methodology we used for the report on Islamophobia has combined both methods of analysis. I have examined policies undertaken since 9/11 in fields such as immigration, security, and religion, and here I simultaneously assess the influence of these policies on Muslims. I also address the structural causes of discrimination, such as the socioeconomic status of Muslim populations and the legal status of racial and ethnic minorities. In doing so, I differentiate my approach from that of the dominant view, which defines Islamophobia solely in terms of acts or speeches that explicitly target Muslims.

It is important to shed light on the several levels of discrimination that Muslims encounter. This phenomenon cannot simply be subsumed under the term *Islamophobia*. Indeed, the term can be misleading, as it presupposes the preeminence of religious discrimination when other forms of discrimination (such as racial or class) may be more relevant. I therefore intend to use the term *Islamophobia* as a starting point for analyzing the different dimensions that define the political situation of Muslim minorities in Europe and the United States. I do not to take the term for granted by assigning it only one meaning, such as anti-Islamic discourse.

It is particularly difficult to identify Islamophobia because of two major features of Muslims in Europe that stand in sharp contrast to the features of Muslims in the United States:

- European Muslims are mostly immigrants.
- European Muslims are socioeconomically marginalized.

For these reasons, Islamophobia overlaps with other forms of discrimination, such as xenophobia, anti-immigration policies, political discourses, and rejection of cultural differences. However, European and American Muslims share the same international situation with regard to events that may trigger Islamophobia.

Most Muslims in Europe are Immigrants or Have an Immigrant Background

According to the best estimates, Muslims currently constitute approximately 5 percent of the European Union's 425 million inhabitants. There are about 4.5 million Muslims in France, followed by Germany's 3 million, 1.6 million in the United Kingdom, and more than half a million in Italy and the Netherlands. Although other nations have populations of less than 500,000, these can be substantial minorities in small countries such as Austria, Sweden, and Belgium. Approximately half are foreign born. In general, the population is younger and more fertile than the domestic populations.[6]

In France and the United Kingdom, Muslim populations began arriving in the middle of the 20th century largely from former colonies, leading to a predominately North African ethnicity in France and a South Asian one in the United Kingdom. In Germany, the community began with an influx of "guest workers" during the postwar economic boom, largely from Turkey. In the Netherlands, immigration of guest workers led to a largely Moroccan and Turkish population. Along with the other nations in the European Union, all of these groups have been substantially augmented by continued immigration during the last twenty years. Although immigrants have come from all over the world, those countries with existing populations tend to attract more of the same ethnic background. Among current European Union member states, only Greece has a significant indigenous population of Muslims, who reside primarily in Thrace. Greece also has a substantial population of non-permanent residents from Albania, most of whom are nominally Muslim but do not practice regularly. This makes it difficult to estimate the total number.

This situation, in which the categories "immigrant" and "Muslim" overlap, is particular to Western Europe, as a comparison with the United States indicates. In 2006 particularly, immigration became an important political issue in America. At the margins of the discourse, the issue can be connected to terrorism. The long, unprotected border with Mexico can be seen as pushing the effective U.S. boundary to Mexican authorities, with the implication that it would be easier for suspect individuals to gain access. However, this is not the central issue in the immigration debate, which instead centers on economic and social concerns such as wages, assimilation, and language. In the United States, the prototypical immigrant is a low-skilled Mexican or Central American worker rather than a conservative Muslim. Of the 15.5 million legal immigrants who entered the United States between 1989 and 2004, only 1.2 million were from predominantly Muslim countries. The number of new arrivals dropped sharply, from more than 100,000 per year prior to 2002 to approximately 60,000 in 2003, but in 2004 this number recovered somewhat by increasing to 90,000.[7] Thus, Islam and terrorism are at best marginal components of the issue of immigration in the United States.

Muslims as Part of the European Underclass

Because European Muslims tend to be socioeconomically marginalized, much of the discrimination against them may be due to their class situation rather than their religion. Religion and discrimination may also interact in the formation of "class"—for example, in the formation of underprivileged classes of British Asian Muslims or French North African Muslims.[8]

The EUMC completes regular summaries of its findings in this sphere. In 2003 the EUMC released a report on employment. In the United Kingdom, the unemployment rates of Pakistanis and Bangladeshis was greater than 20 percent, relative to only 6 percent in the broader population. Immigrants in general had a 13 percent unemployment rate. In Germany, the largest Muslim group of Turks had unemployment rates of 21 percent, contrasted with only 8 percent among others in Germany. Nationality statistics were unavailable for France, but immigrants there had a 22 percent unemployment rate, compared to 13 percent for the country as a whole. Immigrant unemployment rates tend to be at least twice that of natives. In the Netherlands, non-Western immigrants had an unemployment rate of 9 percent; Western immigrants, 4 percent; and native Dutch, 3 percent. In Spain, the numbers were closer to equal, while in Italy migrants had only a 7 percent unemployment rate compared to 11 percent in the broader population.

In France, Spain, Germany, and the Netherlands, OECD data show that individuals from majority Muslim countries have substantially poorer educational outcomes, while they are more equivalent in Italy and the United Kingdom. In Germany, about 70 percent of those from majority Muslim countries have a secondary education or less, while this is true for only about 25 percent of the rest of the population. Only 5 percent have advanced degrees, compared to 19 percent of the broader population. In France, 56 percent of those from majority Muslim countries have a secondary education or less, compared to 46 percent in the broader population. Higher degrees are more equally distributed in France. In Spain, 76 percent have less than a secondary education, compared to 63 percent for others, while only 11 percent have advanced degrees, relative to 20 percent nationwide. The Netherlands' numbers are divergent as well, with 50 percent of those of Muslim ancestry having less than a secondary education, with the balance going the other way in advanced degrees—31 percent to 20 percent. In Italy, the numbers are roughly equal among the wider population. In the United Kingdom, the statistics are also relatively equal, although this conceals the difficulties of those of Pakistani and Bangladeshi heritage.

The EUMC 2006 report on housing shows that, although some improvements have occurred, housing is overall much poorer for immigrants, and they often face discrimination and sometimes even exclusionary violence. In general, rigorous measures of these trends are not available due to reporting inadequacies in the countries mentioned. In Germany, the report states that minorities clearly live in spatially segregated areas with poorer-quality housing. In Spain, the problem has been recognized by the government, which is taking action to increase public support for housing. France is in a similar situation, although a particular difficulty there is the declining conditions of the available public housing. In Italy, responsibility for housing laws is distributed at various levels, and the resulting patchwork is difficult to analyze; generally, however, adequate housing is more difficult for immigrants to obtain. In the Netherlands, although reports of exclusionary violence have surfaced, the best evidence available suggests that state policy on housing has worked fairly well in decreasing the significance of discrimination. The EUMC states that the United Kingdom has dealt with the housing problem particularly well relative to other European states in that it has provided better support for public housing and implemented more effective antidiscrimination initiatives. However, the largest groups of Muslims come from Pakistan and Bangladesh, and statistics show that they live in much poorer conditions than the average Briton. More than two-thirds live in low-income households.[9] Nearly a quarter live in overcrowded houses, while only 2 percent of white Britons do.[10]

The situation in Europe contrasts sharply with that in the United States, where Muslims tend to have more education and a higher income than the non-Muslim population. Because the U.S. Census does not ask about religion and Muslims are too small a proportion of the population to be reliably measured in general national surveys, exact information on their status is not easy to obtain. Special surveys done by Zogby International Polling in 2001 and 2004 provide the best demographic data. These surveys show that more than half of American Muslims earn at least $50,000 per year relative to a nationwide average of $43,000. Some of this difference may be due to the greater likelihood that Muslims live in urban areas with higher incomes and standards of living, but it is clear that they are doing at least as well as non-Muslims in the labor market. Fifty-eight percent of American Muslims are college graduates, while according to the Census Bureau that number was only 27 percent among the population as a whole.[11]

International Constraints that Trigger Islamophobia

Muslim integration in Europe is occurring under the international constraint of the battle against Islamist terrorism. Over the last several years, as the states under review have responded to the threat of terrorism, most have updated and strengthened their security and antiterrorism laws while placing further restrictions on immigration. It often appears as if immigration and internal and external security policies are conflated. Terrorism can be characterized as neither entirely foreign nor entirely domestic. If international terrorists based in foreign countries are recruiting among the disaffected populations of Europe, this becomes both an internal and an external security problem simultaneously. There is little in the way of systematic evidence, but suggestive clues exist. The plots of September 11 were at least partially planned in Hamburg, and among the individuals imprisoned by the United States in Guantanamo Bay are at least twenty Europeans.[12] Since 9/11, the nations of the EU have arrested more than twenty times the number of terrorist suspects as the United States.[13] Because of this threat, states can view domestic Muslims as foreign enemies, a classification that implies a much lower level of legal and social rights and privileges than those to which ordinary citizens are entitled.

Although France did not substantially change its antiterrorism framework after September 11, the Law on Everyday Security was passed on November 15, 2001. This measure expanded police powers by allowing stops and searches of vehicles in the context of terrorism investigations, as well as searches of unoccupied premises at night with a warrant but without notification, and undertaking much more extensive monitoring and recording of electronic transactions. A new immigration law in 2003 made it substantially easier to deport individuals who "have committed acts justifying a criminal trial" or whose behavior "threatens public order," along with increased penalties for illegal immigration, more temporary detention centers, and new limits on family reunification.

Germany developed new policies on civil liberties, immigrant rights, the freedom of churches, and law enforcement powers. These new policies were passed in two large packages, the first on September 19, 2001, and the second on January 1, 2002. It thus became possible to ban religious groups for threatening the democratic order, and the idea of a threatening group was redefined to take more account of foreign concerns. Financial records, electronic and postal communications, and most forms of transportation records became available to the police. Authorities were allowed to use a previously extremely controversial data-mining search method called the "grid search." The new laws also allowed a certain amount of eavesdropping and wiretapping in the course of an investigation. Police can now track the location and numbers of cellular phones. Military intelligence has received substantially more domestic powers, with easier searches, access to communication records, and the legal ability to communicate its findings to other law enforcement agencies. Since September 11, Germany has substantially tightened its asylum-granting procedures and established the legal principle that foreigners who are considered a threat to German democracy and security can be barred from entry and deported.

On November 13, 2001, the United Kingdom passed the Anti-terrorism, Crime, and Security Act, which allows the indefinite detention of foreign nationals who are not considered safe enough to deport to their country of origin, the freezing and confiscation of funds associated with terrorist or other prohibited groups, and requires individuals not to associate with suspected terrorists or forbidden organizations and to report any suspicious activities or individuals to the police. Individuals can be detained and interrogated in anticipation of violence rather than in response to the action. After the bombings on the London subway on July 7, 2005, the government introduced an updated Prevention of Terrorism Act (UK Report), which bans several groups, criminalizes the condoning of terrorism, allows for the detention of terrorism suspects for up to ninety days without charges, and proposes the possibility of stripping naturalized Britons accused of terrorism of their citizenship. A study by the Institute of Race Relations suggests that the antiterrorism statutes have been used overwhelmingly against Muslim defendants.[14] Few arrests have led to convictions, and the statutes have been used to cover routine criminal acts and immigration violations. Of the cases reviewed, one in eight involved a Muslim arrested for terrorism violations; the suspects were turned over to the immigration authorities without any prosecution for the alleged initial offenses. Several Muslims have been arrested for crimes such as credit card fraud due to the expanded police powers provided by the antiterrorism statutes.

Despite the attacks on the Madrid railway system in 2004, Spain made no significant changes to its security and antiterrorism laws. These had been well codified over the years as the Spanish government faced terrorism at the hands of Basque separatists. However, preventive detention of alleged conspirators increased dramatically. Most of these individuals are held for some time and later released due to lack of evidence (Spain Report). Immigration laws have undergone several changes. Over the years in which the conservative government was in power, restrictions on the immigration of foreigners who were considered undesirable were tightened, and the ability of foreign nationals to exercise basic rights such as that of assembly was restricted (Spain Report). However, since the advent of leftist control of the national government, a proposal was adopted in January 2005 to regularize the status of the immigrants in the country. Efforts have been under way to improve social and economic conditions as well (Spain Report).

The Italian government passed what was known as the Pisanu package in 2005 to combat the threat of terrorism. This law expanded police detention powers and loosened the definition of terrorism to include training. The use of the military in emergency situations was legalized, and new record-keeping methods for electronic communications were mandated (Italy Report). Italian immigration law was somewhat unorganized prior to the 2002 passing of the Bossi-Fini law, which tightly regulates the entry and residency of immigrants. In 2003 an amendment created tighter penalties for illegal immigration, mandated the building of more detention centers, and limited family reunification.[15]

The Netherlands has increased its focus on the threat of terrorism, although to date there have been no major legal changes (Netherlands Report). The

increased focus has had two major goals: security and prevention of the radicalization of the domestic populations. The government proposed new antiterrorism laws to make it easier to arrest terrorist suspects and to hold them for
up to two years prior to court dates. It has also responded with new policies on
financial reporting, better intelligence coordination, and a stronger police and
military. The government plans to make laws that will weaken the protections
against searches of mosques and legalize the ability to search outside databases
in order to profile suspects. Although numerous such proposals have been discussed, little legislative action has actually been completed (Netherlands
Report). After much debate, various new immigration policies now emphasize
the assimilation of immigrants to a common set of values rather than focusing
on multiculturalism as in the past. Laws passed in 2001 and 2004 have made
the reuniting of families more difficult by creating age and income restrictions,
and proposals are now under review to facilitate the expulsion of foreigners. In
2001 the Netherlands passed the Aliens Act, which aims at reducing the tremendous flow of asylum seekers that the country had accepted during the
1990s. This policy has been successful, as asylum requests have now dropped
to one-quarter of their previous number (Netherlands Report).

When considering the role of international terrorism in influencing the
situation of Muslims in Europe, it is useful to compare Europe to the United
States. Since the attacks of September 11, 2001, the United States has substantially changed its legal framework for dealing with terrorism and pursued various policies of questionable constitutionality and legality. The Patriot Act
lessened the restrictions on surveillance, allowed various personal records to be
obtained by authorities, reduced the privacy of attorney-client conversation,
and broadened the definition of terrorism to include "material support," a concept that has not been fully defined. Along with these changes in the law, U.S.
citizens have been imprisoned without judicial review, mosques have been
searched for radiation without warrants, phone calls and phone records have
been obtained without court approval, and individuals have been abducted and
sent to secret prisons, as well as to foreign prisons, where they could be interrogated with more violent methods. The severity of these policies compared to
the European response does not seem, however, to have made the situation for
Muslims worse in the United States than in Europe.

Due to this complexity of the situation of Muslims in Europe, it is difficult
and perhaps impossible to untangle the threads of motivation behind them.
Although an anti-immigrant sentiment is clearly growing in Western Europe,
one wonders to what degree this is a result of the fact that so many of the
immigrants are Muslims and whether a different group of immigrants would
have provoked such a strong reaction. It has been theorized that Islam is a

particular threat to European national identities in a way that it is not in the United States, where language difference is considered more problematic to national solidarity.[16]

In general, we can see that, aside from anti-Muslim sentiment, the primary factors driving discrimination in Europe are policies toward ethnic minorities in general, antiterrorism policies, and legal changes in the immigration and naturalization frameworks. This discrimination is expressed in physical abuse; in political, media, and intellectual discourse; and in obstacles to religious practices. Both the public discourse on Islam by politicians, intellectuals, and the news media and the status of Muslims' religious practices are more likely to lead to Islamophobic practices.

Role of Political Leaders and Political Parties

In Europe, the pressures of increasing immigrant populations and the erosion of national boundaries through the transnational force of the European Union have led to a rising incidence of nationalist rhetoric and policies and an essentializing approach to identity. In its more severe forms, this can be classified as xenophobia, a fear and hatred of the foreign. Sometimes, as in Italy, this is represented by claims such as that by Forza Nuova, that Italy is essentially Catholic, which naturally leads to the conclusion that Muslims cannot be good citizens (Italy Report). In Terrassa, Spain, in 1999, after riots between immigrant Maghrebis and local youths led to several injuries, there were two responses. The Socialists proposed better ways of integrating the immigrants to lessen the social pressure, but the center-right Popular Party diagnosed the problem as one of the immigrants' presence rather than of Spanish society's difficulty in coping with them. As these types of incidents pile up, the public mood shifts, and the problems are interpreted as based in Islam (Spain Report).

Anti-immigrant sentiment is common in many countries that face the difficulties of integrating culturally different populations. However, in European countries, this predicament can slide into what can more accurately be termed Islamophobia. Over the years since immigration became an issue in Europe, extreme right-wing parties have found some success in pushing racist and anti-immigrant rhetoric. However, it seems clear that in recent years this has become more anti-Muslim, as the parties have taken advantage of more negative attitudes in the broader population. In the United Kingdom, the British National Party (BNP) attributed the Bradford riots, which could have been presented as a racial issue, to the problems of international terrorism. In a continuing campaign, Chris Allen documents that the BNP enlisted fringe Sikh and Hindu allies in its anti-Muslim campaign, a dramatic shift from the general antiforeign attitudes of years past. Similarly, Le Pen and the National Front in France have played up fears of Muslims linked to fears of terrorism to push themselves into a much more prominent place in French politics. The Lega Nord in Italy has switched its rhetoric to take advantage of anti-Muslim sentiment, deploying slightly modified versions of traditional anti-Semitic devices as weapons against Islam. The German DVO party has increased in strength as well.

This shift in the Far Right and its growing strength inevitably affect the more central public discourse on the issues. In Germany, the use of the term *Leitkultur*, which had been taboo for many years, has come back into regular politics, and its use is accepted by members of the Center Right. In the United Kingdom, former prime minister Margaret Thatcher stated that all Muslims were responsible for terrorism, while the government under Tony Blair made it a criminal offense to condone terrorism in speech either at home or abroad. Many Muslims (and non-Muslims) fear that the label of "terrorist" is being used to criminalize what they consider to be resistance or liberation movements. The definition of terrorism is highly controversial and more often results from political decisions than from objective facts about movements or groups.

Italy's Silvio Berlusconi has made his famous comments about the superiority of Western civilization and the backwardness of Islam. Even in Spain, which has had fewer of these problems, former president of the Catalan Autonomous Government Jordi Pujol stated that "in Catalonia, as in any European country, it is easy to integrate the Polish, Italians, or Germans, but that is difficult to achieve with Arab Muslims, even not being fundamentalists." In France, local politicians have used antimosque campaigns to drum up support. Perhaps the most dramatic change has been in the political culture of the Netherlands, where violence and death threats have become increasingly common in an acrimonious debate (Netherlands Report). Although policy has not yet followed, public debate now incorporates drastic ideas such as the forbidding of Islam, the deportation of second-generation Moroccans, and the banning of gender-segregated mosques (Netherlands Report). The Netherlands is a prime example of the political changes across Europe. It is now increasingly possible to make anti-Muslim and anti-immigrant statements in common politics that would have been entirely inappropriate in previous years.

Two other trends in political discourse are worth mentioning. First, a distinction between radical (bad) Islam and law-abiding (good) Islam has become a common political framing of the difficulties. This has been led particularly by

Nicolas Sarkozy in France and has become widespread in German politics (Germany Report). As Alexandre Caeiro astutely points out in the report on France, this is not a neutral characterization. The fact that Muslims must be named as good or law abiding means that there is an underlying assumption that Muslims are potential troublemakers. The second trend has been the use of Muslim spokespeople to criticize Islam and Muslims. As members of the minority, they can voice criticisms that would seem unduly harsh from the majority population. Probably the most famous of these is Ayaan Hirsi Ali, a Dutch legislator and former Muslim born in Somalia. She is positioned in Dutch discourse as an expert on Islam and thus a plausible critic. She has moved her political alliances from Left to Right as her prominence in this debate has increased. She has declared even more moderate forms of Islam fundamentally incompatible with liberal democracy and called the Prophet Muhammad "a pedophile" and "a perverse tyrant."

Media Coverage of Islam

The country reports display several broad themes in the media coverage of Islam in Europe. Most mainstream media are not openly Islamophobic, as noted in each of the country reports. Some extreme examples of anti-Muslim speech can be found in the reports as well, but these do not seem to typify the media environment. However, events have driven an increase in coverage along with more sensationalist reports that can be portrayed as being about the threat of terrorism. This trend is evident in all of the country reports. In these sensationalist news stories especially, but also across the media overall, there is a tendency to mix foreign and domestic Islam together, thus extending the entire trope of politically radical Islam to immigrant Muslim populations. The European news media also seem to show a particular interest in questions of gender power and politics, often a cultural flashpoint between secularized Europeans and more conservative Muslim immigrant populations.

Quantitative data cited in the UK report show the dramatic increase in stories about Muslims and Islam. A study by Poole identifies different patterns for "British Muslims" and "global Muslims" in the *London Times* and the *Guardian*.[17] As she states, however, "the associative negative behavior [of global Muslims] is seen to evolve out of something inherent in the religion, rendering any Muslim [global or British] a potential terrorist."[18] Similarly, in Germany, the topic of Islam is often an international story, but it is woven into domestic contexts in which international events are seen as probative on the attitudes and behaviors of German Muslims (Germany Report). Italian research in 1999 showed that the news media tend to confuse "Islam as religion" with "the Muslim world," to portray the Muslim world as homogeneous and monolithic, and to simplify and define Islam with largely negative ideas such as the status of women's rights, the rise of fundamentalism, and certain practices that some Europeans would find offensive, such as the sacrifice feast (Italy Report).

The sensationalism of many of the stories means that there are far fewer discussions of the successes of Muslim integration than of the problems. As noted in the report on Germany, honor killings are a large controversial topic despite the fact that they are rare and not representative of the population as a whole. The oppression of females in general and a strong focus on the practice of forced marriages is notable. This means that German viewers may develop a skewed picture of the prevalence of objectionable practices among Muslims. The daily life of Muslim migrant families is generally not portrayed. However, in 2006, a few new TV series placed both Muslim and German characters in realistic situations and have been lauded as a corrective to the media environment (Germany Report).

Islam has become a major media topic in the Netherlands (Netherlands Report). In December 2000, the opera *Aisha and the Women of Medina* was canceled in Rotterdam because of threats by offended Muslims. This led to a debate about the influence of conservative Muslim associations and artistic freedom. Another notable media moment was the May 2001 broadcast of an interview with a Moroccan imam who argued that "homosexuality was a contagious disease," which if spread among Dutch youth would mean the end of the Netherlands, for "if men marry men and women marry women, who will take care of procreation?"[19] Complaints were filed alleging discrimination against gays, but the judge ruled against them, stating that the imam had expressed his religious beliefs.[20] However, this incident was followed by public debates about Islam, freedom of speech and religion, and anti-gay prejudice and violence. A number of more detailed media studies have been done in France and are well documented by Alexandre Caeiro in the French country report. He cites a study by Geisser, which notes that the news media tend to adopt public attitudes and prejudices rather than being informative and typically presents Islam and Muslims in frameworks that suggest danger. A detailed study by Pierre Tévanian shows how the media helped construct the "problem of the hijab" by deciding which voices would be included in the public debate. Social scientists, feminists, teachers, and civil actors who did not oppose the hijab were excluded, helping to construct a narrative in which bearded foreign religious men defended the Muslim headscarf against women who had rejected the hijab, supported by native or emancipated male intellectuals.

Role of Intellectuals

Along with the aforementioned changes in political and media discourse, intellectuals in the various countries have also been part of the difficulties facing
Muslims in Europe. As with the political dialogue, increasingly harsh rhetoric
has become acceptable. Probably the most notable has been the work of the
famous political commentator Oriana Fallaci, whose book *The Rage and the
Pride* attacks Muslims as members of a warlike religion bent on destroying
Italy's Christian society (Italy Report). Her book sold at least 1.5 million copies
and was adopted by various right-wing political movements (Italy Report). In
Spain, political science professor Antonio Elorza argues that Islam is a "religion of combat" that defends terrorism as a "legitimate defense,"[21] a position
shared by Fernando Reinares, a professor of political science and security
studies at King Juan Carlos University in Madrid who opposes Muslim migration since it may allow the entrance of Islamist terrorists.[22] In the Netherlands,
the prominent philosophy professor, Herman Philipse, has frequently stated
that Islam is a violent tribal culture incompatible with modernity and democracy, and ethics professor Paul Cliteur claims that religion causes violence and
that the only solution is secularization (Netherlands Report). In Germany, an
academic area has been developed that focuses on the delegitimation of practices such as the wearing of the hijab and moving them from the area of protected religious expression to that of antistate minority nationalism. In France,
a pamphlet by Caroline Fourest warning of the fascination of the Left with radical Islam won an award from the French Assembly (France Report). As Alexandre Caeiro points out in the report on France, this kind of speech is presented
as courageous truth telling in the face of moral relativists and dangerous
Muslims (France Report).

As in the realm of politics, Muslim academics who repudiate aspects of
Islam have prominent voices in the discussion on Islam in Europe. In
Germany, Bassam Tibi, a professor of international relations at the University
of Göttingen and a Muslim of Syrian origin, launched the term *Euro-Islam* in
1998 to express an understanding of Islam in a "European culture of reference" (Leitkultur).[23] Although Tibi does not himself promote essentialist
visions of Islam, his ideas about the incompatibility of Islam and Europe contribute to an understanding of Islam as foreign and dangerous (Germany
Report). Turkish-born sociologist Necla Kelek has criticized traditional marriage practices in a way that few non-Islamic intellectuals would dare (Germany
Report). In the Netherlands, Iranian refugee and professor of law Afshin Elian
has become an important voice warning of the dangers of Islamist radicalism

due to his status as an "expert witness" (Netherlands Report). Chahdortt Djavann, born in Iran in 1967, wrote two critical books in France, titled *Bas les voiles* (Down with the Veils) and *Que pense Allah de l'Europe?* (What Does Allah Think of Europe?).[24]

Other authors and intellectuals have also made notable contributions. In the Netherlands, the beginning of the questioning of multiculturalism is often attributed to an article in 2000 by a leftist intellectual, Paul Scheffer, who argued that the Netherlands policies were simply not working and cited as evidence the poor socioeconomic condition of immigrants, the growing neighborhood tensions, and the increasing influence of more conservative strains of Islam (Netherlands Report). In France, a literary genre of anti-Muslim literature has become more popular in the last few years. The report on France lists titles such as "Les islamistes sont déjà là: Enquête sur une guerre secrète," "La France malade de l'islamisme: Menaces terroristes sur l'Hexagone," "La tentation du Jihad: Islam radical en France," and "Sentinelle: Contagion islamiste en Europe, le vaccin." The question of Islam has become a central part of the battles over contemporary French identity (France Report).

Religious Practices

Although religious freedom extends across Western Europe, Muslims have encountered difficulties. The country reports indicate that most of the nations studied here have tried to adjust to the practices of Islam. However, they have done so largely within legal and social frameworks formed to accommodate the place of Christianity in European society. These frameworks have not always functioned as well in accommodating Islam. Several areas of difficulty include the conflict over the hijab, which, in Germany and France particularly, has been interpreted as a political rather than a religious practice. Attempts to build mosques often run into resistance from local communities. Particular problems have also arisen with extending the practice of religious instruction in public schools to Muslims. Another significant problem has been the fear of international terrorism, which is associated with conservative and radical imams in domestic contexts.

Policies against the hijab can be couched in general terms, as in the French ban on religious symbols, but are still widely understood by Muslims as a move against Islam—in particular after the approval of a law prohibiting all religious signs in public schools (France Report). The case is different in Germany, where the hijab is allowed for public school students but may be banned for public school teachers. In July 1998 the minister of Baden-Württemberg upheld the decision made by a Stuttgart school not to recruit a Muslim woman as a teacher because she wore a veil. The minister declared that in Islam the hijab was a political symbol of female submission rather than an actual religious requirement.[25] Since then, discussion of the legitimacy of the hijab has grown even more polemical. Based on a 2003 federal constitutional court decision that acknowledged the right of German states to enact such bans, seven German states, in October of that year, declared their support of legislation barring teachers from wearing the headscarf. This declaration occurred at a meeting of sixteen regional ministers of culture, education, and religious affairs in the German city of Darmstadt.[26] In late March 2004 the regional government in Berlin agreed to outlaw the use of all religious symbols by civil servants. On April 1, 2004, the southern state of Baden-Württemberg became the first German state to ban teachers from wearing the hijab. Another five out of sixteen states, including Bavaria and Lower Saxony, are now in the process of enacting similar bans. An obstacle to such bans has recently arisen, however. On July 7, 2006, the state court of Baden-Württemberg rejected the state's headscarf ban as discriminatory against Muslims since veiled Catholic nuns were not forbidden to teach in the state's schools.[27]

Mosques are often opposed on the grounds of pragmatic complaints about traffic and noise, but as the church bells ring across European cities, it seems inevitable that Muslims will see these kinds of complaints as Islamophobic in nature. In Spain, the fear of terrorism has been deployed in campaigns against mosques in a way that it had not been prior to the Islamist international terrorism of recent years. After the attacks of March 2004 in Spain, local community members in Seville organized a slaughter of pigs on the prospective site of a new mosque, and the site itself was also vandalized (Spain Report). Reports of these types of problems have also been noted in the Netherlands, France, and Germany.

In addition, countries that provide religious education in schools have also experienced ongoing problems. Part of this is due to the lack of an official hierarchical clergy that can speak for Muslims as a whole. Accustomed to the organization of European Christian churches, negotiations stall when states cannot find representatives acceptable both to the community and to the state. In Germany, this has been a particular problem and has coincided with controversies over the unwillingness of some Muslim girls to participate in physical education in the public schools (Germany Report). In Spain, the problem was thought to have been solved in the 1990s as the state came to an agreement for the provision of classes by Muslim teachers in the schools. However, in practice, the program has not been implemented across much of the country. There have been accusations of bad faith from Muslim leaders (Spain Report).

Although the Netherlands was formerly seen as a model in this regard, in the wild rhetorical climate of contemporary Dutch politics, extreme ideas such as banning Muslim schools have been proposed (Netherlands Report).

Throughout Europe, the worry about radical preaching in the mosques has led to some impositions on the practice of Islam. For instance, after the attacks of March 2004, the Spanish minister of the interior proposed a law to control the sermons of imams. The proposal was greeted with mixed reviews, denounced by the president of the Islamic Commission of Spain, Mansur Escudero, but welcomed by the Maghrebi union ATIME (Asociación de Trabajadores e Inmigrantes Marroquiés en España) (Spain Report). Both France and the Netherlands have been deporting imams for radical speech. Were this incitement to terrorism, it might be seen as simple law enforcement, but it has been extended to cases where the primary complaint is about attitudes toward women.

Islam and European Secularism

Secularization means that political power is defined by its neutral interactions with religious institutions. We should remember that, with the exception of France, this principle of neutrality is not synonymous with separation of church and state. In fact, it is realized within a range of institutional structures, from a state religion or a concordat to strict separation. It is striking to notice that, throughout Europe, Islam's arrival has reopened a case previously considered closed: the relationship between the state and religions. The multiplicity of situations involving European Islam sheds more light on the specific political and cultural characters of individual European countries than it does on the supposedly monolithic nature of Islam. The secularization profile specific to Europe can be divided into three types: cooperation between the state and the churches, the existence of a state religion, and separation between the state and religion.

The institutional agreements between Islamic organizations and the secular state are only one aspect of the status of religions within Europe and the United States. Beyond the differentiation of the political and religious spheres and the notion of neutrality lies an ideological meaning of secularization, the origins of which lie in the philosophy of the Enlightenment. A common denominator of Western European countries is their tendency to consider that the sacred is misplaced and illegitimate within the civic context. The idea that religion cannot play a role in the general well-being of societies—a mark of the secularized mind—is, in fact, common throughout all of Europe despite differences among the national contracts between states and organized religions. It is important to note here that certain non-Muslim religious groups do question particular tenets of mainstream secularism. Germany, for example, has seen some debate over Christian values in the public sphere, while the display of the crucifix in the classroom has sparked controversy in Italy. However, the main strands of public culture in politics, the news media, and intellectual spheres are highly secularized and tend to ignore religious dimensions and references that are still meaningful to some segments of society.

The consequence of the invalidation of the religious is that the various manifestations of Islam in Europe have become troublesome or even unacceptable. The hijab controversy, the cartoons crisis, and the Rushdie affair shed light on the tension between Islamic claims and European conceptions of secularism.

Demands and requests made by Muslims are immediately perceived as suspect and sometimes even as backward. As such, they provoke highly emotional reactions. The Islamic headscarf worn by women is interpreted as a sign that indicates a rejection of progress and individual female emancipation and provokes the wrath of those groups spearheading the defense of secular ideology: teachers, intellectuals, feminists, civil servants, and so forth. The French law prohibiting religious signs in public schools (March 2004) illustrates this secular ideology at its peak, although there are instances of hijab and niqab all over Europe, as shown in the country reports. The arrival of Islam inside the boundaries of Europe relaunched the dispute over religion in general, as shown by the example of a Norwegian atheist association that sought the right to proclaim for several minutes daily the nonexistence of God in order to compete with Oslo's muezzin.[28]

Throughout Europe, the presence of Islam has called into question the norms of the dominant secular culture. In France, the controversy surrounding the veil has renewed a long-dormant debate over the definition of a secular society. In the United Kingdom, the Rushdie affair sparked a new critique of British public culture. Until then, the British debate over multiculturalism had been dominated by members of the majority population and had treated integration as all but synonymous with minority adjustment to majority standards. As a result of that incident, integration came to be understood as a mutually effective process that would necessarily transform the majority population as well.[29] After the Rushdie affair, British Muslim leaders, for example, expressed their desire to extend British blasphemy laws to protect Islam and all other non-Anglican faiths. In the terms of this request, political integration is understood as a bilateral relationship, in which the host society must negotiate a consensus respectful of the fundamentals of the minority's way of life. For

British Muslims, conflating political adhesion with cultural adhesion constituted an attack on their moral and cultural integrity.

The protests of European Muslims against the cartoons of the Prophet Muhammad also illustrate the tension between the dominant secular public culture and the resistance of a religious minority. Of course, other religious groups (including Western Christians) are also at odds with the idea of a secular public space, but their dissatisfaction tends to receive less media attention than that of Muslims and rarely has the same international dimensions.

Although conflicts with incoming non-European migrants may have been inevitable in any case, cultural differences between immigrants from Muslim countries and often-secularized European populations have tended to make these disputes more dramatic. Interestingly, in contradiction to Huntington's thesis on the political clash between Islam and the West, the conflict does not occur over the nature of the state in Europe, Islamic governance, or the accommodation of Shari'a in the common law. Rather, it concerns lifestyles, gender equality, and the question of homosexuality. In this regard, Inglehart and Norris are right to emphasize that the fight is over Eros and not over politics.[30]

Probably the most explicit case of cultural conflict has taken place in the Netherlands over homosexuality. Prior to his assassination, openly gay politician Pim Fortuyn ran a highly successful political movement against Muslim immigration on the grounds of what he described as Muslims' un-Dutch intolerance. Recently the Netherlands has introduced a video for the socialization of immigrants into Dutch society. The video is clearly intended to press these cultural differences, with its emphases on homosexuality and portrayals of nude sunbathing. Although the Dutch case has been the most prominent, the work of Inglehart and Norris, which analyzes the social attitudes of Western and Islamic societies, shows that the differences are broad in scope. Even controlling for numerous other potentially relevant factors, they find that attitudes in Muslim countries are notably more conservative with regard to abortion, homosexuality, gender equality, and divorce. They attribute this to differences in economic development rather than to core cultural attributes. However, for European societies attempting to integrate Muslim minorities, this difference is likely hard to note, leading to further conflation of cultural conflicts with an anti-Muslim sentiment.

The differences in religiosity and social attitudes between the incoming Muslim immigrants and the European host societies are often substantial. Although data on the social views of Muslims in Europe are hard to come by, the World Values Survey produces polling on useful questions in the countries of origin and the host countries. Seventy-seven percent of Turks, the largest group in Germany, consider themselves to be religious, while the number is only 49 percent in German society as a whole. Moroccans, of whom 95 percent consider themselves religious, are the largest group in the Netherlands, Spain, and Italy, with proportions amounting to 64 percent, 65 percent, and 85 percent, respectively. These numbers are even more pronounced in France, where only 49 percent of the population considers itself religious. Algerians also are more religious at 59 percent.

Substantially more conservative social views are normal in the Muslim countries. One difference can be seen in the number of people who considered a gay person an unacceptable neighbor. In the major countries of Muslim immigration to Europe, 80 percent of Algerians, 92 percent of Moroccans, and 88 percent of Turks felt this was unacceptable, while only 19 percent in France, 23 percent in Germany and Spain, 27 percent in the United Kingdom, 32 percent in Italy, and 8 percent in the Netherlands felt the same. Majorities in France, Germany, and the Netherlands considered homosexuality acceptable, and near majorities in Spain, Italy, and the United Kingdom agreed. In Turkey, Algeria, Morocco, Pakistan, Bangladesh, Albania, and Bosnia, substantial majorities felt that homosexuality was not acceptable. Attitudes toward abortion were slightly more mixed, although Algerians and Moroccans were extreme in their disapproval. Attitudes toward divorce were also mixed, although South Asians were likely to find it unjustifiable. When asked whether males should have more rights to jobs than females, 79 percent of Pakistanis said yes; 77 percent of Algerians, 87 percent of Moroccans, 62 percent of Turks, 56 percent of Albanians, 76 percent of Bangladeshis, and 44 percent of Bosnians agreed. In the European countries under review, these numbers were 29 percent for France, 32 percent for Germany, 39 percent for Italy, 20 for the Netherlands, and 29 percent for Spain.

This conflict between the European secular mind and Muslim religious values highlights a broader challenge. Islam makes it necessary to rethink and to contextualize the principle of equality between cultures, thus bestowing on the principles of tolerance and pluralism a whole other resonance. The multicultural policies that predominate in European societies do not really allow for equality and pluralism to be rethought along the lines of an incorporation of the minority culture's values. In order to create a place for different minority cultures, one solution would be the emergence of a "societal culture," that is, a culture that is organized around a shared language to be used in many institutions (both public and private). Such a society would not imply that religious beliefs, family customs, or lifestyles would have to be shared. Since 1965, American society has presented certain elements of such a culture insofar as the plurality of lifestyles and religious beliefs is no longer considered an obstacle to successful integration within the nation. In such conditions, we might wonder whether agreement on shared cultural and social values is still possible.

NOTES

1. Étienne Dinet, "L'Orient vu de l'Occident," (Paris: Paul Guethner, Rue Jacob, 1922).

2. These confrontations were often phrased in terms of religion—Islam v. Christianity—as demonstrated by Daniel, *Islam and the West*; Maxime Rodinson, *La fascination de l'Islam* (Paris: La Découverte, 1978); and Edward Said, *Orientalism* (New York: Pantheon, 1978).

3. Runnymede Trust, *Islamophobia: A Challenge for Us All.* (London: Runneymede Trust, 1997.

4. Pnina Werbner, "Islamophobia: Incitement to Religious Hatred – Legislating for a New Fear?" *Anthropology Today* 21, no. 1 (2005): 5–9; Tariq Modood, "The Place of Muslims in British Secular Multiculturalism," in *Muslim Europe or Euro-Islam: Politics, Culture, and Citizenship in the Age of Globalization*, eds. N. Alsayyad and M. Castells (New York: Lexington, 2002), 113–130; Steven Vertovec, "Islamophobia and Muslim Recognition in Britain," *in Muslims in the West: From Sojourners to Citizens*, ed. Yvonne Yazbeck Haddad (New York: Oxford University Press, 2002), 19–35; Fred Halliday, "Islamophobia Reconsidered," Ethnic and Racial Studies 22 no. 5 (September 1999): 892–902.

5. Chris Allen and Jorgen Nielsen. *Summary Report on Islamophobia in the EU after 9/11*, Prepared on behalf of the European Monitoring Centre on Racism and Xenophobia (EUMC) (Vienna, 2002); EUMC, *The Impact of 7 July 2005 London Bomb Attacks on Muslim Communities in the EU* (Vienna, 2005).

6. Timothy M. Savage, "Europe and Islam: Crescent Waxing, Cultures Clashing," *Washington Quarterly* 27, no. 3 (2004): 25–50.

7. *Yearbook of Immigration Statistics 2004*, U.S. Office of Immigration Statistics (January 2006).

8. Tariq Modood, "The Place of Muslims in British Secular Society," 113–130; Jocelyne Cesari, *When Islam and Democracy Met: Muslims in Europe and in the United States* (New York: Palgrave Macmillan, 2004).

9. *Household Below Average Income Series*, Department of Work and Pensions, 2003.

10. Malcolm Harrison and Deborah Phillips, *Housing and Black and Minority Ethnic Communities: Review of the Evidence Base* (London: Office of the Deputy Prime Minister, 2003).

11. U.S. Census Bureau News, "High School Graduation Rates Reach All-time High; Non-Hispanic White and Black Graduates at Record Levels," June 29, 2004, http://www.census.gov/Press-Release/www/releases/archives/education/001863.html.

12. Timothy M. Savage, "Europe and Islam: Crescent Waxing, Cultures Clashing," 25–50.

13. Jocelyne Cesari, *When Islam and Democracy Meet: Muslims in Europe and in the United States.*

14. Arun Kundnani, "Stop and Search: Police Step Up Targeting of Blacks and Asians," Institute of Race Relations (Mar. 26, 2003).

15. International Helsinki Federation, Report on Intolerance (March 2005).

16. Aristide R. Zolberg and Litt Woon Long, "Why Islam Is like Spanish: Cultural Incorporation in Europe and the United States," *Politics and Society* 27, no. 1 (1999): 5–38.

17. Elizabeth Poole, *Reporting Islam: Media Representations of British Muslims* (London: Tauris, 2002).

18. Ibid., 4.

19. Baukje Prins, *Voorbij de onschuld: Het debat over de multiculturele samenleving* (Amsterdam: Van Gennep, 2004).

20. Ibid.

21. Antonio Elorza, "Terrorismo islámico: Las raíces doctrinales," in *El nuevo terrorismo islamista*, ed. Antonio Elorza and Fernando Reinares Nestares, 156–57 (Madrid: Temas de Hoy, 2004). See also "Maniqueos e integristas," *El País*, Sept. 28, 2001, and "El círculo," *El País*, Nov. 23, 2001, among others.

22. Fernando Reinares, "Al Qaeda, neosalafistas magrebíes y 11-M: sobre el nuevo terrorismo islamista en España," in Elorza and Reinares Nestares, in *El nuevo terrorismo islamista*, 40–41.

23. According to Tibi, Euro-Islam incorporates pluralism, tolerance, secularity, civil society, and individual human rights.

24. Chahdortt Djavann, *Down with the Veils* (Paris: Gallimard, 2003) and *What Does Allah Think of Europe* (Paris: Gallimard, 2004). Djavann has also published another book, a novel suggestively titled *Comment peut-on être français? Roman* (Paris: Flammarion, 2006), which has, however, failed to produce as much media interest.

25. Germany Country Report on Human Rights Practices 1998 (U.S. Department of State, 1998).

26. "Seven German States Back Hijab Ban, Eight Refuse," IslamOnline.Net and News Agencies, http://www.islamonline.net/English/News/2003–10/11/article08.shtml.

27. This ruling was made even though the federal administrative court had ruled in 2004 that such legislation did in fact apply to nuns.

28. The government authorized the group's request at the same time it authorized the request made by the Islamic association known as World Islamic Mission to sound a call to prayer (BBC News, "Oslo's Rooftop Religious Rivalry," Mar. 30, 2002).

29. Bhikhu Parekh, "Integrating Minorities," in *Race Relations in Britain: A Developing Agenda*, ed. Tessa Blackstone, Bhikhu Parekh, and Peter Sanders, 19–21 (New York: Routledge, 1998).

30. Pippa Norris and Ronald Inglehart, *Sacred and Secular: Religion and Politics Worldwide* (New York: Cambridge University Press, 2004).

II

Case Studies

3

An Obsession Renewed: Islamophobia in the Netherlands, Austria, and Germany

Sam Cherribi

In his seminal book *The Outsider*, Paul Sniderman identifies two structural characteristics that have developed in Europe since the 1980s: a deep strain of intolerance of immigrants or foreigners and the emergence of at least one political party committed to mobilizing public resentment of immigrants or foreigners. Mazzoleni, Stewart, and Horsfield[1] and Norris[2] add a third characteristic: a populist media that consolidates the negative characteristics of migrants and enlarges the sphere of fear. The populist media's coverage of Islam in Europe may be the primary factor in creating Islamophobia.

Ian Buruma has described the effect of such media coverage on the prominence of anti-Islamist Dutch politician Geert Wilders, a man who rose to fame on the wings of the inflammatory film *Fitna*. In an opinion piece published in the *New York Times* on January 29, 2009, Buruma wrote, "If it were not for his hatred of Islam, Geert Wilders would have remained a provincial Dutch parliamentarian of little note. He is now world-famous, mainly for wanting the Koran to be banned in his country, 'like Mein Kampf is banned,' and for making a crude short film that depicted Islam as a terrorist faith—or, as he puts it, 'that sick ideology of Allah and Muhammad.'"

Who made Wilders so famous? According to Otto Scholten et al., "For four months, the attention of the Dutch newspapers was seized by a movie no one had seen. The movie in question was 'Fitna,' a political pamphlet by Dutch right-wing politician and Islam critic Geert Wilders. His aim was to visualize the 'threat' of Islam, which, he claims, originates from the 'rancorous' and 'violent' texts within parts of the Koran":

> In the period between the announcement in November 2007 and March 27, 2008, the day Wilders made Fitna available on the Internet, the case evolved into a remarkable media event. . . . The movie would appear on television in January, Wilders stated. Ultimately, this wasn't the case and the politician repeatedly postponed the "launch" of Fitna. However, somehow the attention didn't fade away. From then on, Wilders, Fitna, and Islam became the subject of a fierce, highly negative debate in Dutch society and— given the democratic function of journalism—in the news media.[3]

This chapter explores how the Dutch discussion in the public sphere, particularly in the media, has impacted Germany and Austria since 2000. Islamophobia is apparent in these three European countries. Analysis of this phenomenon is based on data from the Eurobarometer, the European Commission against Racism and Intolerance (ECRI), the European Union Agency for Fundamental Rights, the European Network against Racism, Media Tenor, and the Racism and Extremism Monitor of the Anne Frank Foundation.

The Netherlands

In early 2008 – just two years after controversial Muhammad cartoons were published in the Danish newspaper *Jyllands-Posten* – *Fitna*, the much-dreaded and anticipated film produced by Dutch parliamentarian Geert Wilders, was released on the Internet.

In *Fitna*, Wilders intersperses footage of imams reading the Quran with scenes from famous terrorist acts, including those of September 11. Veiled Muslim women are shown in stunning contrast against the backdrop of secular Europe. Wilders presents Muslims as backwards, temporally imprisoned in a vision of the world as presented by early verses of the Quran. For Wilders, there is no place for Muslims in modern Europe.

Fitna garnered intense media attention, especially in Europe, but theaters refused to show the film, and Wilders ran into difficulty finding a web host. YouTube only hosted the film for a day and as a result of the film, Pakistan banned YouTube. Dutch cartoonists and pundits ridiculed Wilders. However, according to surveys, the majority of the Netherlands – his target audience – watched the film and found its premise plausible. The day after the film debuted on the Internet, the Dutch polling organization Peil found that nearly half of those who saw the film believed that it was accurate. As for Wilders, his popularity increased. According to a poll by the Maurice de Hond agency, published in NRC Handelsblad on April 6, 2008, if Wilders had run for office the day after *Fitna* hit the Internet, his party would have garnered six more seats than it had actually won during the previous election. Wilders's Freedoms Party gained an impressive number of seats in three consecutive elections: the June 2009 European Parliament elections (4 seats), March 2010 municipal elections in two cities (The Hague and Almere), and the June 2010 legislative elections (24 seats).

Jytte Klausen, in an opinion piece published in Germany's *Der Spiegel* on March 28, 2008, noted that Wilders followed the model of the Danish cartoons in releasing his film. However, Klausen illustrated the differences more clearly than the similarities in *how Fitna* and the cartoons were brought to public light. This is important because much of the criticism of all works that might be labeled "anti-Muslim" has rested on the canard that each work is simply more of the same. Both in substance and in spirit, *Fitna* was not simply more of the Danish cartoons. For example, Klausen herself notes that "the newspaper's idea was to test whether Muslims were attempting to dictate to the general public what could or could not be said about Islam." This was not Wilders's intent, since he already anticipated the climate of response his film would produce. He had at least two prior and vivid models of that response—*Submission* and the Danish cartoons themselves. *Fitna*, for Wilders, was not an experiment in public response.

Klausen goes on to explain that, in the case of the Danish cartoons, two-thirds of the members of the Danish caricaturists association "didn't want to contribute anything at all, and among those who did, several made fun of the Danes for complaining about Muslims and others took shots at the *Jyllands-Posten* editors. Many didn't bother to portray the Prophet at all." There was no such introspective debate within Wilders's party. While the Danes may have questioned and needled the whole oeuvre of cartooning under the folds of Westergaard's bomb turban, Wilders was humorlessly confident in his intentions, squashing any productive public debate before it could even begin.

Further, Klausen states that "*Jyllands-Posten* was targeting a group of Danish imams who had complained about the press, and the paper never intended for the cartoons to travel the world." Wilders, for his part, certainly did intend for *Fitna* to travel the world. He sought and received coverage throughout Europe and in the United States prior to the release of *Fitna*. He was a guest on both CNN International and Al-Jazeera prior to the release. There is no question that not only did he intend for the world to see his film, but especially the Muslim world.

Klausen points to the government of Egypt as using the cartoons to inflame tensions between Europeans and Muslim immigrants. "Nothing happened until the Egyptian government—upset that Copenhagen had not responded to Cairo's diplomatic requests that it address the problem of growing Islamophobia in Denmark—took action by stirring up the religious authorities and considering a boycott of Danish products [. . . At that point] the scandal gained steam," she writes. But *Fitna* came to light only through the efforts of Wilders, not because any outside government needed it to further an agenda.

The two, however, do have something in common, much to Westergaard's chagrin: an interest in cartoons depicting bomblike turbans. In March 2008 the Danish branch of Wilders's "Stop the Islamization of Europe" movement was enjoined to stop using Westergaard's cartoon. Westergaard later won his copyright infringement case.

For his part, Wilders told *Washington Times* columnist Diana West on July 11, 2008, that "I'm not saying that every Muslim in the Netherlands is a criminal or a terrorist . . . We know the majority is not. Still, there is good reason to stop the immigration because the more we have an influx of Muslims in the Netherlands, the [more the] strength of the (Islamic) culture will grow, and [the more] the change of our societies will increase." He sees his efforts as "a fight against an ideology that I believe at the end of the day will kill our freedom, kill our societies and change everything we stand for."

Neither the Danish cartoons nor Wilder's *Fitna* would have been possible without the precedent of *Submission*, which raised the provocative specter of what could be made of the Western free press among Islamic fundamentalists. After *Submission*, Europe simply could not leave the topic of the free press and Islam alone.

A report by the European Commission against Racism and Intolerance on the Netherlands was adopted by the Council of Europe in June 2007 and made public in February 2008. It states that "the Muslim, and notably the Moroccan and Turkish communities have been particularly affected by these developments [mentioned earlier], which have resulted in a substantial increase of Islamophobia in both the political arena and other contexts."[4] This commission is an independent human rights monitoring body established by the Council of Europe. Its members are independent and impartial individuals "who are appointed on the basis of their moral authority and recognized expertise in dealing with racism, xenophobia, anti-Semitism, and intolerance."

In its annual report covering the period from January 1 to December 31, 2007, the European Commission against Racism and Intolerance notes its concern for

the continuing climate of hostility towards persons who are
Muslim or are perceived to be Muslim and deplores the fact that
Islamophobia continues to manifest itself in different guises within
European societies. Muslim communities and their members
continue to face prejudice, negative attitudes and discrimination. The
discourse of certain political figures or some of the media contributes
to this negative climate, which can sometimes lead to acts of violence
against Muslim communities. To deal with this situation, legislation
against incitement to hatred and other relevant laws must be fully
applied. Special efforts should be made to eradicate discriminatory
practices in access to nationality, education, and employment.[5]

A follow-up report titled "Racism in the Netherlands,"[6] compiled by the
European Network against Racism (ENAR), a group of more than six hundred
European organizations devoted to fighting racism, xenophobia, anti-Semitism,
and Islamophobia, reveals that for each year between 2004 and 2007 an average
of four hundred complaints of racial discrimination in the labor market were
submitted to the authorities. Almost half of those were about experiences at the
workplace and a quarter concerned entry into the labor market. Most of the
complaints were submitted by Moroccans, and many had to do with wearing
headscarves. From 2004 to 2006 the Equal Treatment Commission (ETC)
issued ninety-three rulings on racial discrimination in the Dutch labor market,
and in more than half of those cases, the complaints were deemed valid.

In the Netherlands, discrimination in housing and education is much less
pronounced. In 2007 only 1.9 percent of 4,307 complaints received on the
grounds of discrimination were related to housing (in 2006 this figure was
also 1.9 percent). The number of complaints relating to discrimination in
education also remained stable: around 5.5 percent of the total, or around 250
complaints per year.[7] Most complaints about educational programs or institutions were related to enrollment, admission, clothing rules, suspension, and
the relationship between teacher and student, parent, and/or guardian. In
2007, authorities received 2,229 complaints about discrimination on the
grounds of race, religion, or nationality.[8]

Exporting Islamophobia to the Rest of Europe

Within the discussion of immigration, the alleged lack of integration of legal
immigrants – especially Muslim migrants from North Africa and Turkey –
and the ways they lived in Europe became increasingly important issues in

the media. Consequently, Europe in the 1990s and the early 21st century saw an emphasis on populist appeals and the growth of support for populist political parties with strong anti-immigrant policies, including List Pim Fortuyn (LPF) in the Netherlands, Filip de Winter's Vlaams Belang in Belgium, the Freedom Party of Jörg Haider (who died in 2008) in Austria, Pia Kjaersgaard's Danish People's Party (DPP), the Republican Party (REP) in Denmark, the German People's Union (DVU), the National Democratic Party (NPD) in Germany, Jean-Marie Le Pen's National Front in France, Makis Voridis's Hellenic Front in Greece, and Umberto Bossi's Northern League and the National Alliance in Italy.

Politicians often take their cue from the media and shape public policy accordingly. The increase in public support for Far Right parties cannot be considered in isolation from the demographic changes in Europe's major cities over the past two decades and the subsequent media coverage of those changes. A recent world-wide comparative study of neopopulism shows that the news media are instrumental in the rise and fall of populist parties and leaders.[9] Some researchers have found a connection between support for the Far Right and one's daily news diet. In particular, there is a correlation between anti-Islam sentiments and the amount of crime coverage in the news.[10] In Austria, for example, scholars have been able to predict support for the Far Right, such Jörg Haider's Freedom Partry, based on the newspapers one reads.[11]

Mazzoleni, Stewart, and Horsfield identify three phases in the neopopulist movements and their relationship with the media[12]: the insurgent phase, the establishment phase, and the decline phase. The first phase is characterized by "intense media attention to the newly born political force."[13] The second phase occurs when the movement achieves "public legitimacy" and "has become a more durable feature of the national political scene." In this phase, neopopulist leaders "find it more difficult to maintain the levels of attention of the news media." The second phase may be "simultaneous with the fading of the neo-populist party or movement from the media scene." The decline phase does not apply to all movements, and some, such as the National Front in France, continue to thrive.[14] This succession of phases serves as a mechanism whereby distrust of Muslims becomes normalized and institutionalized unless it is counteracted by some movement. In certain cases, backlash occurs because of overexposure of the issue. For example, in February 2009 Geert Wilders was denied entry into the United Kingdom even though he had been invited by a member of Parliament to give a presentation on Islam and his Islamophobic film. His fame, fed by Islamophobia, had, it seemed, run its course.

Post-Haider Austria

Austrian Far-right leader *Jörg* Haider, whom Reuters news agency described as "a charismatic populist who helped bring anti-immigrant politics into the European mainstream," was killed in a car accident in October 2008 at the age of fifty-eight. "Haider, who led the right into a coalition government from 2000 to 2006, polarized Austria and drew condemnation abroad with anti-foreigner outbursts and for appearing to endorse some Nazi policies," Reuters continued. "But he avoided such rhetoric in later years."[15]

In the month before his death, Haider helped Austria's Far Right win about 30 percent of the national parliamentary seats, "mining discontent over feuding centrist governing parties, inflation and immigration. . . . Along with France's Jean Marie Le Pen, Haider was instrumental in moving the far right from the political fringes toward the mainstream, tapping into fears over rising immigration from the Muslim world and a perceived loss of national identity through European integration."[16]

In *Anti-Semitism and Islamophobia: Hatreds Old and New in Europe*, anthropologist Matti Bunzl explains that, by discussing Turkey's inclusion in the EU, Jörg Haider's Freedom Party put the issue of Muslim migrants in Europe center stage. Bunzl writes that the party's main slogan was "Turkey into the EU? Not with me!" He goes on to examine the party's position as stated in its pamphlets: "It is a fact that there was no Enlightenment and no Renaissance in Turkey, those bases of European culture that form the standards for all member states of the EU. In addition, one of the most important values of Europeans, tolerance, does not count in Turkey: here, Christians are hassled in any possible way. . . . Turkey's State Institute for Statistics forecasts a population of 95 million for the year 2050. The country with the highest population in the EU would then be Islamic!"[17]

Haider's Freedom Party pamphlet continued:

Not without reason did Libya's head of state, Muammar Gadaffi, note that Europe would accept an Islamic Trojan Horse if Turkey became a member of the EU. This Trojan Horse will not only cause social tensions of never-anticipated proportions—also the question of Europe's Islamization is being kept quiet by the fanatics for membership. Today, an estimated 15 million Muslims already live in the member states of the EU. Europe can save a lot if it spares itself. Turkey's EU accession would certainly be the end of this community, and it would also foil the basic idea of the process of European unification.[18]

Bunzl describes how, when the Freedom Party abandoned its nationalistic stance in the 1990s, it took on the role of self-appointed protector of Europe, targeting a host of new "others" and casting Jews as allies against the new invaders. Among these others were Africans and Asians, he writes, but "it was the Muslims who now appeared as a potential threat." The Freedom Party's new platform "identified 'radical Islam' as the greatest threat. It was 'penetrating Europe' and had to be stopped both at the national and European level."[19]

In Austria, the political establishment was viewed as a calcified entity, and it was into this stagnant, intractable environment that Haider burst. According to Fritz Plasser and Peter Ulram in their contribution to the book of Mazzoleni, Stewart, and Horsfeld in *The Media and Neo-populism: A Contemporary Analysis*, Haider rose to power on an antiestablishment message. A majority of his votes in 1986 came from young people and the urban middle class: "Haider's personality—or rather, his media image—came first." He offered "hope for 'a breath of fresh air in politics' and the ousting of established politics.[20]

In the 1990s, as Muslim migration placed more pressure on Austria's educational resources and economy, the Freedom Party "redirected its oppositional focus from political renewal to 'politics of resentment,' combining fear with ever-aggressive attacks upon the traditional political class." Pippa Norris point out that "Haider's slogan—'*Stop* der *Überfremdung*" or 'overforeign-ization'—could have been well received where Austrians were already afraid of losing their jobs to Central and East European migrants, or of seeing their children attending schools with many Muslim immigrants."

The European press was only too happy to carry such a divisive and attention-getting message of fear. According to the 2006 EUMC report titled *Muslims in the European Union: Discrimination and Islamophobia*, the news presenters themselves were "mostly Austrian," and Austrians interviewed for the report attested that "if you see the police or you see the people working in the civil service [they were also Austrian], so it doesn't have the mixture like in many multicultural societies such as the Netherlands or the United Kingdom, where you see a Muslim reading the news."

Another interviewee added: "We have, you know, the discussion about this new antidiscrimination law, and it is a real problem that people don't even know about this law. There was no information in the media. . . . The Government hasn't reported it."

Moreover, with Haider providing a charismatic voice for the anti-Islamic sentiment, the sentiment grew. Three surveys carried out by Denz in 1994, 1999, and 2002 on the development of the rejection of different groups as neighbors showed that this negative response went from 19 percent in 1994 to 15 percent in 1999 but grew to 25 percent in 2002.

Before his death, Haider moved on to found the Association for Austria's Future. Now, although Haider is dead, his legacy promises to live on in Freedom Party politician Susanne Winter. In January 2008 Winter drew international criticism for anti-Muslim remarks. In an interview with the daily *Österreich*, Winter said child abuse is "widespread" among Muslim men and that Graz— the city in which she was campaigning for city council—is in the path of a "tsunami of Muslim immigration." She said that in twenty to thirty years, half of Austria's population would be Muslim.[21]

At present, there are approximately 200,000 Muslims in Austria, just over 4 percent of the population, of which the two major ethnic groups are of Turkish descent (about 120,000) and Bosnian (about 50,000).

In late November 2008, according to the *Austrian Times*, a public prosecutor charged Winter with "hate-mongering and vilification of religious teaching" for remarks she made during her city council campaign. "Winter said that she would welcome the lifting of her immunity since only court proceedings would enable her to clear her name. She called the imposition of charges against her an exercise in 'political hatred by crazy, self-proclaimed thought-police'" and added that it could "not be that a person could be tried for expression of opinion in a democracy."

Germany: Roland Koch's Campaign against "Criminal Young Foreigners"

Even as Winter was campaigning for Graz's city council, in neighboring Germany, Roland Koch, governor of Hesse and a member of Chancellor Angela Merkel's Christian Democratic Party, won praise from the Far Right for his comments against Muslims.

On January 4, 2008, *Der Spiegel* reported the following:

> Seizing on the brutal attack by two youths, a Turk and a Greek, on a German pensioner two weeks ago, Koch called for tougher laws on youth crime. He said Germany had "too many criminal young foreigners" and that immigrants must abide by the rules enshrined in the country's Christian culture.
>
> He followed up his call for tougher youth sentencing with a six-point list of values, which included respect towards the elderly, punctuality, hard work, politeness and the following guideline for immigrants:

'In residential estates with a high proportion of immigrants there must be clear rules and of course consequences if they are not respected," wrote Koch. "German must be the language in everyday life and it must be clear that the slaughtering (of animals) in the kitchen or unusual ideas about waste disposal run counter to our principles.'[22]

Germany has a Muslim population of more than 3 million, and Muslims make up a third of all foreigners in the country. Most are of Turkish origin—about a third of all naturalizations involve Turkish migrants.

According to a representative survey of German Muslims in 2002, the majority of Germany's Muslim population regarded itself as German: of the respondents, 82 percent wanted to stay in Germany, and two-thirds wanted to be naturalized (*Survey of the Islamic Archive*, 2002). The same survey, conducted two years later, found that 89 percent believed that it is important to integrate, while only 5 percent opposed doing so. Also, according to a survey conducted by Pew in 2008 "56% express a negative view of Muslims, compared with 42% of those on the left and 45% of those in the center."[23] However, naturalizations of Muslims in general have steadily decreased since 2001 due in no small way to discouraging public discourse mostly surrounding terrorism – discourse that became amplified following later terrorist attacks in Madrid in March 2004 and London in July 2005.

Following the London bombings, Christian Wulff, the head of Germany's Christian Democratic Union party in Lower Saxony, proposed video surveillance of mosques to prevent a similar attack in Germany. His response to the London attack and its support by many Germans illustrated how closely terrorism and Islam are linked in Germany. In the small towns of Osnabrück and Braunschweig in his province, the identities of all attendees of the Friday services at mosques were checked. The mosques were searched, entry and exit from a predominantly Muslim neighborhood were blocked, and identities of its residents were checked. Similar measures were not explicitly enacted in the United Kingdom after the London bombings.

A 2006 study conducted by the University of Bielefeld's Institute for Interdisciplinary Research on Conflict and Violence, revealed that 39 percent of respondents agreed with the following statement: "Due to the many Muslims living here I sometimes feel like a foreigner in my own country"—an increase from the 35 percent who felt that way in 2004. According to the Pew Research Center, the proportion of Germans who believe that relations between Muslims and Western countries are generally bad is the highest of all Western countries, 70 percent.

In the article "Der unheimliche Muslim," published in the journal *Soziale Welt- Sonderband* in 2006, Werner Schiffauer explains that a "growing number of naturalizations turn Ausländer [foreigners] into citizens and threaten to change the balance of power between the 'established' and the 'outsiders.'" He refers to the idea of "moral panic" raised by Stanley Cohen in the early 1970s and points out that such extreme reaction is characterized by an "exaggerated presentation of the threats for society, by a generalized atmosphere of distrust, and by a widespread tendency to witch-hunt."

In an effort to close the widening gap between migrants and natural Germans, in July 2007, Chancellor Andrea Merkel unveiled her country's National Integration Plan (NIP), designed to give officials throughout the government, from the smallest hamlets to the major metropolitan areas, a framework for conducting migrant programs. The NIP is based on the EU's Common Basic Principles, and like it and most other government documents, it does not mention Muslims per se, but Germany did officially address the issue of Muslim immigration in the *Islamkonferenz* (Islamic Conference), which met for the first time in September 2006. According to the Washington, D.C.–based nonprofit Migration Policy Institute, Germany's Islamic Conference identified specific needs that would have to be addressed in order to promote immigration. They include language courses geared toward the specialized needs of targeted immigrant groups—such as separate classes for women—and better educational opportunities for immigrant youth, with the specific goal of ensuring that more immigrants enter the upper educational tracks and have a better chance to go to colleges and universities.

In neighboring Austria, the Muslim population has been recognized by public law since 1912. According to a 2008 Media Tenor report, in German public TV news, only one in ten reports refers to an Islamic organization—56 percent focus on the Roman-Catholic Church and the "German pope." Muslim organizations are framed in the context of conflict and terrorism; only 3 percent of reports have a positive tone.

Conclusion

Since the 1990s, three significant transformations have taken place in Germany, Austria, and the Netherlands: the German reunification in 1990, the accession of Austria to the EU in 1992, and the first high-profile, ethnic-related murder of Dutch filmmaker Theo Van Gogh by a Muslim Dutch citizen in 2002.

These three developments fed into Islamophobia like this: First, without the Soviet Union next door to inspire unity in opposition to a common enemy,

Europe experienced a unity vacuum and needed a new *bête noire* against which to align; Islam filled that gap. The most dramatic example of this was the ethnic cleansing that broke out in Bosnia.

Second, with Austria's inclusion in the EU, Europeans, now grappling with the threat of losing their individual national identities, were given a sort of nationalist template in the form of Haider: essentially, "oppose what is not yourself." In this context, any changes in what was perceived as the traditional population were deemed a threat. Believing this required a denial of the historical presence of Muslims in Europe at least since the beginning of the influx of guest workers in the 1960s. Haider accommodated that denial.

Finally, the murder of Theo Van Gogh gave flesh to the myth of the threat. Here was the nephew of a European icon—Vincent Van Gogh, almost a symbol of Western culture, his paintings expressions of a triumphant Europe—murdered by a Muslim extremist. The incident gave breath to a chorus of I-told-you-so's, and won over Europeans to an Islamophobic mindset, even those who had not previously felt any particular animosity toward Muslims.

To be more specific, in 1989, the fall the Berlin Wall and the subsequent mass exodus of East Germans to the West led to the collapse of the Honecker regime in Germany and a long winter of economic and political discontent. Then free elections were held for the reunification of Germany in an enlarged Europe. These 1990 elections were the first free elections since 1932.[24]

With the half-century-old image of Europe shattering and European identity seemingly under siege, any outside pressure would be seen as a threat. The murder of Van Gogh became a convenient scapegoat for frightened Europeans. The fact that his murderer was a Muslim overshadowed the fact that he was also a European citizen, born in the Netherlands, employed and educated in the cradle of the Enlightenment. The problem then, as framed by the news media, was his Muslimness.

Islam's Dissonance with Traditional Western Journalism

Islam in the West satisfies important criteria for getting into the news. It is rich in the characteristics that determine newsworthiness: timeliness, human interest, conflict, proximity, and—depending on who is speaking out about it—prominence.

As a topic in European news outlets, Islam tends to be inherently conflict ridden.[25] It is a topic that can often induce emotional responses that have been found to be advantageous to program makers who want to retain their audiences.[26]

Even descriptive reporting about Islamic holidays and accompanying rituals, such as the slaughtering of sheep in traditional style for human-interest stories, has been the focus of what could be described as sensational reporting on a fairly neutral topic. Reporting the large numbers of sheep slaughtered in one day by Muslims in the country – which is common in French, Belgian, and Dutch news reports when special abattoirs are set up for the religious feasts – can trigger a range of reactions from non-Muslim audiences. Brigitte Bardot, the famous French actress and animal rights activist, has been the subject of much reporting on these occasions. She is in fact simply describing what is happening when she uses the term "Muslim slaughterers" (*bouchers* in French). This topic already has some news value in terms of timeliness, proximity, and human interest, but throw in Bardot, and add the values of prominence and conflict, and all five criteria for newsworthiness are satisfied, virtually ensuring placement on the front page or the front of a section of the newspaper. For those unaccustomed to the (sometimes gruesome) visuals of lambs' throats being cut, such a report can be a highly charged viewing experience—the feedback to such stories creates another layer of conflict and perpetuates the topic in the news cycle.

Islamic religious practices and a European society's social norms may conflict in ways that have not been the subject of much discussion in the public space, that is, until journalists bring the topic into the news. For example, during the Muslim month of Ramadan, if a Frenchman leaves a bar and hails a taxi, the Muslim driver may decide not to take him if he smells of alcohol. This may be just an occasional incident, but once reported in the news, it may become perceived as "the tip of the iceberg." Inevitably, the public begins to see similarities in other everyday transactions. It is not only issues of conflict, but also the novelty of Islamic religious practices that can be of interest to reporters. The ritual of ablution (washing one's hands, face, and feet before praying), for example, attracted the cameras when Muslims demonstrating in front of the French Embassy in The Hague on a cold day in the late 1980s used snow instead of water.

On some Fridays in the early 1990s, when religious Muslims wanted to get to Amsterdam's largest mosque, located on the Amstel River, during a time when the main bridge there was closed for construction, the cameras captured some unusual pictures. They were unusual because, if they had been cropped closely, viewers might think that they were looking at a picture of an Oriental society rather than a European one. On a bright and sunny day, gender-segregated crowds of Muslims in religious white were standing on the deck of a flat-topped ferry that was taking them and some of their bicycles from one side of the Amstel River to the other. Everyone was looking toward the large door at the entrance of the mosque.

In *The Sociology of News*, Michael Schudson discusses the processes by which the news is manufactured.[27] He points out that journalists not only construct but also create reality, albeit with constraints: "Journalists normally work with materials that real people and real events provide. But by selecting, highlighting, framing, shading, and shaping in reportage, they create an impression that real people—readers and viewers—then take to be real and to which they respond in their lives."[28]

An old axiom says that in every stereotype there is a splinter of truth. That splinter acts as an irritant to existing insecurities until the initial wound becomes an infected, swollen hazard. The splinter that has caused Islamophobia, an entire swollen oeuvre of fear, is "jihadism." Any intellectually honest exploration of Islamophobia requires that we acknowledge the splinter of jihadism as the cause of Islamophobia in order to separate the truth from the lie, the reality from the dark fantasy.

There are those who would argue for an ancient opposition between Islam and Christianity, an entirely valid argument, but we concern ourselves today with a fear of all things Muslim that resides within the modern context, a context of immigration and geopolitical conflict, as well as of technologically advanced, socially liberal societies in tension with Islam's old wall of moral dogma.

Islamophobia is the infected and swollen reaction of a body of thought to a foreign object, the splinter of jihadism, and to truly examine and heal the wound we must pluck out jihadism, separate it from the damaged tissue around it, and hold it up to the light—but we cannot do that if we are so afraid of the thing that we refuse to see all of it, the good, as well as the bad.

Many of the extreme political debates about Islam that can be easily characterized as Islamophobic were incubated in the Netherlands and replicated in other European countries, including Germany and Austria. The extreme opinions of Holland's Party of Freedom, led by Geert Wilders, are mimicked by other politicians across Europe, such as Susanne Winter, who is affiliated with the Freedom Party of Austria, Udo Voigt of Germany's National Democratic Party, and Gerhard Frey of the German Peoples' Union.

NOTES

1. Gianpietro Mazzoleni, Julianne Stewart, and Bruce Horsfield, eds. *The Media and Neo-populism: A Contemporary Analysis* (Westport, CT: Praeger, 2003).

2. Pippa Norris, *Radical Right: Voters and Parties in the Electoral Market* (Cambridge: Cambridge University Press, 2005).

3. Otto Scholten, et. al., *Fitna and the Media: An Investigation of Attention and Role Patterns* (Netherlands: Netherlands New Monitor, 2008), www.nieuwsmonitor.net/d/4/wilders_report_en.pdf.

4. See http://www.coe.int/t/e/human_rights/ecri/1-ecri/2-country-by-country_approach/netherlands/Netherlands%20third%20report%20-%20cri08–3.pdf.

5. See http://www.coe.int/t/e/human_rights/ecri/1-ecri/1-presentation of ecri/4-annual_report_2007/Annual%20report%202007.pdf.

6. ENAR Shadow Report 2007, "Racism in the Netherlands." See also Frank Bovenkerk, "Islamophobia," *Annefrank.org.* http://www.annefrank.org/upload/Downloads/Mon7-UK-Ch5.pdf. For more details about xenophobia and its history in the Netherlands, Austria, and Germany, see the following sources. Robert A. Bauer, *Austrian Solution: International Conflict and Cooperation* (Virginia: University of Virginia Press, 1988); Anton Pelinka and Gunter Bischof, *Austria in the New Europe* (New Jersey: Transaction Publishers: 1992); John Fitzmaurice, *Austrian Politics and Society Today: In Defense of Austria* (New York: Palgrave Macmillan, 1991); Abraham Foxman, *Never Again?: The Threat of the New Anti-Semitism* (New York: HarperCollins, 2003); Jean-Paul Sartre, *Anti-Semite and Jew: An Exploration of the Etiology of Hate* (New York: Schocken Books Inc, 1948); Daniel Sibony, *L'énigme antisémite* (France: Seuil, 2004); Sara Grunenberg and Jaap van Donselaar, "Deradicalization: Lessons from Germany, Options for the Netherlands?" http://www.annefrank.org/uploads/Downloads/Mon7-UK-Ch8.pdf; Frank Letchner, *The Netherlands : Globalization and National Identity* (New York: Routledge, 2008); Hella Pick, *Guilty Victim* (New York: Tauris, 2000); Jehuda Reinharz, ed., *Living with Antisemitism: Modern Jewish Responses* (London: University Press of New England, 1987); Sophie Hofbauer, ed., "The Impact of Immigration on Austria's Society: A Survey of Recent Austrian Migration Research," (Vienna, 2008); Peter Thaler, *The Ambivalence of Identity : The Austrian Experience of Nation-building in a Modern Society* (West Lafayette: Purdue University Press, 2001); Christopher M. Hutton, *Race and the Third Reich* (Malden: Polity, 2005); Reinhold Wagnleitner, ed., *Understanding Austria: The Political Reports and Analyses of Martin F. Herz, Political Officer of the US Legation in Vienna, 1945–1948* (Salzburg: Neugebauer, 1984); Guillaume Erner, *Expliquer l'antisémitisme* (Paris: Presses Universitaires de France, 2005); Ingrid Galster, *Sartre et les juifs: Actes du collique international* (Paris: La Decouverte, 2005); Manfred Gerstenfeld and Shmuel Trigano, *Les habits neufs de l'antisémitisme en Europe* (Paris: Editions Cafe Noir, 2004); Albert S. Lindemann, *Anti-Semitism before the Holocaust* (New York: Longman, 2000); Nicholas Goodrick-Clarke, *The Occult Roots of Nazism: The Ariosophists of Austria and Germany 1890–1935* (Wellingborough, Northamptonshire: Aquarian, 1985); Anne Goujon, et al., "New Times, Old Beliefs: Projecting the Future Size of Religions in Austria." In *Vienna Yearbook of Population Research*, (Vienna: Vienna Institute of Demography, 2007): 237-270; and Rudolph Loewenstein, *Psychanalyse de 'antisémitisme* (Paris: Presses Universitaires de France, 2001).

7. ENAR Shadow Report 2007.

8. Ibid.

9. Norris, *Radical Right.*

10. Stefaan Walgrave and Peter van Aelst. "The Contingent Nature of Agenda-Setting: Different Agenda-Setting Dynamics in Election and Non-Election Times?" Paper Presented at the Third Annual Pre-APSA Conference on Political Communication: Faith, Fun, and Futuramas, September 1, 2004.

11. Mazzoleni, Stewart, and Horsfield, *Media and Neo-populism*, 24.

12. See Gianpietro Massoleni, "The *Media and the Growth of Neo-Populism* in Contemporary Democracies," in Media and Neo-Populism, 1–20; Stewart, Mazzoleni, and Horsfield, "Conclusion: Power to the Media Managers," *Media and Neo-Populism*, 217–237.

13. Ibid., 223.

14. Fritz Plasser and Peter A. Ulram, "Striking a Responsive Chord," in *Media and Neo-Populism*, 21–24.

15. Alexandra Zawadil, "Austrian Far-Right Leader Haider Killed in Crash," Reuters, (October 11, 2008), http://www.reuters.com/article.idUSTRE49A2IM20081011.

16. Ibid.

17. Matti Bunzl, *Anti-Semitism and Islamophobia: Hatred Old and New In Europe.* (Chicago: Prickly Paradigm, 2007).

18. Ibid., 33.

19. Ibid., 34.

20. *Media and Neo-Populism*, 12, 25.

21. David Crossland, "Far-Right NPD Praises Koch's Tough Talk on Immigration," *Der Spiegel* (Jan. 4, 2008), http://www.spiegel.de/international/germany/0,1518,526724,00. html.

22. Pew Global Attitudes Survey. *Unfavorable Views of Jews and Muslims on the Increase in Europe* (September 2008), http://www.pewglobal.org/files /pdf/262.pdf.

23. Pew Global Attitudes Survey. *The Great Divide: How Westerners and Muslims View Each Other* (June 2006): http://pewglobal.org/files/pdf/253.pdf.

24. Dirk Verheyen, *The German Question: A Cultural, Historical, and Geographical Exploration* (Boulder: Westview, 1991), 189.

25. W. Lance Bennet, *News: The Politics of Illusion*, 4th ed. (New York: Addison-Wesley Longman, 2001).

26. Ibid.

27. Michael Schudson, *The Sociology of News* (New York: Norton, 2003).

28. Ibid., 2.

4

Islamophobia in the United Kingdom: Historical and Contemporary Political and Media Discourses in the Framing of a 21st-Century Anti-Muslim Racism

Tahir Abbas

The concept of Islamophobia has become established academic, practitioner, and societal parlance in the last two decades, developing an especially malevolent form after the end of the Cold War and the beginning of the "clash of civilizations" thesis. In Britain, the term took on a well-accepted meaning and application after the events of the "Rushdie affair" of the late 1980s and developments to state-orchestrated analysis of social and cultural exclusion facing ethnic minorities, differentiated by virtue of "race," ethnicity, class, gender, and religion in the mid-1990s. In the post-9/11 and post-7/7 climate, Islamophobia has gathered pace not only as a lived experience but also in the way it is utilized as an analytical concept in various research and policy development arenas, instrumentalized both negatively and positively depending on the predilection of the definers. This chapter explores the nature and orientation of this phenomenon and the extent and limit of its theoretical and conceptual reach by using a case study methodological approach.

   As part of this analysis, it is important to explore the ways in which the state relates to its citizens and defines its roles and responsibilities in relation to them. That is, how is the problem of Islamophobia stated, and what are its precise characteristics? What can be done to alleviate it? To this end, the 1997 Runnymede Trust commission on Islamophobia is used as a starting point. Case studies based on the publication of *The Satanic Verses* by Salman Rushdie in 1988, the more recent examples relating to the Danish cartoons controversy of 2006, and the comments and debate made in relation to the veil by former home secretary Jack Straw, also in 2006, are used to explore the ways in which the discourse has shifted during this period. In conclusion, it is argued that there are changing notions in relation to the ways in which ethnicized and racialized minorities are now regarded, with religio-cultural characteristics at the fore in how they are "othered" by wider society. In this regard, Islam and Muslims have the greatest exposure. This experience has implications for human social relations in the context of a flailing global war on terror, developments in international information communication technologies, and the ways in which the state (i.e., thorough "elite racism")[1] regards its minority citizens in the context of devolution, Europeanization, and the "problem" of Muslim minority youth radical identity politics. This new racism takes the form of an assault on groups through the lens of culture and language rather than direct forms of color discrimination.[2] It is subtle yet sophisticated, new yet age old.

I argue that Muslims in Britain and in Western Europe in general are facing significant challenges that are compounded by the ways in which the state and the Western world at large regards Muslims as somehow the central feature of the "problems" experienced. This is particularly noticeable with reference to the experiences of Muslim young men, for example in relation to the northern disturbances in 2001 and since.[3] Although it is apparent that Islamophobia is a useful term, it does have its range of problems. For some, it is ill defined, and it does not always say anything about degree, scope, or magnitude. It can hide internal practices within Muslim communities where accusations of Islamophobia can mask gender inequalities, regressive cultural practices, and significant power imbalances within the domestic sphere or community context. Further, it conflates Islam and Muslim into single entities, hiding tremendous variations in ideology and praxis. In operating effectively as a normative concept but not without its limitations, it also covers tremendous ground by including those who have limited or no knowledge of Islam and fear it as a whole with those who are seemingly fighting against radical Islamism, which would also include many Muslims. There is also confusion in how some would focus on aspects of discrimination with a deliberate concentration on anti-Islamic rhetoric or doublespeak. All the same, the idea of Islamophobia has significant purchase among intellectuals, scholars, influential think tanks, and government departments. It captures a certain social momentum, and it is therefore important to discuss it as a social concept with real-world implications.

Definitions

It is true that, historically, notions of cultural and social identification of the "Muslim other" stem from an understanding and experience of imperialism and colonialism, and this fear or dread of Islam or Muslims is conceivably described as Islamophobia in the current period. It has been expedient for the established powers to portray Islam and Muslims in the worst imaginable light in order to prevent conversion, as well as to encourage Europeans to resist forces at their borders throughout the history of Western European contact with Islam. Over time, there have been episodes of genuine scholarship and awareness on the part of the English, but ignorance, conflict, and demonization have also been present, namely through the Crusades, imperialism, and colonialism.[4] Throughout this time, Muslims have been portrayed as "savage," "moronic," "small minded," or "fanatical religious militants." These negative characterizations of Muslims are still present today in the sometimes damaging representation and treatment of the Muslim other, which exists as part of an effort to aggrandize established powers and, in the process, to legitimize existing modes of domination and subordination in social, economic, and political life.[5]

As much as present-day Islamophobia relies on history to fill the substance of its stereotypes, the current fear of Muslims has its own idiosyncratic features that connect it with more recent experiences of neocolonialism, decolonization, immigration, and postwar racism. In 1997, the Runnymede Trust, an influential think tank, stated that Islamophobia is created analogously to xenophobia, which is the disdain or dislike of all things "foreign." Seven features of Islamophobia were identified in the initial Runnymede Trust report (1997):

1. Muslim cultures are seen as monolithic.
2. Islamic cultures are substantially different from other cultures.
3. Islam is perceived as implacably threatening.
4. Adherents of Islam use their faith to gain political or military advantage.
5. Muslim criticism of Western cultures and societies is rejected out of hand.
6. The fear of Islam is mixed with racist hostility to immigration.
7. Islamophobia is assumed to be natural and unproblematic.

This typology conveniently provides a range of descriptors in relation to Islamophobia, where the concept captures primary functions that are historical, cultural, and policy oriented in scope. The characteristics of Islamophobia relate to how it is defined by "the other" so as to become further "othered" by the very same "otherer," where this "othering" is related to racist fear and hostility, as well as to the apparently irredeemable nature of Islam and Muslims themselves. Though it is important not to treat Muslims as an undifferentiated mass, as there are very many ethnic, cultural, social, economic, and political differences between individuals and groups, the characteristics of Islamophobia defined by the Runnymede Trust are still relevant today. While racism on the basis of "race" is still present, the anti-Muslim shift suggests markers of difference of a social and religio-cultural nature. Furthermore, while certain signifiers of "race" are now protected by legislation, it is not the case for religious markers where protection is limited to religious communities who are also ethnically defined through case law, namely people from Jewish and Sikh community backgrounds in Britain (however, a European directorate outlawing religious discrimination in employment went into effect in December 2003).

Muslims' being targeted by right-wing groups, with more subtle forms of racist prejudice and hatred after 9/11 and 7/7, nevertheless remain outside the domain of antiracist legislation.[6] The social and religious foundations of Islam, as well as Muslims in general, have attained such a degree of notoriety that their presence is immediately associated with entirely negative and detrimental frames of reference. Since 9/11, the situation has both deteriorated and intensified. Islamophobia has gained greater discursive pervasiveness to the extent that Western European society has become uncritically receptive to an array of negative images and perceptions of Islam and Muslims, such is the power and force of the dominant hegemony, particularly when a host of Western nations are at "war" against terrorism.

While it is possible to demonstrate Islamophobia in its physical, cultural, and emotional manifestations, many social commentators have questioned the very idea of Islamophobia, suggesting that the concept can be one that polices or censors opinion, as would the notion that anti-Semitism may well be used to stifle disapproval of negative actions by the state of Israel. Many of these observers reflect on the example of the liberal feminist journalist Polly Toynbee, nominated for the title of "most Islamophobic media personality of the year" in 2003 at the somewhat sardonic Annual Islamophobia Awards, administered by the Islamic Human Rights Commission (IHRC). The prize was founded on remarks made in an article published in the *Guardian* newspaper a few weeks after the 9/11 attacks: "[R]eligious politics scar India, Kashmir, Northern Ireland,

Sri Lanka, Sudan . . . the list of countries wrecked by religion is long. But the present danger is caused by Islamist theocracy . . . There is no point in pretending it is not so."[7] She continued: "[W]herever Islam either is the government or bears down upon the government, it imposes harsh regimes that deny the most basic human rights." Toynbee rejected the label of "Islamophobe," arguing that her comments must be judged on their truth or falsity, not on the offense they might give to some members of the Muslim community.

Political activist and social commentator Kenan Malik has also rejected the idea of Islamophobia in the influential essay "The Islamophobia Myth."[8] Malik argues that care is required when utilizing Islamophobia as the essential *raison d'être* behind any apparent anti-Muslim event. The charge of Islamophobia can be potentially utilized as a vehicle to suppress discussion, as well as disapproval, of the cultural traditions of certain Muslims and their societies. Although antisocial activities and delinquency may well be behind a number of experiences described as Islamophobic attacks, clearly Islamophobia is not merely about the number of people who have reported physical violence or the number of Muslims who have been stopped and searched by the police. There are, undoubtedly, wider, historically significant, culturally embedded institutions, practices, and individual and group behaviors that are more important than merely the idea that Islamophobia is no more than random but increasingly numerous, physical, or verbal attacks on Muslims and the religion of Islam itself.

Problematizing Multiculturalism: Freedom of Speech versus the Freedom to Offend

While for some the Rushdie affair signaled an irrational response to a legitimate expression of disgust at an offensive publication, it also led many in the liberal intelligentsia to see it as a problem of multiculturalism; that is, too great an emphasis was placed upon diversity at the expense of unity. At present, this suggestion has taken further hold, and many right-of-center individuals and institutions are expressly focusing on Muslims as somehow delimiting the potential of multiculturalism, while others principally see Islam itself as the problem. This shift is a function of the role of global media technologies and the apparent threat of "global Islam" with its increasingly visible Muslim minority presence in secular Western European liberal nation-states.[9] In the context of multiculturalism, it is possible to explore specific media case studies, namely the Salman Rushdie affair and the Danish cartoons controversy.

Contemporary Britain prides itself on its liberal ideologies that encourage multicultural integration, freedom of speech, and equality of opportunity. The British government repeatedly states that policy has moved away from its inherently postwar assimilationist principles and now seeks to develop a multicultural society in which the term *British* can simultaneously refer to all cultures. Even so, over the past twenty years, Britain has witnessed disputes between these cultures on several occasions, including the Muslim protests of 1989 after the publication of Salman Rushdie's *Satanic Verses* and, in recent periods, after the publication (originally in September 2005 and again in February 2006) of several cartoons by Danish right-wing newspaper *Jyllands-Posten*, again negatively depicting the Prophet Muhammad. The concept of political correctness has gradually emerged in Britain as a result of an increasingly liberal state.

According to S. D. Gaede,[10] contemporary society has several "bases for discrimination," including "race," gender, sexual orientation, and cultural background. Political correctness aims to implement a standard tolerance level that transcends each discriminating basis. It is clear that these tolerance levels vary, but political correctness eradicates this problem by implying a wholesale restriction on any behavior that may be deemed offensive. It results in the emergence of categorized groups in society that offer no consideration for the individual. Political correctness poses further problems for society because there cannot be a measurement of offensiveness. At the level of the individual, the definition of "offensive" will undoubtedly vary considerably; therefore, it is impossible to implement a blanket ban on offensive discourse. If a select few, invariably the ruling elite, are to decide on a scale and determine what constitutes offensiveness, then society would witness what Gaede describes as "the privatization of conviction."[11] Interestingly, many advocates of freedom of speech argue that the Muslim reaction to *The Satanic Verses* and the cartoon depictions of the Prophet Muhammad are clear examples of excessive political correctness that assert the rights of people to express their freedom of speech. However, they fail to realize the distinct differences between freedom of speech and blasphemy. Britain represents a democratic, liberal society in which equality is promoted regardless of ethnicity, culture, or religion, but, crucially, British laws on blasphemy are anachronistic and fail to accommodate such principles in reality.[12]

In *The Satanic Verses*, Rushdie presented a story that directly questioned significant aspects of the Islamic religion. The most controversial elements of the book were the use of the name "Mahound" to refer to the Prophet Muhammad, the depiction of the Prophet's wives as courtesans, and the suggestion that the Quran lacks all authenticity. The novel, which was written to appeal to Western audiences, presented and reinforced an Orientalist appreciation of Islam; "sex and violence not only sell books, they can also shape the images of other people, other societies, and other civilizations."[13] The novel caused outrage in the global Muslim community, and the book was banned in India and South Africa; some Muslims even burned the book in protest. Furthermore, Ayatollah Khomeini issued a *fatwa* (religious edict) against Rushdie for his apostasy, and it remained in effect for a decade. Throughout its history, the Western world has seen capital punishment inflicted for acts of treason. Islam has a similar concept of "treason." However, it is not, as in the West, based on treachery toward the state but towards the *ummah* (community of Muslim believers). In the case of treason against the *ummah*, capital punishment is the ultimate penalty (as interpreted by some). Within this frame of reasoning, blasphemy is considered an act of treason, and Rushdie was thus regarded as a "traitor." Blasphemy law in Britain, however, was restricted to Christianity, and it did not incorporate profanity against other minority religions.

Ultimately, the relationship between law and religion differs considerably in Islam and Christianity. Western societies that project secularism (but still find it virtually impossible to abandon Christian symbols and principles) have witnessed the containment of apparently blasphemous texts and the altering of law with regard to issues such as homosexuality. Christianity has developed simultaneously with a society that accepts the importance of not enforcing laws that attempt to regulate religious belief and inhibit freedom of speech. In contrast, Muslims believe that the law as revealed to the Prophet Muhammad is perfect in form and should be abided by all and strictly maintained. Therefore, a few puritan Muslims believe that "classical Jurists divided the world into Dar al Islam and Dar al Harb, the abode of Islam and the abode of war."[14] Nonetheless, regardless of the rulers, the law should remain the same. However, it is also true that this very same episode gave Islamophobia the impetus it needed to achieve greater acceptance among the many, reifying its capacity to capture the imagination of the unenlightened.

It is this puritan understanding that the British media depicts as the general Muslim ideology when, in fact, the majority of Muslims believe that it is possible to live perfectly peacefully in the West *and* remain wholly contented as a Muslim.[15] *The Satanic Verses* portrays this Orientalist understanding of Islam to Western audiences. The appeal of the book was increased by the fact that Rushdie was a Muslim born into an Indian family (he has since renounced his faith). As such, many Westerners believed that his writings were a credible source of historical fact. Furthermore, the West appeared to adopt Rushdie as an accepted voice of Islam and Muslims; however, this only served to reinforce the stereotypes present in Western minds. Rushdie is primarily a novelist, not a scholar.

Similarly, the Danish cartoons were arguably an offensive attack on the Islamic religion and, in particular, the Prophet Muhammad. The Danish newspaper was quite possibly aware of the fact that depictions of the Prophet Muhammad of any kind are prohibited in Sunni Islam and that they are an affront to Muslims; yet it published them, not once but twice. In Britain, five thousand Muslims participated in a "unity rally" in Trafalgar Square, "United against Islamophobia, united against incitement, united in our love of the Prophet." The peaceful assembly was not only a demonstration against the cartoons but also an antidote to previous protests by angry young radicals that had resulted both in an exasperated response by civil society and the government. Ultimately, it resulted in the proscription of the Muslim organization Al-Ghuraba (The Strangers), which was responsible for the initial angry demonstration consisting of merely two hundred people or so.

Following the original printing of the caricatures of the Prophet Muhammad, the Muslim reaction was relatively subdued, with small groups peacefully appealing for censorship of the images. When the petitions proved unsuccessful, the protest grew, and messages were transferred throughout the global Muslim community asserting the necessity to suppress the images. After newspapers in Germany, Italy, France, Holland, and Norway reprinted the pictures in February 2006, some extremist Muslim groups responded with violent protests, most notably against the Danish embassies in Lebanon and Syria. These aggressive outbursts were then depicted throughout the Western media as the generalized reaction of the Muslim community as a whole. As such, the local event became national as a result of the intensification and acceleration of efforts by global media technologies. Did the British news media refuse to print the cartoons out of respect for their Muslim readers, or was it because a negative Muslim response was feared? Nevertheless, the portrayal of the Muslim protests primarily focused on volatile attacks on various Danish embassies around the world, thereby disseminating the stereotype of Muslims as terrorists and radicals. Muslim action or reaction that is confrontational, whatever the degree or purpose, is often instrumentalized by current political and media discourses and used as evidence to support the increasingly popular negative views in relation to Islam.[16] There was minimal reporting of peaceful rallies that represented the principles of the majority of the Muslim community. Clearly, the processes of globalization and transnationalism played significant roles in increasing the visibility of the responses to *The Satanic Verses* and the caricatures of the Prophet Muhammad. After the *fatwa* against Rushdie was issued, Khomeini was portrayed in the West as a symbol of evil, similar to

Osama bin Laden in contemporary Western societies. The image of a mad-
dened Muslim zealot and potentially a menace to the West's own (Christian)
existence came to signify a particular ideological standpoint presented to the
West by the media. Globalization has dramatically advanced since the Rushdie
affair, and with the introduction of the Internet and twenty-four-hour news, the
transmission of information (which is not always knowledge or understanding)
is instantaneous.

The accepted awareness of Islam by the West is one that is manipulated
and spoon-fed by the media to unassuming audiences. The consequences of
this are significant for Muslim representation in the West and ultimately for
social cohesion. The managed reality that is depicted by the media is transferred onto society. When interacting with Muslims, Westerners will automati-
cally perceive them as the stereotypes formulated by the media regardless of
the way Muslim people actually are. As a result of the events of 9/11 and 7/7,
this stereotype includes characteristics such as "terrorists," "suicide bombers,"
people who are "anti-West," and "oppressors." It appears that Western societies
are witnessing a cyclical process that cannot be broken unless, potentially,
equality within the law is implemented. Political correctness fails to provide a
solution because the problem is not the offensive opinions of individuals—it
goes beyond that. Muslims argue that freedom of speech is essential in society;
however, the publicizing of deliberately offensive material that offers a misrep-
resentation of a religion does not constitute free speech. The Orientalist ideology of the past is equally evident in contemporary society. This perspective is
continually sustained by globalized Western media as demonstrated in 2006,
with the engineered representation of Muslim reactions to the cartoon depictions of Prophet Muhammad. The arguments that such texts constitute freedom of speech emerge from an Orientalization of Islam that neglects to
adequately consider the Muslim perspective.[17]

British Muslim Women and the Veil: Reexoticizing
the Female Other

One example of the interest in women in Islam occurred in October 2006,
when Jack Straw, former home secretary, commented on the wearing of the
face veil (the *niqab*) by Muslim women who sought his advice in his constitu-
ency surgery of Blackburn. Writing in the *Lancashire Telegraph* (October 5,
2006), Straw simplistically painted a picture of unwanted difference being
exercised by British Muslim women who wished to wear the niqab when
seeking his counsel. Straw argued that it was a "visible statement of separation

and of difference." His comments created a national debate that at the time prompted other notable political figures to make similar claims, including not only Tony Blair, who was still prime minister, but also then chancellor Gordon Brown and then deputy prime minister John Prescott, as well as the shadow leader of the opposition, David Cameron, and his then shadow home secretary, David Davies. The remarks made by Straw and others reflect the exoticization of the Muslim woman, which had its apex in the colonial periods of the nineteenth century but has reemerged in the neo-Orientalist and neoconservative times we live in now. European men infatuated by the infamous but principally imaginary harems of the Mughals or Ottomans see Muslim women as mysterious but altogether alluring "prisoners" in need of "rescuing." In reality, the *chador, burqa,* and the veil constitute an attempt to limit the potential menace to Muslim women posed by unfamiliar men, not, as many people argue, to prevent women from expressing their true physical nature. In the vast majority of cases, Muslim women make their own decisions in relation to covering up. As such, for those who do not follow the practice of their own free will, it is certainly a problem for society, of which Muslims are an important constituent. However, an alternative notion is that British Muslim women born or brought up in a free and open society don the niqab as a reaction to colonialism, particularly in relation to how Muslims in distant lands are being treated by external antagonists. It is a symbol of defiance and an expression of resistance to attempts to forcibly assimilate Muslim minorities without providing adequate resources or generating the capacities of individuals and communities to integrate on their own.[18]

For many, it is simply not appropriate to dictate how people ought to dress in a still relatively tolerant liberal society. However, even so, there are concerns with the niqab as it masks the face, making it difficult to directly communicate with others (i.e., by nonverbal cues). In certain circumstances, however, some might argue that it has the potential to create barriers and further isolate the very people with whom British Muslim minorities need to better engage. This is a practical argument that has a great deal of purchase. However, what was more worrying about Straw was that a well-informed person in a position of power and influence had reignited such a sensitive issue. Utterances repeated, reinforced, and enhanced by senior politicians and public officials, including Trevor Phillips, who, as the last chair of the Commission for Racial Equality, bizarrely predicted "blood on the streets" if matters did not change in relation to Muslim women. His words served only to fuel the existing and rampant Islamophobia in society. In this way, license is given to uncompromising, electioneering political figures to argue that Muslim practice encourages separate lives, destroys multiculturalism, breeds intolerance, and potentially creates "suicide bombers." There is no sense of how the state continues its assault on basic liberties or how it abuses the notions of freedom and democracy in far-away lands. The state pronounces a "fear psychosis" pertaining to the "war on terror," thereby absolving itself of its historical involvement in establishing the concerns in the first instance and then, when opportunity arises, turns the attention toward the "inward-looking" lives that Muslims live at home.[19]

The problems in Britain have been created in part by the complete lack of appreciation of the needs of inner-city Muslim minority communities, who experience deepening economic marginalization and widening social inequality. Public attention is focused away from structure and toward culture, enforcing a debate in relation to "Britishness": a red herring that is an attempt to shift the focus from cultural pluralism or multiculturalism and toward monoculturalism or cultural imperialism. Meanwhile, mosques are fire-bombed, and Muslim graves are desecrated. Niqab-clad women are assaulted in public places, while Muslims feel ever beleaguered and harassed by the workings of state and society. The other aspect of this debate is the focus on women per se: That is, Muslim women are somehow prevented from exercising the freedoms enjoyed by all other women. However, Muslim women argue that the uniformity that wearing the niqab provides is a source of independence and egalitarianism before Allah. In many respects, the niqab is a reactionary "symbol of separateness" enforced by government and media rhetoric that has spun the "war on terror" (before the phraseology was officially dropped in 2007) while emphasizing the presumed unassimilability of Muslims. Many politicians support the idea that the niqab leads to "segregated communities," "parallel lives," or "voluntary apartheid," but what they often forget is the extent of exclusion and alienation that many Muslim minorities already experience. For some women, appropriating certain religiously inspired garb is a response to continued onslaught, while for other women it is an expression of confidence and a form of empowerment against currently hostile media and political discourses. At the same time, this discussion is necessary inasmuch as, internal to Islam, there is also tremendous debate about "what to wear or not" for "modern Muslim women."[20] This is also an important consideration with regard to integration into society and the continuing contributions Muslim minorities can make.

Concluding Remarks

The allegations of media bias need to be taken seriously as the extent of coverage of "extremist Muslims" and "Islamic terrorism" has dramatically increased in recent periods and especially since the events of 9/11 and 7/7. The language used to describe Muslims is often violent, thereby implying that Islam is violent, too. Arabic words have been appropriated into universal journalistic vocabulary and invested with new meaning that is generally exaggerated and aggressive. "Jihad," for example, has been used to signify a military war waged by Islamists against the West. Invariably, the deeper Quranic meaning of the term is, in fact, far broader and refers more to the idea of a "struggle." Words and concepts such as "extremist," "anti-integrationist," "radical," and "fundamentalist" are repeatedly employed in ominous headlines across the entire range of press in Britain. In the post-9/11 era, politicians have used people's fear of Islam for their own political ends. By focusing on the "war on terror," the existing anti-Muslim frame of reference is replaced with the idea of "terror." This reporting is compounded by a concentration on the "enemy within" or the "loyalty" of Muslims to Britain. The examples of *The Satanic Verses* affair of 1989, the Danish cartoons fiasco of September 2005 and February 2006, and the Jack Straw "what not to wear" debate of October 2006 all confirm the importance and the relationship of the news media to the experiences of contemporary forms of Orientalism and Islamophobia.[21]

Historically, Islamophobia had pro-Christian and anti-Muslim features, namely at the time of the Crusades, empire, and colonialism. In the modern era, religious characteristics have been replaced by secular notions, namely a focus on the ideas of freedom, democracy, and global values. Meanwhile, Muslim women are further exoticized, while Muslim men are even more "irrationalized." In relation to political discourse, a form of liberal political correctness that does not explicitly target the religion of Islam has been replaced by a fear of multiculturalism. Meanwhile, the traditional Left is waning, and the Far Right is gaining electoral ground and, in the process, therefore, greater cultural and political acceptability in certain parts of Britain. There are tremendous identity disputes internal to the Muslim community defined and redefined by economic, social, and political challenges, as well as by the external contexts in which groups find themselves. Intergenerational differences within Muslim communities create a vacuum easily filled by hate, anger, and, ultimately, disdain (both in minorities and majorities). In the case of Muslims, the space is seized by managed communitarian political elites and pro–New Labour Muslim groups who legitimize the status quo and existing modes of domination and subordination. Islamophobia is a complex, multifaceted, economic, political, and cultural phenomenon, and its impact on Muslim/non-Muslim relations will remain an important feature of social life in Britain for some time.[22]

NOTES

1. Teun A. van Dijk, *Elite Discourse and Racism* (New York: Sage, 1993).

2. Adrian Blackledge, "The Racialization of Language in British Political Discourse," *Critical Discourse Studies* 3, no. 1 (2006): 61–79.

3. Claire Dwyer, Bindi Shah, and Gurchathen Sanghera, " 'From Cricket Lover to Terror Suspect' — Challenging Representations of Young British Muslim Men," *Gender, Place, and Culture* 15, no. 2 (2008): 117–36.

4. Clinton Bennet, *Victorian Images of Islam* (London: Grey Seal, 1992); Carole Hillenbrand, *The Crusades: Islamic Perspectives* (London: Routledge, 2000).

5. Edward Said, *Orientalism* (London: Routledge and Kegan Paul, 1978).

6. Tariq Modood, *Multicultural Politics: Racism, Ethnicity, and Muslims in Britain* (Edinburgh: Edinburgh University Press, 2005); Pnina Werbner, "Islamophobia: Incitement to Religious Hatred—Legislating for a New Fear?" *Anthropology Today* 21, no. 1 (2005): 5–9.

7. Polly Toynbee, "Last Chance to Speak Out," *Guardian* (October 5, 2001).

8. Kenan Malik, "The Islamophobia Myth," *Prospect* 107 (February 2005).

9. Gabriele Marranci, "Multiculturalism, Islam, and the Clash of Civilisations Theory: Rethinking Islamophobia," *Culture and Religion* 5, no. 1 (2004): 105–17.

10. Stan D. Gaede, *When Tolerance Is No Virtue: Political Correctness, Multiculturalism, and the Future of Truth and Justice* (Downers Grove: InterVarsity, 1994), 21.

11. Ibid., 22.

12. Bassam Tibi, *Islam and the Cultural Accommodation of Social Change*, trans. Clare Krojzl (Boulder: Westview, 1990).

13. Ziauddin Sardar, and Merryl Wyn-Davies, *Distorted Imagination: Lessons from the Rushdie Affair* (London: Grey Seal, 1990), 34.

14. Malise A. Ruthven, *Satanic Affair: Salman Rushdie and the Rage of Islam* (London: Hogarth, 1991), 51.

15. Ed Husain, *The Islamist* (London: Penguin, 2007); Ziauddin Sardar, *Balti Britain: A Journey through the British Asian Experience* (London: Granta, 2008).

16. Elizabeth Poole and John E. Richardson, eds., *Muslims and the News Media* (New York: Tauris, 2006).

17. Shabbir Akhtar, *Be Careful with Muhammad! The Salman Rushdie Affair* (London: Bellew, 1989); Kai Hafiz, ed., *Islam and the West in the Mass Media: Fragmented Images in a Globalizing World* (Cresskill: Hampton, 1999).

18. Haleh Afshar, Rob Aitken, and Myfanwy Franks, "Feminisms, Islamophobia, and Identities," *Political Studies* 53, no. 2 (2005): 262–83.

19. Frank Furedi, *Invitation to Terror: The Expanding Empire of the Unknown* (London: Continuum, 2006); Arun Kundnani, *The End of Tolerance: Racism in 21st Century Britain* (London: Pluto, 2007); Arun Kundnani, "Islamism and the Roots of Liberal Rage," *Race and Class* 50, no. 2 (2008): 40–68.

20. Haleh Afshar, "Can I See Your Hair? Choice, Agency, and Attitudes of Faith and Feminism for Muslim Women Who Cover," *Ethnic and Racial Studies* 31, no. 2 (2008): 411–27.

21. "What Not to Wear" is a fashion makeover reality television program that has aired in the UK since 2001 and was watched by more than six million people at the height of its popularity. The term is used in this chapter to represent the ironic nature of a well-heeled, middle-class, middle-aged English gentleman giving advice about Muslim women's clothing.

22. Tahir Abbas, *Islamic Radicalism and Multicultural Politics: The British Experience* (New York: Routledge, 2010).

5

Islamophobia and Anti-Americanism: Measurements, Dynamics, and Consequences

Mohamed Nimer

Islamophobia and anti-Americanism denote hatred of a faith community or a people because they are Muslim or American. Such hatred is expressed through vitriolic rhetoric and/or physical acts of violence and discrimination against objects or persons because of their association with Islam, Muslims, the United States, or Americans. To appreciate the grave dangers of Islamophobia and anti-Americanism, one must be clear about their essence—what they are and what they are not. A critical study of Islam or Muslims is not Islamophobic. Likewise, a disapproving analysis of U.S. history and government is not anti-American. One can disagree with Islam or with what some Muslims do without ill feelings. Similarly, one can oppose U.S. policies without detesting the United States as a nation.

These demarcations may sound clear and simple, and yet both Islamophobia and anti-Americanism are on the rise. Anti-Muslim feelings in the United States have increased, especially after the terrorists' attacks of September 11, 2001 (hereafter referred to as 9/11). Between one-fourth and one-third of Americans hold negative views of Islam and Muslims.[1] Opinion leaders, especially on Internet blogs, talk radio, and cable television, are increasingly using harsh language to refer to the Islamic faith. Franklin Graham, Jerry Falwell, and Pat Robertson, religious leaders often courted by elected officials and politicians, have called Islam "a wicked religion," the Prophet Muhammad "a terrorist," and Muslims "worse than Nazis."

Rising Awareness

Islamophobia has received more attention as intellectuals have begun question-ing the conventional stereotypical portrayals of Arabs and Muslims. Perhaps the earliest work to tackle the intellectual sources of such prejudice is Edward Said's *Orientalism*. Published in 1978, it illustrated how Islam is "otherized" as a religion that is very different from Christianity and Judaism and a culture that is inferior, violent, static, monolithic, and irrational.

In 1980 the American-Arab Anti-Discrimination Committee (ADC) was founded to raise public awareness of anti-Arab stereotypes in popular culture. Quite often the ADC and its leaders found themselves confused with Islam and Muslims. A decade later, the Council on American-Islamic Relations (CAIR) began organizing public challenges to anti-Muslim bias. The state of this prejudice became shockingly clear hours after the 1995 bombing of the Murrah Federal Building in Oklahoma City. Politicians, former officials, and self-styled terrorism and Middle East experts falsely blamed Middle Easterners and Islamic fundamentalists for the attack. The accusations were widely reported in the media, inflaming an anti-Arab, anti-Muslim mood that ignited 220 reported incidents of intimidation and hate crimes across the country.[2]

A CAIR report documenting this episode of glaring prejudice became a front-page story in the *New York Times*—a first in the history of media coverage of bias against Muslims in the United States.[3] Since then, CAIR has published an annual report, *The Status of Muslim Civil Rights in the United States*, which tracks complaints of anti-Muslim harassment, discrimination, and violence. Although such reports have received scant public attention, media reporting on anti-Muslim incidents has generally, though modestly, increased.

Despite growing awareness, Muslims remain strangers to most Americans: Nearly two-thirds of those polled told pollsters they do not have a Muslim friend, classmate, or coworker.[4] After the Oklahoma City bombing, media outlets identified the emerging domestic terrorist threat in right-wing militias. How-ever, these are American extremists, while the radicals of 9/11 were foreigners. This distinction, however, was not extended to the radicals involved in the London subway attacks. They were not seen as nationals who had gone to the dark side. Rather, they were seen as Muslims who had attacked Britain because of religion. Indeed, some religious ideas are part of the story in the three cases, but only in the instance involving Christians was religion decoupled from terror. This double standard lies at the heart of the current manifestations of Islamophobia.

Measuring Prejudice

Anti-Muslim sentiment can be measured by monitoring public views on Islam and Muslims. While European pollsters have not tracked public attitudes about Islam and Muslims, American pollsters have consistently provided data since 9/11. They have found no steady pattern of hostility. As table 5.1 shows, the favorability rating of Islam stayed within the close range of 38–40 percent from 2002 to 2005. But, as the wars in Iraq and Afghanistan dragged on and the insurgencies and terrorist attacks continued, the favorability rating dropped sharply to 15 percent in 2007. However, Americans' unfavorable view of Islam increased from 33 percent in 2002 to 37 percent in 2005 but decreased to 30 percent in 2007. How could both favorable and unfavorable views decline? American public opinion is increasingly polarized at a time of growing U.S. involvement in the Muslim world. The rising intensity of feelings on the far ends of the political/ideological spectrum may have produced such seemingly contradictory outcomes.

Other polls measured public responses to extreme feelings about Muslims. More than one-fourth of survey respondents agreed with the statements "Muslims teach their children to hate" and "Muslims value life less than other people."[5] In 2004, about 44 percent of respondents said they believe that some curtailment of civil liberties for Muslim Americans is necessary.[6] Yet, more recent opinion polls show that most Americans believe Muslim extremists distort rather than represent the teachings of Islam.[7] Those with the most negative attitudes toward Islam and Muslims tend to be less-educated, politically conservative, white males.[8] To sum up, while Americans harbor substantial fear and suspicion of Islam and Muslims, such sentiment is

TABLE 5.1. American Public Opinion Views of Islam

	Favorable	Unfavorable	Don't Know
March 2002	38	33	29
July 2003	40	34	26
July 2004	39	37	24
July 2005	39	36	25
September 2007	15	30	23

Source: Pew Research Center, various surveys. See http://pewforum.org/surveys/religionviews07/#section1 (accessed March 16, 2008). The question in the 2007 poll was open ended. Responses were classified as positive, negative, or neutral. http://pewforum.org/docs/index.php?DocID=89 (accessed March 16, 2008).

not pervasive; it is a minority sentiment that either did not change or slightly receded.

(Islamophobia can also be measured by the frequency of anti-Muslim incidents. Table 5.2 presents FBI data that officially documents that anti-Muslim violence has risen dramatically in the United States since 9/11.) Although the number of offenses decreased after a sharp peak in the year of the attacks, the overall upward trend continued. The five-year average of the number of hate-crime offenses before and after 2001 increased from 30.6 to 171—nearly a sixfold jump.

The Council on American-Islamic Relations has developed a community-based reporting of discrimination incidents, which include not only physical violence but also harassment and denial of equal rights in different walks of life. The statistical tracking of these reports shows an acute rise in the number of incidents. From 1996 to 2000 CAIR received a total of 1,497 reports.[9] The number increased to 7,582 from 2002 to 2006, or a fourfold increase. Assaults on mosques in the West have become routine.[10] Additionally, post-9/11 discriminatory government policies have impacted tens of thousands of immigrants.

(Are fear and bias against Muslims justifiable reactions to 9/11 and subsequent terrorism in the name of Islam? Fear is a natural emotional reaction whenever people feel danger. However, when such an emotion is expressed in a discriminatory action or in the form of rhetoric against a whole faith community or against persons because they are or appear to be Muslim, then natural fear will have morphed into Islamophobia) Likewise, for Muslims impacted

TABLE 5.2. FBI Statistics on Anti-Islamic Hate Crimes: 1996–2006

Year	Number of Offenses
1996	33
1997	31
1998	22
1999	34
2000	33
2001	546
2002	170
2003	155
2004	193
2005	146
2006	191

http://www.fbi.gov/ucr/hate96.pdf, December 15, 2008 http://www.fbi.gov/ucr/hc97all.pdf, December 15, 2008 http://www.fbi.gov/ucr/98hate.pdf, December 15, 2008 http://www.fbi.gov/ucr/99hate.pdf, December 15, 2008 http://www.fbi.gov/ucr/cius_00/hate00.pdf, December 15, 2008 http://www.fbi.gov/ucr/01hate.pdf, December 15, 2008 http://www.fbi.gov/ucr/hatecrime2002.pdf, December 15, 2008 http://www.fbi.gov/ucr/03hc.pdf, December 15, 2008 http://www.fbi.gov/ucr/hc2004/hctable1.htm, December 15, 2008 http://www.fbi.gov/ucr/hc2005/table1.htm, December 15, 2008 http://www.fbi.gov/ucr/hc2006/table1.html, December 15, 2008 negatively by U.S. policies, frustration with and anger toward the United States is a natural reaction, but attacking Western-looking persons because they appear American is an expression of anti-Americanism.

There is no systematic tracking of anti-American incidents. The U.S. annual report on global terrorism includes politically motivated acts of violence worldwide. Most of the attacks described in this annual release do not involve U.S. targets—actual or perceived. Polling data offer some clues. A global survey of world public opinion in November 2005 revealed that many Muslims maintain a negative view of the United States. In five major Muslim-majority countries, respondents with an unfavorable view of the United States ranged from 51–79 percent.[11] Favorable opinion declined sharply from 2002 to 2006: from 61 percent to 30 percent in Indonesia, from 25 percent to 15 percent in Jordan, and from 30 percent to 12 percent in Turkey.[12] One must note that studies show that anti-American feelings have spread well beyond the Muslim world and even among America's NATO allies, such as Germany.[13] In other Western nations, the average favorable rating of the United States in Canada, Britain, France, and Spain decreased from 67 percent in 2000 to 50 percent in 2005.[14]

Politics of Prejudice

When ignorance and stereotypes prevail in an age of great terror, it is not hard to imagine how the notion that the "other" is the enemy can gain currency. American ultraconservatives use fear of Islam to gather support for their position on identity discourse. Free Congress Foundation (FCF), a major advocate of an exclusivist Christian identity, states: "[O]ur main focus is on the Culture War. Will America return to the culture that made it great, our traditional, Judeo-Christian, Western culture? Or will we continue the long slide into the cultural and moral decay of political correctness?"[15] The FCF holds weekly meetings, which include briefings by members of Congress and White House officials. The meeting is attended by many leaders of conservative organizations.[16]

The leaders of FCF believe that the United States is facing a cultural disintegration. Their main concerns revolve around social issues and the role of Christianity in shaping society. To widen their appeal, they use Islam and Muslims, categories that are easy to pick on, as scapegoats. Former director of the Center for Cultural Conservatism at the FCF William Lind writes: "While many average Americans recognize American Muslims as a dangerous fifth column, the multiculturalist elite demands a 'tolerance of diversity' that Islam itself does not know. A Republican administration invites mullahs to the

White House to celebrate Islamic holidays. That multiculturalism preaches the suicide of the West."[17] (Samuel Huntington, conservative political thinker and author of the well-known *Clash of Civilizations*, shares the essence of such lamentation, although he attributes the perceived threats to American national identity to broader factors, including the growth of minority groups— particularly Hispanics—and the diluting effect of globalization on American corporate culture.)[18]

Richard Cizik, former leader of the National Association of Evangelicals, points out that Christian Right voices receive disproportionate press coverage, although the whole religious Right, including the fundamentalists, represents at most 25–30 percent of the evangelical movement.[19] Cizik warns against ste-reotyping evangelicals on the basis of the intolerant views of certain religious conservatives. The misperception of evangelicals is compounded every time politicians engage in posturing that validates extreme voices.

A case in point is John McCain's relationship with televangelist Rod Parsley of Columbus, Ohio, who believes Christians and Christianity are under attack by what he calls "the forces of secularism and humanism."[20] He coupled his political mobilization of religious conservative voters with a campaign of vilifi-cation against Islam. After publishing *Silent No More*, a book with extreme anti-Muslim views, he referred to 9/11 as a "war that has raged in nations around the world [and] merely exploded onto our Western landscape—the war between Islam and Christian civilization."[21] A leader of a megachurch that is rising in religious Right circles, Parsley has been courted by conservative politicians. Prominent conservative figures, like former attorney general John Ashcroft, have spoken in Parsley's church. In addition, GOP candidate John McCain vis-ited Parsley in Cincinnati and called him a "spiritual guide."[22] Collin Powell, former Bush administration secretary of state, split from his party in 2008 in part because of what he described as an intolerable level of intolerance: "I have heard senior members of my own [Republican] party drop the suggestion [that Obama] is a Muslim and might be associated with terrorists."[23]

In political seasons, fear of Islam and Muslims has proven to be a useful mobilizer across party lines. The rumor about Senator Obama's being Muslim serves as a vivid illustration. No sooner was it made public than it became major national news. It turned out that Obama's father has a Muslim heritage, but Obama's parents divorced when he was two, and he was reared by his Christian mother. A Clinton campaign volunteer was fired after revelations that she was behind the rumor.[24] Instead of using his old Muslim ties as an added advantage for any future president who might be dealing heavily with the Muslim world, the senator mobilized supporters, including his church pastor, to provide witness that he is a not a Muslim but a practicing Christian.[25]

Islamophobia often goes hand in hand with anti-Arab racism, which, too, has been used to cultivate votes. Conservative radio talk-show host Rush Limbaugh, aiming at listeners who might not be swayed to reject Obama because of his blackness, suggested he is an Arab:

> These polls on how one-third of blue-collar white Democrats won't vote for Obama because he's black, and—but he's not black. Do you know he has not one shred of African-American blood? He doesn't have any African—that's why when they asked whether he was authentic, whether he's down for the struggle. He's Arab. You know, he's from Africa. He's from Arab parts of Africa. He's not—his father was—he's not African-American. The last thing that he is is African-American. I guess that's splitting hairs, I don't—it's just all these little things, everything seems upside-down today in this country.[26]

Politically motivated Islamophobia has also taken the form of well-funded, well-planned, ambitious campaigns. *Obsession: Radical Islam's War against the West* is a stereotype-filled propaganda film with extensive usage of images of Arab and Iranian military activity. It was produced by a start-up organization, the Clarion Fund, to coincide with the 2008 U.S. election. The cover of the DVD notes: "The threat of radical Islam is the most important issue facing us today. But it's a topic that neither the presidential candidates nor the media are discussing openly. It's our responsibility to ensure we can all make an informed vote in November." Robin Saul, president and publisher of the North Carolina *News and Record* decided against distributing the DVDs: "We were told its purpose was educational. We didn't see it as educational at all. It was fear-mongering and divisive."[27] It has been widely reported that 28 million free *Obsession* DVDs were distributed by direct mail and in U.S. newspapers in swing states. The message of the film is inescapable: Vote for a president (i.e., a Republican) who will confront the Muslim threat.

While the intensity and the volume of Islamophobic politics increased after 9/11, evidence of it existed during election seasons before the disaster. However, that usually took the form of maligning Arab or Muslim candidates for public office, pressuring congressional and presidential hopefuls to stay away from Arab and Muslim groups, and demanding that politicians refuse contributions from Arab or Muslim Americans. Yielding to such forces, candidate Hillary Clinton returned money raised by members of the American Muslim Alliance in 2000, when Clinton's opponent accused the group of sympathy with terrorism for advocating a Palestinian state.[28] Ironically, this happened in the same year when the American Muslim Political Coordination Council, an alliance of American Muslim groups, endorsed republican George W. Bush for president.

Evidence of organized Islamophobia extends beyond electoral politics. Outfits such as Frontpagemag.com, Jihadwatch.com, Worldnetdaily.com, Danielpipes.org, the Middle East Forum, and Campus Watch promote the premise that Islam and Muslims are the threatening other. They actively work to malign organizations, political and civic leaders, and academics who counter their Islamophobic rhetoric. Their leaders, including Daniel Pipes, David Horowitz, and Robert Spencer, have teamed up with conservative pundits like Michael Ledeen, Sean Hannity, and Ann Coulter to woo Republican college students, asking them to host events dubbed Islamofascism Awareness Week—curiously countering the Muslim Student Association's long-held program Islam Awareness Week.[29]

Mutually Reinforcing Dynamics

A circular cause-and-effect relationship exists between Islamophobia and anti-Americanism. Consider the following sequence of events, starting arbitrarily with 9/11: The strike by Al-Qaeda left thousands of people dead and injured and triggered the most noticeable anti-Muslim violence in U.S. history and the most vocal wave of anti-Islamic rhetoric in the West. The attack is then used to justify the invasion of two Muslim-majority countries, Afghanistan and Iraq, where hundreds of thousands of people have been killed or injured. This then unleashed a wave of terrorist attacks against vulnerable targets of U.S. allies around the world (the bombing of establishments frequented by nationals of U.S. allies in Bali, Casablanca, Riyadh, Istanbul, Madrid, and London.

These attacks have been followed by increased U.S. pressures on Muslims in the United States and abroad, including human rights abuses and the use of torture in the name of national security. Revelations about such practices at Abu-Ghraib and other U.S. holding facilities in Afghanistan and Guantanamo Bay, Cuba, have inflamed anti-American sentiments.

So the pattern is clear: Terrorist attacks against Americans are followed by anti-Muslim rhetoric and policy. This in turn reinforces anti-American sentiment and provokes a new round of terrorist attacks. For those who promote reconciliation, it is pointless to ask which of the two phenomena began first. What is more important is to recognize the symmetrical relationship between the two, namely, as Islamophobia increases, anti-Americanism is strengthened, and vice versa.

Anti-Americanism is usually dismissed as unimportant rhetoric. Some call it an irrational disposition; others say it is inevitable because many people around the world feel envious of America's power and prosperity, which have been assumed for so long that it does not matter what others feel so long as they respect the United States. This attitude, however, is self-defeating in a world that is becoming increasingly interdependent and highly impacted by the dynamics of communication.

What factors have led to this unfortunate state of affairs? What remedies should be sought to ameliorate prejudice? In this chapter I discuss the most salient misconceptions and real grievances fueling the current vicious cycle. I also outline the basic ingredients of solutions that may bring about its end.

Misconceptions

There is a mirror-image effect in American Islamic relations. While Hollywood movies reduce Muslims to what Jack Shaheen calls the three Bs (billionaires, bombers, and belly dancers), many in the Muslim world view Americans in terms of three Rs: rich, ruthless, and raunchy. Evidence shows that many Muslims do hold strong negative stereotypes of Westerners in general and Americans in particular. A June 2006 Pew Research Center poll found that "pluralities in all of the predominantly Muslim countries surveyed associate Westerners with being greedy, arrogant, immoral, selfish, and violent. And solid majorities in Jordan, Turkey, and Egypt—as well as a plurality of Muslims in Nigeria—view Westerners as being fanatical."[30]

The problem lies in the broad-brush generalization of Muslims and Americans as morally lax people who have ample means and will to harm others. This sweeping notion, which constitutes the crux of anti-Americanism and Islamophobia, is usually accompanied by demonization and justification of hostility.

Beyond agreeing with negative statements about Americans and Muslims, there is agitation that invokes antagonistic emotions. Pat Robertson has repeatedly said on national television that al-Qaeda militants are only carrying out Quranic commands to kill Jews and Christians. Such accusations were echoed in other forums beyond the so-called Christian Right. For example, in December 2004 the Simon Wiesenthal Center hosted an event at the University of Toronto to counter the UN secretary general's seminar on Islamophobia. The Canadian event featured Bruce Tefft, a former CIA official, who blamed Islam for terrorism: "Islamic terrorism is based on Islam as revealed through the Qu'ran. . . . To pretend that Islam has nothing to do with Sept. 11 is to willfully ignore the obvious and to forever misinterpret events. . . . There is no difference between Islam and Islamic fundamentalism, which is a totalitarian construct."[31]

This extreme form of associating Islam with violence also suggests treating Islam not as a religion but as an aggressive ideology. This message has had resonance in some conservative circles. Most recently Oklahoma state legislator Rex Duncan (who is a Republican) refused a gift of Islam's holy book. He said, "Most Oklahomans do not endorse the idea of killing innocent women and children in the name of ideology."[32]

Anti-American agitation by Muslim radicals often takes the form of blaming the United States for most of the Muslim world's problems, even in areas where America is not a player. For example, Bin Laden repeatedly held U.S. imperialism responsible for the persecution of Muslims in the Indian state of Assam. Bin Laden's faulty rationale goes like this: The exercise of U.S. power has left Muslims unable to support vulnerable Muslim minorities, such as those in India. However, there is no link between the rise of U.S. power and the persecution of Muslims in Assam. In fact, the general weakness of Muslim-majority countries predates the rise of the United States in global affairs.[33]

This spurious association is also evident in linking Iraq to 9/11, where the broad demographic characteristics of religion and ethnicity are the real connection. Perhaps mindful of the sensitivity of this linkage, the Bush administration first said that, in the post-9/11 world, the United States could not afford to let Iraq keep weapons of mass destruction. The administration also accused the Iraqi government under Saddam of having had links with al-Qaeda. Of course, evidence for such claims was lacking from the start. However, U.S. government officials testified in U.S. and international forums that the United States possessed intelligence confirming these reports.

In both cases—the invasion of Iraq and the attacks on Americans and their allies—the justification of violence is made via ideology-based views of history and world affairs, assigning responsibility for events not by relating actors to actions but by selectively mixing geopolitical analyses and visions with ethnic, religious, and/or national affiliations. In other words, Bin Laden's stretching the line of logic beyond reason and fact in blaming the United States is clearly anti-American, just as Bush's justification of the war in Iraq as retaliation for 9/11 is Islamophobic.

Real Grievances

In many ways Islamophobia and anti-Americanism reflect the sad state of U.S.-Muslim world relations. The United States has inherited and maintained the status quo of a Muslim world divided by colonial European powers. For many years the United States has invested in relations with key Muslim-majority states ruled by repressive regimes. A 2008 report suggests that the United States readjust its position on internal political disputes in these countries in ways that focus on principle rather than on the parties involved in these conflicts.[34]

Unjust American policies cause anti-American feelings, while terrorism stirs up Islamophobia. Late University of Maryland political scientist Louis Cantori reported astonishment and anger while attending a public meeting in 2004, at which returning members of the U.S. occupation administration in Iraq expressed exhilaration at what they saw as successful U.S. imperialism.[35] However, many of the world's Muslims perceive America's militarism as a modern crusade whose broad aim is to weaken Muslims. By the same token, the vulnerability Americans feel regarding terrorism is justified; the fear is real.

Legitimate grievances must be addressed to dry up the sources of anger. The U.S. government should work to resolve conflicts in the Muslim world or, at the very least, refrain from opposing national liberation movements because its hostility feeds legitimate resentment against the United States. Michael Scheuer, former CIA head of the Bin Laden unit, cautions, however, that this may not happen so long as the U.S. government is in the grip of those who believe in an imperial vision of America's position in the world.[36]

Ultimately, controlling terrorism is a task best handled by security agencies. Muslim-majority countries should not only work to curb terrorist activity but also guarantee freedom of speech and association so that extremist ideas can be recognized and isolated by mainstream Muslim opinion. This prospect could prove more effective than U.S. military ventures. Only the hope of a better future can temper the frustrations of Muslims and Americans who are distressed about reactionary behavior and disastrous outcomes.

Obstacles to and Catalysts for Change

Anti-Muslim sentiment may recede as Americans learn to differentiate Muslim extremists from mainstream Muslims. Moreover, expressions of anti-Americanism may wane as Muslims learn how to separate American national symbols and ideals from the policies of any particular administration. Education and improved communication between Americans and the Muslim world can dispel stereotypes and erroneous perceptions. Yet, re-gardless of how many misconceptions are cleared up, violence involving Americans and Muslims overseas will always reinforce new rounds of anti-Americanism and Islamophobia. Both have also been fueled by clash-ing political agendas.

Serious obstacles limit the chances of a meaningful change. Denial is the major complicating factor. Insisting that the CIA hatched the 9/11 attacks to justify the subsequent wars only widens the gap of understanding. Likewise, seven in ten Americans believed it was likely that Saddam Hussein was personally involved in the 9/11 attacks despite the absence of any evidence to that effect.[37] Some commentators on both sides conveniently use such perceptions as evidence demonstrating that people on the other side are driven by hate and conspiracy theories.

However, Muslim activists of all sorts around the globe condemned 9/11 in no ambiguous terms. American Muslim leaders and major Islamic centers endorsed an antiterror *fatwa* (religious opinion) issued by major Muslim jurists.[38] In addition, Muslim public affairs agencies have maintained regular contacts with law enforcement agencies. American Muslim organizations encourage the recruitment of Muslims in these agencies.

Condescending attitudes toward others eliminate the prospect of building relationships of trust necessary for a fruitful engagement. Muslims who speak of America as a sick culture contribute to the reinforcement of mistrust. Another form of denigration is common among pundits who use the views of former Muslims as a yardstick for "moderate Islam," which implies the intolerant position that one can dialogue with Muslims only when they renounce their faith. Neither Islamophobia nor anti-Americanism is destined to dominate American Islamic relations. However, if mainstream voices acquiesce to the loud noises of fanatics and zealots, then the self-fulfilling prophecy of the clash of civilizations will become the order of the day.

Dialogue and Reform

Dialogue for the purpose of exposing myths and forging a common understanding is a must to ensure a peaceful future. Charting the way out of stereotyping and communication based on profiling, Muslims, Christians, and Jews must acknowledge and build on their shared religious heritage. Beyond members of the Abrahamic family of faiths, scriptures of all of the world's major religions enunciate the golden rule, which simply recommends treating others as one would like to be treated. This universal principle offers a solid moral ground for peaceful coexistence.

Political realists may think such a lofty idea will not change the nature of international relations, which, in their view, is based on mistrust, power, and interest. But those who believe in the free will of humankind may disagree. Therefore, there is reason to support a global discourse premised on a shared future. Within this framework, various subdiscourses may prove fruitful. One conversation should deal with the notion of world domination.[39] Neither the Quran nor the Bible justifies domination and oppression. Princeton scholar Richard Bulliet argues that Islamic and Western civilizations are more inter-linked than many are prepared to acknowledge.[40]

Another exchange in the global dialogue revolves around interfaith relations. There are some who criticize conventional, feel-good interfaith meetings, believing they have produced few tangible results. They believe fruitful engagements must appreciate differences, as well as agreements, between faith communities. Yet contacts between American Muslims on the one hand and Catholics and mainline Protestants on the other have gone beyond pleasant exchanges of good ideas and intentions. There have been joint responses to crises, including political alliances to defend civil rights and oppose unjust wars. Still, relations between Muslims and Jews are very tense and conflict ridden. Furthermore, increasing anti-Muslim sentiment is finding a place in certain segments of the American conservative movement, including some think tanks and Republican politicians and activists.

Unfortunately, many Muslims mix criticism of Israel with ambivalence or even prejudice against Jews. On August 31, 2007, Rabbi Eric Yoffie, president of the Union of Reform Judaism, a movement that claims 1.5 million members, raised this issue in his address to the annual convention of the Islamic Society of North America (ISNA).[41] Such a call would be more effective if coupled with a proper acknowledgment of the faults of organized Jewry, which goes the extra mile in justifying and supporting the Israeli destruction of Palestinian life.

Another discussion involves Muslims in the West and the rest of the *ummah* (worldwide community of believers). Western Muslims are sharing numerous good ideas with their fellow Muslims around the globe—ideas that may contribute to rapprochement between East and West. One of the great communication barriers between the two sides stems from the popular perception that religion accounts for too much in Muslim public life. Jamal Badawi, a reputable North American Muslim scholar and activist, differentiates between secularism and secularity.[42] The former is an antireligion ideology, which Muslims would oppose, whereas the latter is a principle that allows the development of effective political institutions that Muslims may view as good. Badawi argues that the American model of separating church and state follows the secularity concept. If this understanding becomes a basis for political reform in Muslim-majority countries, it would demonstrate that American principles are consistent with Islamic ideals. It would also demonstrate that Muslims can agree on a conception of the public good that includes the views and needs of believers and nonbelievers alike.

Islamic scholar Tariq Ramadan goes even further. He attempts to define a Western Muslim culture in order to facilitate the integration of the growing Muslim population in the West:

> We shall have to liberate ourselves . . . by developing a rich, positive, and participatory presence in the West that must contribute from within to debates about the universality of values, globalization, ethics, and the meaning of life in modern times. In addition, it is time to be committed to forms of religious education that will encourage independence of mind and in-depth consideration of the application of Islamic principles in the West and the meaning of being a European or [an] American Muslim.[43]

American civil society groups should engage their counterparts in Muslim-majority states rather than justify denying them a place at the political table. The debate over Islam and democracy must be seen in a new light: Subscribers to the notion that the two are incompatible are those who would like to see the West clash with the Muslim world. In other words, the question of compatibility is not answerable through a positivist scientific discovery. Rather, it is subject to one's preferences for East-West relations. Those who opt for conflict would welcome the intensification of Islamophobia and anti-Americanism.

NOTES

1. These findings are supported by public opinion polls commissioned by CAIR in 2004 and 2005. See Council on American-Islamic Relations (CAIR), *American Public Opinion about Islam and Muslims* (Washington, D.C., 2005). A Gallup/USA Today poll in 2006 found four in ten Americans admitting prejudice against Muslims. See http://www.beliefnet.com/story/197/story_19765_1.html (accessed Nov. 1, 2007).

2. CAIR, *A Rush to Judgment* (Washington, D.C.: Author, 1995).

3. James Brooks, "Attacks on U.S. Muslims Surge Even As Their Faith Takes Hold," *New York Times* (Aug. 28, 1995). See http://www.nytimes.com/1995/08/28/us/attacks-on-us-muslims-surge-even-as-their-faith-takes-hold.html?scp=1&sq=August%2028,%201995,%20Center%20for%20American-Islamic%20Relations&st=cse (accessed June 18, 2010).

4. CAIR, *American Public Opinion about Islam and Muslims*, 2006, 6.

5. Genesis Research Associates, *American Public Opinion about Islam and Muslims*. Descanso, CA., 2005, http://www.cair.com/Portals/0/pdf/american_public_opinion_on_muslims_islam (Dec. 15, 2008).

6. See http://www.comm.cornell.edu/msrg/report1a.pdf (Mar. 30, 2008).

7. Genesis Research Associates, *American Public Opinion about Islam and Muslims*.

8. Ibid.

9. CAIR's reporting years are 1996–1997 and 2000–2001.

10. In 2006 CAIR reported 221 anti-Muslim incidents, or an average of more than four cases per week, involving mosques or community organizations. CAIR, *The Status of Muslim Civil Rights in the United States*, 2007, 15. http://www.cair.com/Portals/0/pdf/2007-Civil-Rights-Report.pdf.

11. See http://pewresearch.org/pubs/6/arab-and-muslim-perceptions-of-the-united-states (Dec. 15, 2008).

12. See http://pewglobal.org/commentary/display.php?AnalysisID=1019, Dec. 15, 2008.

13. See, for example, Michael Werz, *Anti-Americanism and Ambivalence in the New Germany*, German Marshall Fund and the Brookings Institution (Washington, D.C., January 2005).

14. Pew Research Center, the Pew Global Attitudes Project (Washington, D.C., June 23, 2005): http://pewglobal.org/reports/display.php?ReportID=247 (Feb. 18, 2009).

15. Free Congress Foundation, "About Free Congress Foundation," http://www.freecongress.org/aboutfcf.aspx (Dec. 15, 2008).

16. *New York Times* (2008).

17. William Lind, "Multiculturalism Reigns over the West," *Insight Magazine* (Dec. 31, 2001). Nicholas Kristof attributes the following quote about American Muslims to William Lind and Paul Weyrich: "They should be encouraged to leave. They are a fifth column in this country." Kristof cites Paul Weyrich: "Islam is, quite simply, a religion of war." See *New York Times* (July 9, 2002).

18. Samuel Huntington, *Who Are We? The Challenges to American National Identity* (New York: Simon and Schuster, 2004). Contrast Huntington's views with those of Charles Taylor; see James Tully, ed., *Philosophy in an Age of Pluralism: The Philosophy of Charles Taylor in Question* (New York: Cambridge University Press, 1994).

19. Richard Cizik, "Don't Stereotype Evangelicals," in *Islamophobia and Anti-Americanism: Causes and Remedies*, ed. Mohamed Nimer, 115–16 (Beltsville, MD.: Amana, 2007).

20. Rod Parsley, *Culturally Incorrect: How Clashing Worldviews Affect Your Future* (Nashville: Nelson, 2007), 18.

21. Rod Parsley, *Silent No More* (Lake Mary, Fla.: Charisma, 2005). See http://www.WorldNetDaily.com (June 23, 2005).

22. *Mother Jones* (Mar. 12, 2008). Parsley cites "the global war against radical Islamic extremism" as a common-ground issue for Christians. Parsley, *Culturally Incorrect*, 198.

23. *Meet the Press* (NBC, Oct. 19, 2008).

24. See http://Washingtonpost.com (Dec. 5, 2007).

25. *Washington Post* (Nov. 29, 2007).

26. Media Matters carries the audio clip of this Sept. 22, 2008, citation at http://mediamatters.org/items/200809220015 (Feb. 18, 2009); the clip was transcribed by Dan Chmielewski, "Rush Limbaugh: Obama Is Arab, Not African-American," http://www.theliberaloc.com/2008/09/23/rush-limbaugh-obaba-is-arab-not-african-amrican/ (Feb. 18, 2009).

27. John Robinson, Sept. 21, 2008, http://blog.news-record.com/staff/ jrblog/2008/09/why_we_didnt_di.shtml (Feb. 18, 2009).

28. Dean E. Murphy, "Mrs. Clinton Says She Will Return Money Raised by a Muslim Group." *New York Times* (Oct. 26, 2000). See http://www.nytimes. com/2000/10/26/nyregion/ mrs-clinton-says-she-will-return-money-raised-by-a-mus-lim-group.html?scp=1&sq=October% 2026,%202000,%20Hilary%20Clinton&st=cse. See also Muqtedar Khan, "Hillary Clinton Rejects Muslim Support," http://iviews.com, Nov. 2, 2000; http://www.themodernreligion.com/jihad/hilary-mkhan.html (Dec. 15, 2008).

29. For evidence of such activism, see frontpagemag.com, Sept. 21, 2007, http:// frontpagemag.com/Articles/Read.aspx?GUID=5EC88545-3022-47F9-8213- 38314CCA6F09 (Feb. 18, 2009): http://www.terrorismawareness.org/ (Feb. 18, 2009). Also see Robert Spencer, *Stealth Jihad: How Radical Islam Is Subverting America without Guns or Bombs* (Washington, D.C.: Regnery, 2008).

30. See http://pewglobal.org/reports/display.php?PageID=831 (Nov. 2, 2007). Also see Ibrahim Kalin, Kudret Bulbul, and Bekir Berat Ozipek, "A Fragmented Vision: Perceptions of the West in Turkish Society," *Insight Turkey* 10, no. 1 (2008): 129–47.

31. "Islamic Terror Based on Qu'ran: Ex-CIA Official," http://www.freerepublic. com/focus/f-news/1297328/posts (Dec. 9, 2004).

32. See http://www.tulsaworld.com/news/article.aspx?article ID=071023_1_a1_ spanc46170 (Oct. 31, 2007).

33. For an in-depth historical account of Osama bin Laden's thinking and activism, see John Esposito, *Unholy War: Terror in the Name of Islam.* (New York: Oxford University Press, 2003), 3–25; Daniel L. Byman, "Al-Qaeda as an Adversary: Do We Understand Our Enemy?" *World Politics* 56, no. 1 (2003): 139–63.

34. Search for Common Ground, "Changing Course: A New Direction for U.S. Relations with the Muslim World," (Washington, D.C., 2008), 49.

35. Nimer, *Islamophobia and Anti Americanism*, 67–68.

36. Anonymous (pseudonym), *Imperial Hubris* (Washington, D.C.: Brassey's, 2004).

37. See USAToday.com, Sept. 3, 2003, http://www.usatoday.com/news/ washington/2003-09-06-poll-iraq_x.htm (Dec. 14, 2008).

38. See http://www.cair.com/AmericanMuslims/AntiTerrorism/FatwaAgainstTer-rorism.aspx (Nov. 5, 2007).

39. Scott C. Alexander, "We Should Deconstruct Our Supremacist Master Narra-tives," in Nimer, *Islamophobia and Anti Americanism*, 41–54.

40. Richard Bulliet, *The Case for Islamo-Christian Civilization* (New York: Columbia University Press, 2004).

41. See the text of the address at http://www.shalomctr.org/node/1302 (Oct. 29, 2007).

42. Nimer, *Islamophobia and Anti-Americanism*, 56.

43. Tariq Ramadan, *Western Muslims and the Future of Islam* (New York: Oxford University Press, 2004), 225.

6

Muslims, Islam(s), Race, and American Islamophobia

Sherman A. Jackson

At the heart of racism is the religious assertion that God made a creative mistake when He brought some people into being.
—Friedrich Von Otto

No man has ever been born a Negro hater, a Jew hater, or any other kind of hater. Nature refuses to be involved in such suicidal practices.
—Harry Bridges

Without the clue of race [American] history [i]s a nursery tale.
—Henry Adams

America, Immigration, and Race

The question of what it means to be an American, will persist for as long as the American project endures. For America is in a constant state of precarious becoming, as Alisdair MacIntyre put it, "always *not yet*."[1] Part of the reason for this is that, as a child of the Enlightenment, the ideals upon which America was founded and in whose terms it seeks to actualize itself are understood to be universal, essential human values. As such, "anyone and everyone may be summoned to take part in [America's] completion."[2] This is amplified and underscored by another, equally American, fact—the constant flow of new arrivals to the United States. On this fact, as MacIntyre notes, "[T]he American idea can never be just what the Founding Fathers said it was or what any particular later native generation has made of its variety and contradictions: It waits also on what the immigrant has to say about it."[3]

It is not difficult to imagine how the immigrants' awe at the reality and expanse of American freedom and opportunity might be accompanied by a quiet, intermittent moral vexation. For none of the freedoms and opportunities that greet them upon arrival have actually been earned. This becomes particularly problematic in the face of the plight of those prior Americans who do not enjoy the same level of access to these entitlements. Perhaps the most expedient way to assuage these pangs of conscience is to join the chorus of those who vindicate their good fortune by appealing to the "universal" values of equality, freedom, justice, and the like as the simple birthright and common heritage of all. Here, in fact, immigrants come to enjoy a mildly inscrutable advantage over the natives: They retain the advantage of being able to avail themselves of the opportunities born of America's successful pursuit of its ideals, without having to see themselves as sharing any responsibility or ownership for America's moral failures. In this context, America comes to constitute an unstoried, historically empty abstraction, a mere ideological construct, filled not with historical blacks, Chinese, or Native Americans but with universal "human beings" who either do or do not avail themselves of American opportunity. America itself, meanwhile, is imagined to play the singular role of neutral facilitator.

This essentially unstoried perspective on the United States is contrasted with another point of view, what one might call the view of "American realism." From this vantage point, America is the sum total of both its ideals *and* its realities. And close to the very core of American reality is the enduring significance of race.[4] In his seminal work, *Whiteness of a Different Color*, Matthew Frye Jacobson makes the critical observation that "It is America that produced the distinctly racial understanding of 'difference.'"[5] On this understanding, not religion, class, national origin, or even language served as the *sine qua non* for separating authentic from spurious claims to Americanness. Rather, as Toni Morrison observes, "Deep within the word 'American' is its association with race."[6] More specifically, according to Morrison, American whiteness has played a unique and singular role in this regard. As she put it, "To identify someone as South African is to say very little; we need the adjective 'white' or 'black' or 'colored' to make our meaning clear. In this country it is quite the reverse. American means white."[7]

Even before the election of America's first Blackamerican president, one could acknowledge, I think, the unique role of whiteness in the formation of American identity without embracing the seemingly Manichaean dichotomy

Morrison implies, according to which whiteness not only connotes American-ness but does so to the complete exclusion of other races. While it may be true that the *primary* racial connotation of "American" is whiteness, it is not true that whiteness is the *only* racial identity that connotes America. Snoop Dogg, Muhammad Ali, and Martin Luther King, Jr. are equally connotative of America. In fact, not only do these personalities connote America, but they connote *only* America—i.e., not Europe, not "the West," not even Africa at first blush. One is reminded in this context of the insightful declaration of James Baldwin: "Negroes do not . . . exist in any other [country]."[8] All of this is another way of saying that, unlike Europe, the United States is not limited to a *single* racial authenticity. There are, rather, multiple—at least two—racially authentic Americans. And this may be part of what we are witnessing in the fact that it is primarily white people and black people who are not routinely asked the question "Where are you (or your parents) from?"[9]

Muslims, Race, and Racial Agnosia

It would seem, in light of all of this, that any journey to full belongingness in America would imply at least some coming to terms with the reality of race. To date, however, Muslims who have migrated to this country from the Muslim world appear unwilling or unable to take a firm and principled position on the matter of race. On the contrary, even as they continue to nurse old-world racial prejudices and complexes, Muslim immigrants tend to approach the United States through the prism of a certain racial agnosia, especially when it comes to American whiteness. This is all reinforced, moreover, by a tacit commitment to the dictum that Islam simply does not "do race." If, however, as has been suggested, race is integral to the enterprise of American identity formation, indeed, to the very modality and possibilities of how America might actually concretize its ideals, it may be time for Muslims to reconsider this posture. For even if Islam does not "do race" per se, it certainly "does reality," and race continues to constitute an inextricable constituent of American reality.

To be fair, part of the problem here reverts to the different ways in which race is confronted and processed within and without the United States. Within America, whiteness functions as a racial category, doubling as a marker of such qualities as innocence, intelligence, competence, integrity, peacefulness and the like. Outside America, however (e.g., in the Muslim world), this whiteness loses much of its specifically racial tenor and becomes more a marker of civilization (i.e., the West), while continuing to connote many of the afore-mentioned positive qualities. In this civilizational context, the standards and "achievements" of the (white) West come to represent either the antithesis of true Islam or, ironically, the benchmark by which Islam in its truest expression is to be measured and pursued. By contrast, American blackness is seen not only as a racial category but as an identity marker that implies a relationship of subordination (albeit contested), if not inferiority to American whiteness. In this capacity, American blackness is imagined to be both part and not part of the West. On the one hand, it reflects the underbelly of the West, the scarred and pitied victim of its moral bankruptcy and historical sickness. On the other hand and precisely in this capacity, it is imagined to have made no substantive contributions to the West.

All of this is ultimately brought into an awkward and somewhat facile relationship with the dictum that Islam is a racially undifferentiated construct in which all Muslims have an equal claim to the faith and its attendant entitlements. In real terms, of course, the extent to which contemporary Muslim reality reflects this ideal will depend on the outcome of sociopolitical negotiations that take place in real space and time. In this regard, Muslim civilization is as storied as America and the West. And like black and white Americans, Muslim immigrants carry the cumulative effects of their historical victories and failures, all of which place them more or less at peace or war with themselves and their normative ideals. A major difference, however, between modern Islam and modern America is that, as the ascending civilization, America enjoys the luxury of being able to recognize its historical failures and proceed in its quest for historical redemption without having to worry about deflecting the negative claims and insinuations of a superior, competing order. Modern Muslim communities, by contrast, in both the East and the West, are characterized by a severely impoverished discourse on race (and color), and any racial or color prejudices or complexes that Muslim immigrants might have brought to the United States from the Muslim world are buried beneath the myth of Islam's unmitigated success in its historical struggle to live up to its race-neutral ideals.[10] Race, as a consequence, is all but dismissed as either the odd obsession of bigoted American whites or the panacean excuse/explanation of over-sensitive American blacks. As for those who have enjoyed the privilege of being reared in an authentic Muslim society, race-thinking is simply irrelevant where not morally wrong.

What all of this comes down to is not only an imagined Islam but a contrived America as well. Race is treated as some sort of bogeyman in which no reasonable person and certainly no pious, practicing Muslim could justifiably believe. People with black skin exist, but there is nothing historically, civilizationally, or epistemologically valuable or relevant about them other than perhaps their status as nonwhite. As for whiteness, it can be engaged and even occasionally responded to in its 'invisible' form, that is, as a civilization or even as a national identity —"American." As a race, however (i.e., a raw, historically predatory power that results in sociocultural, economic, and political advantages and presuppositions from which nonwhites might be excluded), whiteness is barely recognized. In the end, this racial agnosticism has the effect of reinforcing the invisibility of whiteness as a race, with all that that implies for any attempt to expose the historical and contemporary effects of white supremacy. All of this is done, moreover, in the often self-congratulating name of an ostensibly race-neutral (and thus morally superior) Islam.

The Potential Wages of Racial Agnosia

Given the racial and ethnic makeup of the Muslim American community (Blackamericans being among the major groupings), it will come as no surprise that part of the problem I see in this state of affairs is the extent to which it collaborates, however "innocently," in the subjugation of blacks. If American whiteness, as a privileged and historically exploitative construct, does not exist, it cannot have contributed anything to the status quo. There is thus nothing but (lack of) intelligence, hard work, and ingenuity to explain blacks' station in society. Beyond this, however—and this is the real crux of this chapter—I believe that what I have described as racial agnosticism is bad both for immigrant Muslims *and* for America. For it is only to the extent that America remains conscious of what its most "peculiar institution" (i.e., American whiteness) has done, how and why it has done it, and how it has disguised and continues to sustain it that the dominant group in the United States is likely to be able to sustain anything approaching self-understanding and self-control.[11] Only through sustained awareness and vigilance, in other words, regarding the psychological history of American whiteness is America apt to maintain a commitment to denying itself the comfort of innocence in the face of intentional campaigns to create another "problem people" or "dirty"[12] another group, especially in this, our post-9/11, world.

Of course, Blackamerican Muslims (like Blackamericans in general) have historically struggled to sustain just such recognition even if at times with more self-indulgence than objectivity. The rise of "immigrant Islam," however, has complicated this enterprise in at least two ways. First, immigrant Muslims enjoy the presumption of representing Islam in its most authentic expression. As such, to the extent that *they* dismiss race as Islamically irrelevant, this will be assumed to be the position of Islam in its truest and most informed articulation.

Second, the racial agnosticism nursed by immigrant Muslims appears at times to coincide with a tacit but deeply operative effort within parts of white America to forget or whitewash the past in order to safeguard American innocence and reinforce the status of American ideals as universal and American opportunity as perpetually open to all who are willing to avail themselves. Muslim racial agnosticism, in other words, echoes the ethos of that mentality within the United States that seeks "to cut itself off as far as possible from any consciousness of . . . [American] history and its contradictions."[13] The success of (socially) nonwhite Muslim immigrants brings credence to the claim of universal freedom, equality, and racial neutrality and the idea that America is a level playing field for anyone willing to play hard enough, with all that this contributes to the vindication of the entire American past.

Of course, all of this works to conceal the possibility that to afford America the luxury of innocence through historical amnesia might render it more rather than less likely, under the right circumstances, to produce, without the slightest twinge of guilt, another "problem people," maligned, defined, feared, and detested as were the non-Aryan Jew and the Negro. In fact, it may even be easier to shift responsibility for this new bigotry to this new problem people than it was to blame the Jew and the Negro for being hated. For whereas Jewish induction into American whiteness thoroughly complicated the task of isolating and indicting them as a "discrete and insular class" (which is why even as a 'minority' they never qualified for Affirmative Action) it is precisely their post-9/11 *exclusion* from American whiteness (socially if not legally) that denies Muslim immigrants this kind of insulation. As for the Negro, while every negative stereotype hurled at the him or her could be turned, with a modicum of effort, into an indictment of what America itself had created, no such stigma attaches to warning Americans about "terrorists," "extremists," "Islamofascists," and "threats to national security." This has obvious and far-reaching implications for Islamophobia in America and sets it apart fundamentally from even traditional antiblack racism.

Beyond the direct implications of racial agnosia for American Islamophobia, there is the less direct though equally potent contribution it makes via the alienation it spawns among second- and third-generation "immigrant" Muslims. Many of these people lack the experiential groundedness in a "back-home" culture to provide them with a livable, deeply felt sense of identity-in-difference. Whereas their parents may be able to speak of "the Americans" with a palpable sense of visceral distance and uncomplicated otherness, second- and third-generation immigrant Muslims often grapple what W. E. B. Du Bois referred to as "double consciousness," whereby they struggle both *to be* and *not to be*—American. This is part of the common difficulty they experience in trying to establish a healthy sense of belonging-ness that does not carry a nagging sense of assimilationist guilt. In effect, the racial agnosticism handed down by their parents has effectively left this generation unraced. Yet, as I (and others) have argued, race remains an integral part of American genuineness and identity formation. The net result of all of this is often a deep and vexing alienation from American society, which is often most expediently expressed in some or another form of Islamic radicalism. Let me pause here to give a brief example of what I am trying to get at.

A few years ago I was invited by the Muslim Students' Association of a Midwestern university to give a lecture. After the lecture, the students invited me out to dinner, where I stumbled into a conversation with a Pakistani med-ical student. This young man had a long, beautiful beard but spoke with abso-lutely no accent. He kept complaining, however, about how he could not see himself as "an American" and about how he was Pakistani. Of course, I had heard all of this before, but being a little tired after the lecture, my patience was in short supply. So I decided to let him have it. I fired back at him: "You are *not* Pakistani; you are not socialized as a Pakistani; you could not eat the food, speak the language, or deal with the cultural idiosyncrasies or responsibilities of being a Pakistani in Pakistan. You are an American, and you should simply accept that fact." He strongly protested, however, that, *as a Muslim*, he could not see himself as a bona fide American.

Clearly, this young man knew that *I* was an American, and he respected my Islamic bona fides as he did those of Zaid Shakir, Hamza Yûsuf, Umar Fârûq AbdAllâh, and countless other white and black Muslim-Americans. His real problem was thus not in reconciling *Islam* with America; this was just his trump card, his would-be unassailable justification for his rejectionism. His real problem lay, rather, in his inability to reconcile his *self* with America. But why could he not be an *authentic*, self-validating American? Because he was not *white* and because he was unwilling to be assimilated into some jive, subaltern, "honorary" whiteness, whereby he might end up weighed down by the burden of always having to look upon and measure himself through the eyes of an other. I explained to him that this was not necessary, that America had not one but at least *two* authentic prototypes, one white, the other black. I explained that he did not have to declare himself black but that the existence of multiple American racial authenticities held out the future possibility of alternatives to subaltern whiteness. While whatever identity he chose would invariably be raced, I conceded, he *could* potentially carve out an identity of his own that was not beholden to the dominant group. For, again, I explained, America, unlike Europe, boasted not a single but multiple racial authenticities and thus multiple possibilities. We ended our conversation that night in what I took to be a rather entertaining (and exhausting) waste of time.

The next day, however, as I was being escorted to the airport, this same young man approached me and handed me an envelope. I stuffed it in my jacket pocket, and when I got to the airport I opened it up and found a hand-written letter. This is partly what it read:

> I wanted to thank you for talking with me . . . [T]hese past few
> months I had a lot of radicalness in me. Honestly, its [sic] not because
> I love to fight or something, but I am truly lost. I see no clear path to
> success and then just think of taking out the aggressor of the
> Muslims. I mean, my brother, my brother, you hit a homerun [sic] in
> describing us second generation Muslims. We don't know where to
> go, what to do, how to do it and are getting so lost that all we see is
> jihad. And this isn't just me. I know so many people like this . . . SO
> MANY. And you really shook me down, just by being direct, straight
> to the point and putting me on the spot . . . [T]he youth need your
> approach . . . They need to be questioned and shook [sic], so they snap
> back into reality.

Obviously, neither the color-blind, postracial model of America nor the 'virtual identity' handed down by his parents was working for this young man (nor, I presume, for the many like him, of whom he spoke). What relieved him, however, of his agony was the idea that there were alternatives to whiteness as *the* singular authenticator of genuine Americanness. Ironically, however, it was actually American blackness that both proved this possibility and made it believable. And here we come to the great paradox of both an unraced America and a racially agnostic Islam: We simply cannot have race if we cannot have blackness. And without American blackness, there is no reason to believe in any credible alternative to whiteness as the exclusive authenticator of claims to genuine American-ness. Thus, far from undermining the interests or integrity of the United States or Islam, blackness and race can actually function to the benefit of both.[15]

This, in my view, is part of what the imagined Islam and the contrived America of Muslim immigrants fails to recognize. Furthermore, this oversight ultimately lends traction to the phenomenon of Islamophobia. For, on the one hand, the alienation arching from the uneasy and palpably conflicted quips and struts of Muslim youth is almost certain to confirm for the dominant group the propriety of its own prejudice. After all, as a phobia, Islamophobia is *supposed* to be an irrational and unfounded fear or aversion. But where second- and third-generation Muslim youth evince an unwillingness or inability to accept their status as Americans, fear of and contempt for Islam and Muslims will be looked upon as both rational and founded. Meanwhile, this racial agnosia effectively places Muslim immigrants into a racial noncategory that disqualifies them from the benefits of America's quest for historical redemption. At some level, Muslim immigrants seem to understand this, as suggested by their attempt to highlight and discredit Islamophobia as a species of *racial* profiling. The problem, however, is that the charge of racial profiling becomes most credible when levied against discrimination against people who self-identify as a race.

Between Racial Agnosia and Non-American Race

This brings me to my final point regarding race and blackness. Part of the problem with Muslim immigrants' identifying with race relates to the seeming paucity of racial choices left to their disposal in the aftermath of September 11, 2001. This single act of terrorism has all but preempted the possibility of their being inducted, like the Jews, Irish, Italians and others before them, into the panoply of American whiteness—at least socially (as opposed to legally), where it affects everyday interactions. In such light, any suggestion that Muslim immigrants racialize their identity would seem to entail an invitation to join American blackness. Inasmuch, however, as blackness continues to be perceived as a negative category, given its binary opposition to whiteness, moving from unraced to raced would seem to imply moving not simply from stigma to stigma but from faddish and perhaps temporary stigma to historically grounded, enduring stigma, an unwise, myopic exchange on any sober calculus.

My point, however, has *not* been to invite Muslim immigrants to blackness but merely to a recognition of the importance of race in American identity formation and belongingness *through the prism of American blackness*. To fully appreciate my point, it is important to understand, first of all, that belongingness is not the same as being held in high esteem; nor is being held in high esteem the same as belongingness. The relative importance and priority of these values, as well as the distinction between them, must be kept clear and in proper balance. Particularly in these volatile times (and, I argue, in all times) being held in high esteem is best thought of as a want or desire to be pursued only after the satisfaction and securing of the basic necessity of belonging. In the language of classical Islamic law, being held in high esteem constitutes a casual need (*hâjjah*) or perhaps even a luxury (*tahsîn*), while belongingness constitutes an absolute necessity (*darûrah*). According to

Islamic law, absolute necessities are not to be sacrificed in pursuit of casual needs or luxuries. While the dissociation from race may thus promote the interest of avoiding stigma and enhancing social esteem, it must also be assessed in terms of its costs to the interest of belongingness. Moreover, this assessment must assume a long-term trajectory and include the need to absorb unanticipated calamities on the ground and provide insulation against occasional acts of violence and lamentable rhetoric emanating from Muslims domestically or in far-off places.

Second, it is not at all clear (or necessarily likely) that Blackamericans would admit Muslim immigrants to American blackness even if the latter should desire such admission. Here, however, we might pause to consider what it is that Blackamericans quietly covet even in their marginalized racial identity. Perhaps it relates to a latent power derived from the margin, which includes enough 'partial inclusion' to preempt cries of "Go home!" while also insulating one from the kind of co-optive power and hegemonic influence that the center might deploy in a manner that stifles one's ability to self-authenticate or denies one's ability to self-define. If Muslims want to be included *in* America without becoming imprisoned *by* the dominant socio-political hegemony in America, they might do well to consider the power of the margin.

Finally and perhaps most interestingly, there is evidence that even American whites might be opposed to such a move. This opposition most emphatically underscores the point I have been trying to make regarding the storied-ness of the American project. For it is clearly and directly aimed at disqualifying Muslim immigrants from the kind of collective empathy and belongingness that emerges out of the American story and informs America's quest to redeem itself in light of its past misdeeds. The following example will demonstrate my point.

On September 22, 2008, syndicated radio talk-show host and conservative pundit Rush Limbaugh delivered a message over the airwaves designed to turn white voters away from democratic presidential candidate Barack Obama. Limbaugh pointed out that the Democrats were concerned about white, blue-collar voters not being able to bring themselves to vote for Obama because he was black. Republican strategists knew this, of course, and sought to reinforce and capitalize on it via moves such as the creation of "Joe the plumber." But Limbaugh sensed that the number of whites who might be alienated by Obama's blackness might not be enough to ensure a McCain victory, so he set out to find a more secure basis for turning white voters—Democratic *and* Republican, working-class *and* others—away from Obama. During the course of his radio broadcast, Limbaugh declared Obama to be an *Arab*! Not only, however, did he declare Obama to be an Arab, he categorically insisted that Obama was not black!

> These polls on how one-third of blue-collar white Democrats won't vote for Obama because he's black—but he's not black! Do you know he has not one shred of African American blood? He doesn't have any African—that's why when they asked whether he was authentic, whether he's down for the struggle. He's Arab! You know, he's from Africa. He's from Arab parts of Africa. He's not—his father was—he's not African American. The last thing he is is African American.[16]

This is a remarkable statement. And while it may be laughable in some of its blatant inaccuracies (e.g., "Arab parts of Africa"), this should not detract from the fact that Limbaugh is a shrewd and polished propagandist who knows his audience well. In order to augment the ranks of white—and maybe even some black—voters who would not be willing to vote for Obama, Limbaugh deemed it necessary to do two things. First, he had to *negate* Obama's status as an African American. Second, he had to *affirm* for his listeners—and assure them—that Obama was an Arab, in fact, that he had "not one shred of African American blood." To be sure, Limbaugh knew that he was misrepresenting Obama's genealogy. In an earlier broadcast, on August 19, 2008, Limbaugh had tried to go back to an argument from an earlier era, in which he had impugned Obama's qualifications (traditionally a veiled reference to the purported intellectual inferiority of blacks.) In this broadcast, he explicitly blamed Affirmative Action and the fact that no one in the Democratic Party "had the guts to stand up and say no to *a black guy*."[17] This, according to Limbaugh, was the primary reason Obama got the nomination. By late September, however, this line of argument had come to be recognized as a lost cause, at which time it became necessary to devise a new argument, one in which Obama would be recast as "an Arab."

Limbaugh had come to understand that the United States was much more serious about capitalizing on this opportunity for historical redemption than he had theretofore imagined. In fact, in his August 19 broadcast, he explicitly mentioned "guilt" as playing a role in bringing Obama to the fore. Once he recognized this, however, he also came to recognize that the "redemption vote" might be undermined if he could find a way to negate the very basis of the need for redemption itself. By insisting, in other words, that Obama was *not black*, Limbaugh was implying that there would be no redemption in voting for him. Then, in order to reinforce the implications of this negation, he set out not only to take Obama out of the category of blackness but also to place him in a category that was least likely to elicit any empathy on the part of American voters.

By casting Obama as an Arab, in other words, Limbaugh was seeking to place him in the company of those toward whom "white, blue-collar" and other Americans felt no debt at all.

Less than a month after this recasting of Obama, the pervasiveness of the mentality that Limbaugh had tried to spawn was publicly confirmed on October 10, 2008, when, during a campaign stop in Lakeville, Minnesota, a woman (Gayle Quinnell) addressed Republican presidential candidate John McCain and stated that she did not trust Obama because "he's an Arab." McCain politely corrected the woman (while many in attendance booed in disapproval), stating that Obama was not an Arab but a "decent family man," saying nothing, meanwhile, about the association of Arabness with lack of trustworthiness.[18]

Clearly Limbaugh, like Quinnell and even McCain, had all racialized the Arabs. In this context, in fact, I should perhaps modify my earlier characterization. The attempt to recast Obama as an Arab did not place Arabs *outside* the category of race per se; after all, "Arabness" was being invoked to replace "blackness" as Obama's race. This was a move, rather, that had both the aim and the effect of placing Arabs outside the amorphous but highly operative category of *American* "race." From here, not only could the most ridiculous things be said, believed, and feared about Obama: this could all be executed with a total sense of impunity.

I would like to conclude this chapter where I started, by reiterating the centrality of race to American identity formation and belongingness. Muslim immigrants may choose to maintain their position of racial agnosia, preferring to remain unraced rather than being forced to choose a racialized American identity. It may be, however, that America is a society that racializes all of its people willy-nilly. While the United States may have an abundance of ideological and rhetorical tools with which to continue to extol the dismissal of accidental human traits as irrelevant, it may still lack the concrete, historically grounded, psychological metrics with which to encounter and measure individuals as "just humans." If this is true, it may be to the advantage of Muslim immigrants to exercise their own agency in adopting or crafting an indigenous American racial identity of their own rather than have a non-American—which will invariably be processed as an un-American—racial identity superimposed on them. For while MacIntyre may be right that America waits to see what the immigrant has to say, I doubt that America will wait indefinitely. And even is America is willing to wait, events (e.g., another 9/11, another Fort Hood shooting, another Christmas bomber) may not permit it. I do not purport to know nor do I assume the right to say which direction Muslim immigrants should take in this regard. My fear, however, is that if they should end up shackled to an explicitly non-American racial identity, anti-immigrant Islamophobia in this country may simply, and sadly, come to know no bounds.

NOTES

1. A. MacIntyre, "The American Idea," in *America and Ireland, 1776–1976: The American Identity and the Irish Connection* (Westport: Greenwood, 1976), 61; emphasis in the original.

2. MacIntyre, "Idea," 61.

3. MacIntyre, "Idea," 61.

4. Throughout this chapter I am not speaking of race as a biological reality, a notion that has been thoroughly (and rightly) discredited. Race, as I use it, is a sociohistorical reality, and Americans are racially defined by a particular sociohistorical experience. As for black Americans, as the most "visible" American race, whites, Native Americans, Jews, Hispanics, and other elements all contribute to their biological constitution. None of these elements outweigh, however, black Americans' "discrete and insular" experience as (permanent) nonwhites. For more on my understanding of race as a sociohistorical reality, see my *Islam and the Blackamerican: Looking toward the Third Resurrection* (New York: Oxford University Press, 2005), 13–15.

5. *Whiteness of a Different Color: European Immigrants and the Alchemy of Race* (Cambridge: Harvard University Press, 1998), 143. More recently, S. P. Huntington appears to make a slightly less direct reference to the racial element in American identity when he refers to Americans as "*Anglo*-Protestants" (emphasis mine). See his *Who Are We? The Challenges to America's National Identity* (New York: Simon and Schuster, 2004), xv, xvi, xvii, and passim. It is interesting that Huntington's foil is not blacks as the greatest threat to American identity but Hispanics.

6. See her *Playing in the Dark: Whiteness and the Literary Imagination* (New York: Vintage, 1993), 47.

7. Morrison, *Playing in the Dark*, 47.

8. James Baldwin, *The Fire Next Time* (New York: Dell, 1963), 40.

9. Of course, accent may make a difference, but, even here, a diction distinctly grounded in "Ebonics" will immediately be recognized and identified as American.

10. While race prejudice, and more specifically antiblack sentiment, was known in premodern Islam and persists in the Muslim world today, I do not intend to suggest that these sentiments emerge from the same place psychologically and had the same effect ontologically as has antiblack racism in the West. For one, no formal barriers (e.g., whites-only signs, miscegenation laws) to black inclusion or even leadership ever existed in Islam. Furthermore, slavery was not a formally race-based system. Thus, even as crafty a critic of race prejudice in Islam as Bernard Lewis would acknowledge that "At no time did the Islamic world ever practice the kind of racial exclusivism . . . which has existed until very recently in the United States." See his *Race and Color in Islam* (New York: Harper and Row, 1971), 102.

11. See Theodore Allen, *The Invention of the White Race*, 2 vols. (New York: Verso, 1994), vol. 1: 1–51.

12. I take this notion of "dirtying" people from Toni Morrison, who speaks of someone having such power over you that the person can actually harm your innermost soul, not just kill, jail, or maim you but "dirty" you, "Dirty you so bad you couldn't like yourself any more." See her *Beloved* (New York: Knopf, 1987), 251.

13. MacIntyre, "Idea," 64.

14. This was Toni Morrison's point when she stated, "American means white." Morrison, *Playing in the Dark*, 47.

15. One thinks in this context of the Prophet Muhammad in tribal Arabia. Had he invoked a completely "tribally blind" Islam, he would never have been able to avail himself of the *asabîyah* (group solidarity), which conferred upon him the protection of his uncle, Abû Tâlib, or his clan, Banû Hâshim, during his time in Mecca. Nor would he have been able to appeal to neighboring tribes for protection, which precipitated his migration to Medina.

16. Several websites carry the written transcript of this statement along with an audio clip of Limbaugh's actual broadcast. Visit, for example, http://www.mediamatters.org/items/200809220015.

17. See the written transcript and hear an audio clip of the actual broadcast at http://www.mediamatters.org/items/200808200002; emphasis mine.

18. For a video clip of this exchange, visit http://www.huffingtonpost.com/the-uptake/mccain-responds-to-arab-a_b_133820.html.

III

Manifestations

7

Islamophobia and the War on Terror: Youth, Citizenship, and Dissent

Sunaina Maira

Islamophobia is an increasingly pivotal term in twenty-first-century discourses of racialization, difference, religion, and nationalism in the United States and beyond, as well as in current debates about immigration, globalization, and human rights. The global "war on terror" waged by the United States after 2001 has heightened the scrutiny and suspicion, nationally and globally, of Islam and Muslims, but this historical moment needs to be situated in relation to earlier moments of fear, anxiety, or animosity toward Islam and Muslims. In this chapter, I argue that historicizing the notion of Islamophobia and understanding the political and cultural processes that underwrite the construction of subjects as "Muslim" is important because it reveals the larger political forces that are at work in the war on terror and that are linked to issues of domination, othering, and dissent. However, these political and historical processes are often obscured by a discourse that reduces Islamophobia to an issue of cultural or civilizational difference and multicultural tolerance.

The term *Islamophobia* has gained currency in the United States relatively recently, mainly since the 1980s, in the wake of the Iranian Revolution and the Tehran hostage crisis, which created a backlash in the United States against Islam and Muslims. However, animosity toward and suspicion or fear of Islam and Muslims has a much longer history, one that is intertwined with modernity, colonialism, and globalization and with the relationship of the United States to areas designated as "Muslim" or "Middle Eastern." The genealogy of Islamophobia can be traced to the encounter between European colonialism and Islam, which emerged from the Western colonization of Africa, the Middle East, and Asia and is embedded in the larger context of the construction of the "other" in Western modernity. Islam was constructed as emblematic of "other" peoples, cultures, and civilizations in opposition to Western civilization, Christianity, and also later Judaism in the context of the European Inquisition, the Crusades, and sectarian wars and also in relation to Western capitalism and New World settler colonialism.

Thus, the evolution of historical processes of Islamophobia, even when not named as such, is intertwined with the development of categories of "race" as part of 18th- and 19th-century European systems of classification of peoples and areas of the world that did not deserve freedom and needed European "civilization," thereby justifying Western colonialism. In the New World, Christian missionaries from Europe transplanted ideas of "barbaric infidels" to North America, superimposing them on the "heathen savages" or indigenous peoples of North America, who needed to be civilized, according to divine mandate.[1] American Orientalism and Islamophobia thus have a long history that can be traced to the foundational Holy Land myths of the Christian settlers. Eerily, Native Americans in the U.S. military today have testified that occupying forces in Iraq speak of fighting in "Indian country" and "killing Indians in Iraq," underscoring the ways in which different forms of racialization are superimposed in a palimpsestic notion of Manifest Destiny.[2]

For example, U.S. wars on the so-called Barbary pirates off the coast of North Africa, from the 1780s to the bombardment of Algiers in 1815, figured them as Muslim/Arabs terrorizing the West and disrupting their trade and commerce.[3] Representations of the "Orient" during the late nineteenth and early twentieth century were circulated by American missionaries, tourists, and merchants as the United States ventured into trade with the Middle East.[4] These stereotypes of Muslims and Middle Easterners crystallized in archives of American Orientalism that were shaped by historical events, including U.S. support for the Balfour Declaration of 1917 and the creation of the state of Israel in 1948, the overthrow of Mossadegh in Iran and the installation of the Shah in 1953, the attack on Beirut in 1958, the OPEC oil crisis of the 1970s, the Tehran hostage crisis of 1979, and the two wars in Iraq.

Clearly, there are historical discontinuities, as well as continuities between different moments of Islamophobia and racial formation, but I believe that in each of these historical encounters an interplay of political, economic, and cultural factors is at work that we need to pay attention to in order to understand the suspicion of or hostility to those figured as Muslim. If we take this longer view of the history of Islamophobia, we can understand how it has evolved in relation to European colonialism, Western modernity, and global capital and not apart from these processes, which underlie the ambiguity of current racial thinking about Muslims. Sherene Razack argues that Muslims as a group have been evicted from the modern political community, proving the state of exception of imperial governmentality that has legalized their torture, collective punishment, and dehumanization in the war on terror.[5]

States of Exception/Emergency

The attacks on the United States on 9/11 intensified a discourse about Islam that has congealed a set of historical associations between Islam, the Middle East, terrorism, violence, misogyny, and antimodernity that are integral to Orientalism[6] and are at the center of the new culture wars in the United States focused on Islam, gender, and the Middle East. In the wake of the 9/11 attacks, questions of religion, racialization, national identification, and citizenship have taken on new, urgent meanings for Muslims living in the United States and Arab and Middle Eastern Americans more generally, as well as South Asians and others mistakenly profiled in the post-9/11 backlash, particularly (turbaned, male) Sikh Americans, some of whom were attacked or killed for "looking Muslim." The national allegiances of Muslim, Arab, and South Asian Americans have come under intense scrutiny for signs of betrayal to the nation and for any wavering in allegiance to the project of "freedom" and "democracy" as defined in the neoconservative vision of the "New American Century."

However, the current "state of emergency" affecting Muslims and Arabs, as well as other immigrant and minority communities, in the United States— the suspension of civil rights and the targeting of certain groups by sovereign violence—is in fact not exceptional in the United States; rather, it is constitutive of an imperial governmentality that rests on the exclusion of certain groups from citizenship at various historical moments.[7] The post-9/11 moment is not a radical historical rupture but builds on forms of power already in place that target different groups to varying degrees and in specific ways, particularly in moments of national crisis—this is a state of everyday life in empire. Moreover, while U.S. policies of military, political, and economic domination have reemerged as the focus of public debate with the war on terror, they are rooted in a longer history of U.S. imperial power that has used both direct and indirect methods of control and that has long illustrated the "state of exception."[8] For reasons of space, I do not delve here into the theoretical debates about the concept of "empire," which has been revived in public discourse since 2001, but clearly U.S. imperialism has historically been marked by nebulous, nonterritorial forms of domination that do not resemble traditional forms of territorial "colonialism,"[9] including covert wars and proxy regimes, in addition to the "formal" colonialism evident in the current occupation of Iraq.

(Furthermore, the war on terrorism overseas and the war on terror at home are linked because empire works on two fronts, the domestic and the foreign. Thus, U.S. foreign policy is linked to the "policing of domestic racial tensions" and the disciplining of subordinated populations through racial, gender, and class hierarchies within the nation,[10] including the racialization of Muslims and Arabs as suspect citizens. The national consensus for U.S. foreign policies is strengthened through historical processes of scapegoating "outsiders" and conflating internal and external enemies through racialized and gendered discourses, as evident in the internment of Japanese Americans in World War II and during the Cold War.[11] However, the transnational link between the two realms of imperial power are generally obscured in everyday discussions and representations even if they are alluded to implicitly and sometimes problematically in the suspicion of Muslim communities with overseas ties. This analysis is important for understanding the profiling of Muslims in the United States after 9/11, for it has always been the case that imperial power maintains dominance outside the nation by maintaining dominance over subordinated groups at home.

(Arabs and Middle Easterners in the United States—both Muslim and non-Muslim—have long been subject to racism, repression, and surveillance due to U.S. interventions and strategic interests in "remaking" the Middle East and, in particular, U.S. support for Israel and Zionist policies in Palestine.[12] Processes of exclusion and demonization of Muslims and Middle Easterners began well before 9/11 and have endured in consistent expressions of Islamophobia and anti-Arab racism.[13] Orientalist images of backward, religious, authoritarian, and misogynist Muslims and Middle Easterners have historically provided Americans with "opportunities for creating selves" associated with modernity and with a "foil for the 'progress' that many Americans so assiduously pursued as their birthright and destiny" as part of the everyday cultures of U.S. imperialism.[14] Orientalist images of Muslim "infidels" and "barbaric" Arabs have historically permeated U.S. popular culture, providing an antithesis to U.S. national identity and helping to legitimate the United States' imperial expansion and racial domination, including its military, political, and economic interventions and support for colonialist projects in the Middle East.[15])

Muslim Immigrant Youth and Cultural Citizenship

Images of Muslim youth are central to discourses of Islamophobia and Orientalism and to discussions of profiling, immigration, and national identity. Muslim youth in the United States are coming of age at a moment when their religious and national affiliations are politically charged issues tied to the state's war on terror, both within and beyond the nation's borders. They are often emblematic of the "othering" of Islam and the Middle East; young Muslim men, in particular, are associated in the mainstream media with militancy, fanaticism, and misogyny, and young Muslim women with victimization and the veil (an ever-present signifier of Muslim femininity), as female subjects requiring rescue and liberation by Western civilization and feminism.

This chapter draws on research that focuses on Muslim immigrant youth from South Asia who have been living in the United States after the events of September 11, 2001, and grappling with the implications of Islamophobia for their national, ethnic, religious, racial, and gendered identities. My research uses an ethnographic approach to understand the impact of Islamophobia on the everyday experiences of Muslim youth in the United States and the range of their responses to the war on terror, considering them as active subjects fashioning complex critiques rather than passive objects of Islamophobia, profiling, or even sympathy. The study focuses on a group of working-class students from India, Pakistan, and Bangladesh in a public high school in a small New England city that I call Wellford.[16] The larger project situates the experiences of South Asian Muslim immigrant youth in relation to domestic racism, neoliberal capitalism, and U.S. foreign policy in the Middle East and South Asia both before and after 9/11.[17]

The South Asian immigrant student population in the Wellford high school is predominantly working to lower-middle class, recently arrived (within five to seven years before 2001), and with minimal to moderate fluency in English. Students from India, Pakistan, Bangladesh, and Afghanistan constituted the largest Muslim population at the school, followed by youth from Ethiopia, Somalia, and Morocco. The parents of these youth generally worked in low-income jobs in the service sector, and they themselves worked after school, up to thirty hours a week, as security guards and in fast-food restaurants, gas stations, and retail stores.[18] The majority of the Indian immigrant youth are from Muslim families, most from small towns or villages in Gujarat, in western India. The families of the South Asian (Sunni) Muslim youth are not very involved in local Muslim organizations or mosques in the area, largely because they are so busy struggling with work and survival, and generally do not affiliate with the local Indian American or Pakistani American community organizations, which primarily involve middle- to upper-middle-class, suburban families.[19]

My research explores the impact of 9/11 and the anti-Muslim backlash on notions of cultural citizenship, or everyday experiences of national belonging, for South Asian Muslim immigrant youth. Cultural citizenship, or the cultural dimensions of citizenship and national identification, is a key trope of belonging for Muslim immigrant youth because daily experiences of inclusion and exclusion are shaped by national and ethnic identity, race, religion, gender, and class and not just by legal citizenship.[20] At the same time, formal citizenship remains an important aspect of national belonging and also of the war on terror, which has led to the mass detention and deportation of undocumented Muslim and Arab immigrants. However, even legal citizenship is not enough to guarantee protection under the law with the state's war on terror, as is clear from the profiling, surveillance, and, in some cases, detention of Muslim Americans who are U.S. citizens.[21] These dramatic enactments of exclusion and criminalization are on a continuum of historical practices that have culturally and racially constructed nonwhite groups and particular immigrant communities in the United States, such as Arab Americans, Latinos, and Asian Americans, as "perpetual foreigners" and threats to the nation despite legal citizenship.[22] Religious affiliation is also a marker of inclusion into cultural citizenship, defined in relation to a dominant Protestant or Judeo-Christian identity. This is evident in discourses about Muslims (and Arabs) that view them as inherently opposed to "Western" values that imbue neoliberal democracy and global capitalism, linking citizenship to Islamophobia through a civilizational discourse about subjects who deserve acceptance or are unfit for inclusion into the nation. These questions are especially pertinent to youth, who are viewed as the next generation of citizens and who symbolize the possibility of threat to or support of the existing social order, giving youth a charged ideological significance.

My research situates cultural citizenship in a particular moment of U.S. empire, during the war on terror, and explores how Muslim immigrant youth have grappled with their own and others' understandings of "Muslim identity" in relation to racialization, labor, popular culture, family, cross-ethnic alliances, and urban space. Many of these issues are often neglected in scholarship on Muslim American youth, which has tended to have a narrow focus on issues of religious identity and cultural conflict, gender, and family, generally placing these in the well-worn and often Orientalist frame of "cultural conflict" and often neglecting questions of class, national and global politics, race relations, and popular culture. Not enough research pays attention to the ways in which contemporary Islamophobia and Arabophobia have shaped the identities and experiences of Muslim American youth. Since 2001, the emerging body of work on these young people has (not surprisingly) begun shifting the focus to issues of Islamophobia and racism, but studies of the discrimination and victimhood they have experienced do not always consider the ways in which Muslim American youth, as political actors, resist or challenge these discourses, nor do the studies adequately address the geopolitical or historical context of post-9/11 Islamophobia.

Dissenting Citizenship

The larger research project sheds light on the ways in which Muslim immigrant youth themselves understand, challenge, resist, or rework different notions of cultural citizenship and experiences of belonging and exclusion in relation to transnationalism, multiculturalism, and political dissent. Here, I will briefly explore what makes it possible or impossible for young people from targeted communities to take a dissenting stance in a climate of political repression and express a "dissenting citizenship." The working-class Muslim immigrant youth in my study are not engaged in traditional forms of political activism, nor do they use a formal political vocabulary, but they still offer critiques of racism, Islamophobia, war, and foreign policy and grapple with an ethics of belonging.

Though these Muslim immigrant youth were not involved in political or community organizations, a critique of the state's rationale for the collective punishment of Muslims and the U.S. war on terror was pervasive among them. For example, Ayesha, a young woman whose family was from Gujarat, observed, "Just because one Muslim did it in New York, you can't involve everybody in there, you know what I'm sayin'." A week after the 9/11 attacks, Ayesha chose to write the words "INDIA+ MUSLIM" on her bag. For her, this was a conscious gesture of defiance, for she well knew the possibility of repercussions for those publicly identified as Muslim after September 11 but was not afraid of backlash. She said staunchly, "I'm hard headed. That's how I am." Adil, a Pakistani boy, was critical of the U.S. invasion of Afghanistan in 2001: "You have to look at it in two ways. It's not right that ordinary people over there, like you and me, just doing their work, get killed. They don't have anything to do with the attacks in New York, but they're getting killed. And also the people in New York who got killed, that wasn't right either." Zeenat, a newly arrived immigrant from Gujarat, India, believed that the bombing of Afghanistan in response to the attacks of 9/11 was "wrong" because the United States was attacking people who were not involved in the terrorist attacks. She observed, "After September

11, they [Americans] hate the Muslims. . . . I think they want the government to hate the Muslims, like, all Muslims are [the] same." Zeenat seemed to be distinguishing between civil society and the state, while pointing to both as Islamophobic and responsible for constructing Muslims as a category of collective guilt.

The dissent of these Muslim immigrant youth was clearly driven by two factors: They had been forced to deal with state and civil society discrimination targeting their communities soon after arriving in the United States, and they were from a region that was experiencing a U.S. military invasion (in Afghanistan). Their persistent, if not strengthened, identification as Muslim seemed to be partly a defiant response related to the first factor, resisting Islamophobia, scapegoating, and collective punishment targeting Muslims, Arabs, and "Muslim-looking" people. All of these youth also challenged the state's rhetoric about the "liberation" of Afghanistan and the "collateral" killings of civilians, critiquing the war in terms of human rights and international justice and linking it to nationalisms and state-sponsored terror.

Not all the students were as bold as Ayesha in challenging the profiling of Muslims and publicly claiming a Muslim identity—which Ayesha did without wearing a hijab, contrary to expectations of what religious identification looks like for Muslim girls. After 9/11, South Asians, Arabs, and Muslims across the United States were increasingly hesitant to speak publicly about political issues, given that even legal citizens were worried about expressing their political critique as the state acquired sweeping powers of surveillance with the USA PATRIOT Act. Repression historically works on two levels to silence dissent, as Corey Robin (2004) points out: on a state level and on the level of civil society, where individuals internalize repression and censor themselves.[23]

Interestingly, for these Muslim immigrant youth after 9/11, the high school was one of the few, and perhaps only, public spaces where they felt comfortable discussing politics, mainly because of the liberal political climate and the support of progressive teachers and staff. For example, after an anti-Muslim incident in the high school involving Adil and Walid, another Pakistani boy, the school organized an assembly featuring two Arab American speakers who criticized the war on terrorism and the attack on civil liberties. To an auditorium filled with their peers, Adil, Walid, and an Indian Muslim girl, Shireen, delivered eloquent speeches condemning racism. Adil said that when he was threatened by some young men in the city, "I could have done the same thing, but I don't think it's the right thing to do." Adil was a muscular young man, and his call for nonviolent response was a powerful one at that assembly, especially at a moment when the United States was bombing Afghanistan in retribution for the attacks of September 11, and it implicitly spoke to the larger question of violence, war, and international human rights. Shireen stood up in her salwar kameez and said, "We have to respect each other if we want to change society. You have to stand up for your rights." Even though these working-class immigrant youth did not have the support of (or time to participate in) traditional forms of community or political activism, they seemed to have become spokespersons in the public sphere willing to voice a dissenting view and engaging with the discourse of "rights."

Muslim immigrant youth were being visibly drawn into civil, immigrant, and human rights debates in the local community. In the face of the repression of political speech after 9/11, I found some South Asian Muslim immigrant youths to be engaged in a practice of dissenting citizenship: an engagement with the state that is based on a critique of its disciplining power and national mythologies and that grappled with questions of political justice and human rights. Dissenting citizenship is still a form of citizenship, however, and so it engages with the role and responsibility of the nation-state and the question of belonging and rights for subjects; thus, it encapsulates the contradictions of challenging the state while seeking inclusion within it. However, the notion of dissenting citizenship that I propose is not meant to suggest that dissent by South Asian Muslim immigrant youth or South Asian or Muslim Americans more generally was overt, consistent, or public, let alone that it is inherently guaranteed, given the intensified climate of repression and surveillance. Their dissent was not always expressed as overtly or publicly as political dissent is imagined to be, but it tells us something about the nature of dissent at a time of political repression, which is sometimes subtle and coded or oblique.

Dissenting citizenship is inextricably intertwined with the politics of race, gender, and class for these Muslim immigrant youth. Walid, a Pakistani boy, commented as follows:

> Actually, I think that a lot of black people don't feel like white people about that thing that happened on September 11. I've been thinking something else about white people after that thing happened. 'Cause I've seen a lot of black people talking about how one time they were slaves, so they don't really like white people either. . . . But you know, I feel bad for Americans, this is *their* country. We are immigrants. If something happens back home, and someone did something to us, we're gonna be angry, too, right? So I can see how white people feel upset about September 11.

While responses of various groups in the United States to the events of 9/11 are more complex than the white/black binary that Walid suggests, especially given the multicultural nationalism and hyperpatriotism after 9/11, what is important is that he came to *believe* that African Americans shared his experience of marginalization within the nation, while acknowledging the nationalist sentiments of the majority. It is apparent that 9/11 seems to have drawn these immigrant youth into an understanding of citizenship that is based on racialized fissures in claims to national identity, as well as affiliation with other youth of color. For these Muslim immigrant youth, the war on terror prompted an identification with other groups resisting racism, who provided a model of dissenting citizenship and a larger critique of the exclusion inherent to the nation and it history of settler colonialism, slavery, and exclusion from citizenship.

Cross-ethnic affiliations among youth do not exist either in the absence of interracial tensions between South Asians and other minoritized communities, including antiblack racism in South Asian immigrant communities[24] or, on the other hand, in the absence of multicultural attempts at inclusion and regimes of cultural and religious tolerance. As Wendy Brown points out, U.S. foreign policies are legitimized by supposedly apolitical understandings of tolerance and intolerance in everyday life that produce essentialized notions of "cultural difference" and "civilizational conflict."[25] The explosion of talks, television programs, and books about Islam after 9/11 have in many cases produced a neo-Orientalist perspective on the "Muslim world" and evaded the politics and histories of the Middle East and South Asia, focusing selectively on issues such as gender oppression, religious fundamentalism, and (certain) repressive regimes. Building on Edward Said's work, Asad AbuKhalil points out that much of this neo-Orientalist discussion spotlighting Islam after 9/11 contains a virulent strain of "theologocentrism," making a "direct connection between Islamic theology and the political conditions of the Arab and Muslim world" and providing a problematic explanation for the presumed causes of "Muslim terrorism" in the pages of the Quran.[26]

Dissenting citizenship captures some of the ambivalence toward the United States that these working-class immigrant youth experience, for the nation is simultaneously a place invested with their parents' desire for the American dream and their own hopes of belonging in a new homeland and also the site of alienation, discrimination, fear, frustration, and anxiety about belonging and survival, a tension apparent in Muslim American communities today. A few youths had expectations that the United States would live up to its ideals of freedom and equal rights, but most seemed to emphasize simply that U.S. actions needs to be held to an international standard of justice that should apply to all nation-states, including India and Pakistan.

The process of dissenting citizenship is not without fundamental tensions that animate its expression by these young immigrants, for they implicitly understand the limits of a state-based notion of citizenship and of rights afforded by the state. Muslim immigrants from India, in particular, have had to consider the failures of both home and host states—India and the United States—to guarantee protection and equal rights to Muslim subjects. The anti-Muslim massacres in Gujarat in the spring of 2002, as well as the military standoff between India and Pakistan that preceded it in 1999, reinforce for Indian Muslim youth a sense that they are in an ambiguous zone between religious and national identification, as their national allegiances are questioned in India as well. Right-wing Hindu movements in India and in the United States have also promoted a virulently anti-Muslim rhetoric and hysterical generalizations about "Islamic terrorism" and Pakistani militants that have overlapped, often intentionally, with the Bush regime's rhetoric in the war on terror, especially as India has become the U.S. ally in the region and forged new political, military, and economic alliances with Israel.

Gendering Dissent: Good, Moderate, and Bad Muslims

Performances of dissenting citizenship by Muslim American youth are shaped by religion, class, nationalism, and gender through an uneasy conjoining of liberalism, feminism, and Orientalism that is evident in local spaces as well as the larger national contexts that shape them. A particular space has been constructed for Muslim and Arab women in the post-9/11 debate over the war on terror that is very revealing of the ways in which Muslimness and Arabness are gendered in the public sphere. In the high school, for example, more South Asian Muslim girls than boys spoke at public events in the aftermath of 9/11, even though the boys were the most visible targets of profiling. Beyond the question of invisibility and hypervisibility, what is striking is how Muslim and Arab spokeswomen have both challenged and supported Orientalist perspectives on Muslim and Arab "culture" and on the status of women in particular, in public discourse in the U.S. Arab and South Asian women authors and activists, some promoted by the state and right-wing think tanks, such as Irshad Manji, Wafa Sultan, Brigitte Gabriel (who is a Christian), or even Asra Nomani—began appearing in the mainstream media frequently after 9/11, extolling the individual freedom offered by the "democratic" West and the United States in particular and denouncing the backwardness and repressiveness of "the Muslim world," some more shrilly than others.[27]

The hunger for native informants on Islam and the Middle East has led to state and media promotion of what Hamid Dabashi[28] calls a "new breed of comprador intellectuals," or native Orientalists, who provide authenticity and credibility to reports of atrocities, particularly against Muslim women, "justifying the imperial designs of the U.S. as liberating these nations."[29] The increasing circulation, funding, and promotion of these Muslim and Arab native informants, or "moderate" Muslim spokespersons, who stage public testimonials of their individual "liberation" in the West demonstrate that dissenting citizenship is gendered in ways that are often deeply problematic. Testimonials that selectively focus on the oppressiveness and misogyny of Islam or Muslim societies are shaped by a universalizing feminist discourse about women's rights that often expresses a liberal Orientalism, which Leila Ahmed described as "colonial feminism."[30] In the United States, imperialist feminism is preoccupied with women in hijab or presumably "oppressed" Muslim women requiring liberation from their tradition in order to be brought into the fold of the nation. At the same time, there is a deep anxiety about young Muslim men as potential terrorists and religious fanatics who are, unlike women perhaps, ultimately inassimilable. As Miriam Cooke observes, "Imperial logic genders and separates subject peoples so that the men are the Other and the women are civilizable."[31]

Gendered performances of dissenting or "moderate" Muslim politics are embedded in distinctions between "good" and "bad" Muslim citizens that have been reified by state and media discourse since 2001. Mahmood Mamdani has argued that after 9/11:

> President Bush moved to distinguish between "good Muslims" and "bad Muslims" . . . "bad Muslims" were clearly responsible for terrorism. At the same time, the president seemed to assure Americans that "good Muslims" were anxious to clear their names and consciences of this horrible crime and would undoubtedly support "us" in a war against "them." But this could not hide the central message of such discourse: unless proved to be "good," every Muslim was presumed to be "bad." . . . Judgments of "good" and "bad" refer to Muslim political identities, not to cultural or religious ones.[32]

"Good citizenship" was performed by Muslim Americans after 9/11 in a variety of ways, testifying loyalty to the nation and asserting belief in its democratic ideals. Sometimes dissenting citizenship blurred into "good" Muslim citizenship as antiwar critics who were Muslim made public testimonials that emphasized that Muslims were peaceful, loyal, American citizens while simultaneously critiquing aspects of the government's policies, revealing the contradictions of the narrow registers in which Muslims voice their dissent in the war on terror.

The desire to perform "good" Muslim citizenship has altered the identities and social relations within Muslim American communities after 9/11 and created divisiveness, mistrust, and suspicion related to questions of dissent and complicity. Sally Howell and Andrew Shryock argue that Arab Americans and community leaders who want "to reassert their status as 'good' and 'loyal'" citizens of the United States have tried to distance themselves both from "a strong identification with religious beliefs, political ideologies, or cultural practices that are genuinely alternative to those present in America today" and "from the people who are most likely to suffer from these images and their consequences."[33] This has heightened divisions within the targeted communities and reinforced distinctions between "good" and "bad" Arabs, similar to those between "good" and "bad" Muslim citizenship that I witnessed in Wellford and that are evident in national politics. Furthermore, I argue that the categorization of good, "moderate," or bad Muslims rests on assumptions about the relation of Islam to democracy, violence, and modernity that are themselves Islamophobic and troubling.

The notion of good Muslim citizenship sometimes dovetails with a rhetoric of multicultural inclusion that suggests that Islamophobia can be countered simply by tolerance of religious difference via a form of religious multiculturalism. Orientalist constructions of "the Muslim world" after 9/11 reinscribe the multiculturalist presumption that political injustice can be resolved simply by awareness of religious or cultural difference, ignoring the larger geopolitical and imperial frames of the war on terror. Muslim American youth have also been forced to play the role of educators for the American public, giving speeches at their schools and in community forums about Islam. A coordinator of a Muslim youth group at the local mosque in Wellford pointed out that it is a role that has also brought a certain pressure and fatigue to young Muslim Americans forced to become public spokespersons after 9/11.

Furthermore, focusing on "Muslim" as just another cultural (or ambiguously racial) marker has, in some cases, absorbed Arab/South Asian/Muslim Americans into a discourse of difference and belonging to the pluralistic and tolerant nation-state and subsumed the category "Muslim" into an ethnicized U.S. identity politics. "Muslim Americans," or the trio of "Arab, Muslim, and South Asian Americans," are constructed as belonging to just another, culturally distinct ethnic category whose problems can be contained within a discourse of domestic racism and addressed by inclusion within the multicultural nation.[34] However, the war on terror has highlighted the limitations of liberal multiculturalism as a response to state policies targeting Muslim and Arab Americans after 9/11, although it evades the larger political context and deeper structural racism undergirding Islamophobia as well as anti-Arab racism. The racism and Islamophobia of the domestic war on terror are not simply a problem of religious difference or multicultural tolerance within the nation but are linked to global histories of U.S. involvement in the Middle East and South Asia. Some Muslim Americans, as I found in my research on immigrant youth, understood the anti-Muslim backlash in relation to other forms of subjugation, racialization, and repression in the United States and also globally, including anti-Muslim violence in South Asia, and began forging cross-ethnic or interracial affiliations and alliances based on a deeper critique of oppression and marginality.

Conclusion

An analysis of Islamophobia needs to be situated in the larger historical and political context of empire—tracing it to European colonialism, Western modernity, and, especially for Muslim Americans in the current moment, a deeper exploration of U.S. racism and imperial policies in the Middle East and elsewhere. My own interest in ethnographic research helps me to understand the dissenting responses of Muslim immigrant youth and the contradictions of expressing dissent as it is laced with the politics of multiculturalism, Orientalism, anti-Arab racism, and feminism.

The U.S. presidential campaign of 2008 underscored the ways in which Arabs and Muslims continue to be othered as suspect citizens, as was apparent in the removal of Muslim women in hijab from Barack Obama's campaign rally and the statement by John McCain that implicitly suggested that an Arab could not also be a decent, family man. Arab and Muslim Americans also continue to be demonized as "anti-American" and "pro-terrorist" dissenters, as was illustrated by the attacks on Palestinian professor Rashid Khalidi. As the global war on terror continued, and the then president-elect talked about reviving the war in Afghanistan, targeting Pakistan if necessary, and continuing to support the occupation in Palestine, the linkages between citizenship, dissent, Islam, and U.S. policies in the Middle East and South Asia need to be thoughtfully and rigorously considered. As always, the academy is a site that is also impacted by the repression of dissent and need for knowledge of targeted groups and regions, and so the stakes for our critique of Islamophobia, racism, and Orientalism are very high.

NOTES

1. Steven Salaita, *The Holy Land in Transit: Colonialism and the Quest for Canaan* (Syracuse: Syracuse University Press, 2006b); Roxanne Dunbar-Ortiz, "The Grid of History: Cowboys and Indians," in *Pox Americana: Exposing the American Empire*, ed. John Bellamy Foster and Robert W. McChesney (New York: Monthly Review Press, 2004), 31–40.

2. Eli Painted Crow, a Yaqui soldier who served in the *U.S. military in Iraq* in 2004, cited in an interview by Amy Goodman, *Democracy Now*, Mar. 8, 2007. http://www.democracynow.org/2007/3/8/the_private_war_of_women_soldiers (accessed Dec. 27, 2008). See also Thomas A. Bass, "Counterinsurgency and Torture," *American Quarterly* 60, no. 2 (June 2008): 233–40.

3. Douglas Little, *American Orientalism: The United States and the Middle East since 1945* (Chapel Hill: University of North Carolina Press, 2002), 231.

4. Ibid.; Salaita 2006b.

5. Sherene H. Razack, *Casting Out: The Eviction of Muslims from Western Law and Politics* (Toronto: University of Toronto Press, 2008).

6. Edward Said, *Orientalism* (New York: Vintage/Random House, 1978).

7. Giorgio Agamben, *State of Exception*, trans Kevin Attell (Chicago: University of Chicago Press, 2005); Keya Ganguly, *States of Exception: Everyday Life and Postcolonial Identity* (Minneapolis: University of Minnesota Press, 2001).

8. Derek Gregory, *The Colonial Present* (Malden: Blackwell, 2004); Razack, *Casting Out*.

9. Harry Magdoff, *Imperialism without Colonies* (New York: Monthly Review Press, 2003); Neil Smith, *The Endgame of Globalization* (New York: Routledge, 2005).

10. Donald Pease, "New Perspectives on U.S. Culture and Imperialism," in *Cultures of United States Imperialism*, ed. Amy Kaplan and Donald Pease (Durham: Duke University Press, 1993), 22–37.

11. Ann L. Stoler, "Intimidations of Empire: Predicaments of the Tactile and Unseen" in *Haunted by Empire: Geographies of Intimacy in North American History*, ed. Ann L. Stoler (Durham: Duke University Press, 2006), 12.

12. Nabeel Abraham, "Anti-Arab Racism and Violence in the United States," in *The Development of Arab-American Identity*, ed. Ernest McCarus (Ann Arbor: University of Michigan Press, 1994), 155–214; Said, *Orientalism*.

13. Steven Salaita, *Anti-Arab Racism in the U.S.A.: Where It Comes from and What It Means for Politics Today* (London: Pluto, 2006a).

14. Holly Edwards, "A Million and One Nights: Orientalism in America, 1870–1930," in *Noble Dreams, Wicked Pleasures: Orientalism in America, 1870–1930*, ed. Holly Edwards (Princeton: Princeton University Press, 2000), 28.

15. Said, *Orientalism*.

16. I have changed the name of the location and used pseudonyms to protect the identity of the research subjects. As part of my ethnographic study in Wellford in 2001–2003, I interviewed South Asian Muslim immigrant students, non-Muslim and second-generation South Asian youth, as well as Muslim immigrant students from other countries, parents of both immigrant and nonimmigrant students, teachers,

staff, youth program organizers, community and religious leaders, and activists working on immigrant and civil rights. I did fieldwork at the public high school and a range of sites in Wellford, including homes, workplaces, social gatherings, and cultural and political events. At the time of this research, I was also involved with a volunteer program for South Asian immigrant students in the high school, SAMTA (South Asian Mentoring and Tutoring Association), which organized workshops on academic, social, and career issues.

17. Sunaina Maira, *Missing: Youth, Citizenship, and Empire after 9/11* (Durham: Duke University Press, 2009).

18. These South Asian immigrants are part of a second wave of South Asian labor migrants who began arriving in the 1980s, which has created an urban community of working-class and undocumented immigrants, in contrast to the upwardly mobile, highly educated South Asian immigrants who arrived in the 1960s and 1970s and dispersed to the suburbs.

19. The 2000 Census reported 2,720 Indian immigrants (2.7 percent of the population), 125 Pakistanis, and 120 Bangladeshis in Wellford. This, of course, does not include undocumented immigrants. The "native" population is 74.1 percent, and the foreign-born population is 25.9 percent; 17.7 percent are not citizens, and 31.2 percent speak a language other than English (U.S. Census Bureau, 2000; http:factfinder.census.gov/bf/_lang=en_ . . . 2000, accessed Nov. 13, 2002).

20. Renato Rosaldo, "Cultural Citizenship, Inequality, and Multiculturalism," in *Latino Cultural Citizenship: Claiming Identity, Space, and Rights*, eds. William F. Flores and Rina Benmayor (Boston, Massachusetts: Beacon, 1997), 27–38.

21. David Cole, *Enemy Aliens: Double Standards and Constitutional Freedoms in the War on Terrorism* (New York: New Press, 2003).

22. Abraham, "Anti-Arab Racism."; Louise Cainkar and Sunaina Maira, "Crossing the Boundaries of Asian and Arab American Studies: Criminalization and Cultural Citizenship of Arab/Muslim/South Asian Americans," *Amerasia Journal* 31, no. 3 (2006): 1–27; Mai M. Ngai, *Impossible Subjects: Illegal Aliens and the Making of Modern America* (Princeton: Princeton University Press, 2004).

23. Corey Robin, *Fear: The History of a Political Idea* (New York: Oxford University Press, 2004).

24. Vijay Prashad, *The Karma of Brown Folk* (Minneapolis: University of Minnesota, 2000).

25. Wendy Brown, *Regulating Aversion: Tolerance in the Age of Identity and Empire* (Princeton: Princeton University Press, 2006).

26. As'ad AbuKhalil, *Bin Laden, Islam, and America's New "War on Terrorism"* (New York: Seven Stories, 2002), 29.

27. Irshad Manji, who calls herself a "Muslim refusenik," is of Indian/Egyptian origin and the author of *The Trouble with Islam*, Asra Nomani, the Indian American author of *Standing Alone: An American Woman's Struggle for the Soul of Islam* was catapulted into fame by the death of her friend, journalist Daniel Pearl, and launched a "Muslim women's freedom tour." More shrill spokespersons include Brigitte Gabriel, the Lebanese Christian founder of the American Congress for Truth, and Wafa Sultan,

a Syrian American psychiatrist who became famous for declaring on Al-Jazeera television (Feb. 21, 2006), "There is no clash of civilizations but a clash between . . . civilization and backwardness, between the civilized and the primitive, between barbarity and rationality." See Irshad Manji, *The Trouble with Islam: A Muslim's Call for Reform in Her Faith* (Toronto: Random House Canada, 2003) and Asra Q. Nomani, *Standing Alone: An American Woman's Struggle for the Soul of Islam* (San Francisco: HarperSanFrancisco, 2006).

28. Hamid Dabashi, "Native Informers and the Making of the American Empire," *Al-Ahram Weekly*, 2006, http://weekly.ahram.org.eg/print/2006/797/special.htm (accessed Nov. 16, 2006).

29. Hamid Dabashi, *Iran: A People Interrupted* (New York: New Press, 2007), 8. See also Ali Behdad, "Critical Historicism," *American Literary History* 20, nos. 1–2 (Summer 2007): 286–99.

30. Leila Ahmed, *Women and Gender in Islam: Historical Roots of a Modern Debate* (New Haven: Yale University Press, 1992).

31. Miriam Cooke, "Islamic Feminism before and after September 11," *Duke Journal of Gender Law and Policy* 227, no. 9 (Summer 2002), http://www.law.duke.edu/shell/cite.pl ?9+Duke+J.+Gender+L.+&+Pol'y+227 (accessed June 20, 2010).

32. Mahmood Mamdani, *Good Muslim, Bad Muslim: America, the Cold War, and the Roots of Terror* (New York: Pantheon, 2004), 15.

33. Sally Howell and Andrew Shryock, "Cracking Down on Diaspora: Arab Detroit and America's 'War on Terror,' " *Anthropological Quarterly* 76, no. 3 (2003): 456.

34. Evelyn Alsultany, "Selling American Diversity and Muslim American Identity through Nonprofit Advertising Post-9/11," *American Quarterly* 59, no. 3 (2007): 593–622.

8

Islamophobia and American Foreign Policy Rhetoric: The Bush Years and After

Juan Cole

One of the more pressing foreign policy problems facing the United States is its relations with the Muslim world. In the wake of the September 11 attacks, the administration of U.S. president George W. Bush decided to play the Islam card, making a "war on terror" central to the subsequent political campaigns. By late summer of 2006, as public opinion began turning against the Republican Party in the United States, a desperate Bush led the way in redefining the enemy as "Islamic fascism." This ploy, which failed to excite the American electorate, provoked widespread protests from Middle Eastern governments and newspapers. The phrase nevertheless entered the Republican political lexicon and affected the way the United States was perceived in the region. In the 2007–2008 presidential campaign, Islamophobia emerged as a major campaign issue, with Republican candidates such as Rudi Giuliani and Mike Huckabee regularly saying outrageous things about Islam and Muslims. Even John McCain, who sometimes took a more principled stand, campaigned against "radical Islamic extremism." The campaign of Barack Obama, eager to dissociate its candidate from rumors that he was a secret Muslim, sometimes behaved insensitively on the issue. His administration now faces the task of removing this substantial irritant in U.S. foreign relations with the states that make up the Muslim world.

The Bush administration attempted to have its cake and eat it, too, in identifying a "Green Menace" that could substitute for the old "Red Menace" of the Soviet Union and international communism, which had served U.S. politicians on the Right so well since the late 1940s in their fear mongering and assault on U.S. civil liberties. (Thus, Bush identified Islam as a "religion of peace" and discouraged scapegoating Muslims for the September 11 attacks. Yet at the same time, he continually linked the Muslim world to terrorism and depicted it to the American people as a threat to U.S. national security. He spoke of small, weak countries such as Saddam's Iraq, as well as Syria and Iran, as existential threats to the United States. Two of the three had a secular, nationalist government.) By 2006, Bush's initial attempt to speak out of both sides of his mouth was faltering, as he began engaging more in fear mongering, setting the tone of the 2006 and 2008 elections for the Republicans.

The easy prejudices and bigotry of some in Bush's inner circle are apparent in the memos of former secretary of defense Donald Rumsfeld, a master of misdirection. Robin Wright of the *Washington Post* reported on Rumsfeld's memoranda, or "snowflakes," late in 2007.[1] When, in April 2006, retired generals criticized Rumsfeld for his conduct of the Iraq War, he wrote in a memo, "Talk about Somalia, the Philippines, etc. Make the American people realize they are surrounded in the world by violent extremists." Rumsfeld was apparently referring to the tiny Abu Sayyaf group in the Philippines, which is estimated to have two hundred members. It is more a criminal gang than an Islamic movement. As for Somalia, it is a failed state wracked with tribal violence, little of it explicitly religious in character. It is difficult to see how two hundred people in the Filipino jungles and some warring tribes in the Horn of Africa could have the world's sole superpower "surrounded." The only thing the two phenomena have in common is that the Moro Filipinos and the Somalis are largely Muslim populations. "Muslim" apparently equals "danger." Rumsfeld's effort was classic fear mongering.

Rumsfeld's theory of Muslim radicalism in the Persian Gulf depended on pop sociology of a breathtakingly glib sort. He believed that petroleum wealth had detached Muslims "from the reality of the work, effort and investment that leads to wealth for the rest of the world. Too often Muslims are against physical labor, so they bring in Koreans and Pakistanis while their young people remain unemployed. An unemployed population is easy to recruit to radicalism." He added that if radicals "get a hold of" oil-rich Saudi Arabia, the United States will have "an enormous national security problem."

Most Muslims, of course, do not live in petroleum-rich states. Egypt, with a population of 79 million, has very little petroleum, and the largest Muslim country, Indonesia, has become a net importer of oil. Saudi Arabia does suffer from high male unemployment (30 percent in early 2008), but this has to do with high population growth rates and a distorted economy (oil income hardens the currency and hurts exports of agricultural and manufactured goods). The state-owned oil wealth is very unevenly distributed and difficult to inject into the economy without producing high inflation. The unemployment is not voluntary. Nor is dependence on guest workers for manual labor specific to the Saudis. The United States imports large numbers of foreign workers for manual labor as well, but Rumsfeld does not appear to see this tendency as an indictment of Christianity. The idea that "Muslims" are "against physical labor" is just daft, and Rumsfeld contradicted himself when he said that they "bring in" "Pakistanis." What religion did he think the Pakistanis followed? When American politicians look at the United States or Europe, they explain economic phenomena through economics, but the Muslim world is apparently a mystical realm where national character flaws explain everything.

Rumsfeld's anxiety about terrorists taking over Saudi Arabia was, to say the least, exaggerated. In fact, recent polling in Saudi Arabia found that 88 percent of the population approved of the government security forces pursuing al-Qaeda activists.[2] Some 90 percent say that fighting terrorism is among their top priorities (even the small number of Saudis who still have a favorable view of Osama Bin Laden are worried about terrorism, an indication that they do not believe he is a terrorist, which is why they can still admire him.) Two-thirds of Saudis support stronger relations with the United States, and most say that their view of America would improve dramatically if it withdrew troops from Iraq. The Kingdom of Saudi Arabia looks nothing like Rumsfeld's fantasy.

Rumsfeld's Islamophobia led him to see the United States as "surrounded" by violent Muslim movements, even if those were tiny and without popular support in their own contexts, and even if their focus was on local goals rather than on geopolitics. He depicted Muslims as intrinsically extremist, who were both menacing and "surrounding." At the core of their pathological behavior he found a lack of any Protestant ethic, a moral laziness that created idleness, unemployment, and extremism. This lazy road to terrorism threatens the United States not only through violent attacks but also because it menaces the stability of Saudi Arabia, the world's large exporter of petroleum and therefore a kingpin of America's hydrocarbon economy.

As Republican domestic fortunes began to sink in the run-up to the 2006 midterm elections, party leaders appear to have made a decision to push a new rhetoric, one that replaced the "global war on terror" with a struggle against "Islamic fascism." Rumsfeld accused the Democratic Party's critics of both the Iraq War and the war on terror of trying to "appease" a new form of "fascism."[3]

Bush himself picked up these expressions with alacrity around the same time. In late summer of 2006 he said that arrests of suspected terror suspects in Britain were a "stark reminder that this nation is at war with Islamic fascists who will use any means to destroy those of us who love freedom, to hurt our nation."[4] It was rather grandiose to depict the United States as "at war" with a handful of radicalized British youth, and it was unfortunate that Bush called the problem "Islamic." Putting "Islamic" in front of another word implies that it is intrinsic to or characteristic of the Islamic religion or civilization. Islamic ethics are those of the Muslim scripture and religious teachings, for instance. It would not be objectionable to speak of Muslim failings or Muslim terrorists. However, what follows the word "Islamic," whether most English speakers realize it or not, pertains to the religion itself or to the broader civilization that was deeply influenced by that religion. The term is analogous to "Judaic." Likewise, one would not speak of a "Judaic assassin" but rather a "Jewish" one since "Judaic" has to do with the ideals and accomplishments of a religious civilization.

Saudi Arabia, which has old and warm relations with the Bush dynasty, reacted immediately to the new demagoguery. A cabinet statement carried by the Saudi Press Agency "called on everyone to realize that terrorism has no religion or nationality." It "warned against hurling charges of terrorism and fascism at Muslims without regard to the spotless history of Islamic civilization" and added, "What Islam is being accused of today, like fascism, is primarily a Western cultural product." The Saudi cabinet called for close international cooperation to combat terrorism.[5] A very popular Saudi newspaper ran a vehement opinion piece by Abdallah al-Jafri that noted the cabinet's response and lamented, "Thus, Bush's hatred for Islam has reached this extent!"[6]

Indonesian intellectual Muhamad Ali wrote of the phrase in the *Jakarta Post* soon after it began being deployed and pointed out that "when Islam is attached to an extreme ideology, it may imply that Islam plays a part in the creation of such extremist ideologies." He observed that none of the radical Muslim movements invokes fascism as part of its political genealogy. He deplored a similar tendency in the Iranian press to compare Bush himself to fascist leaders such as Mussolini. He advised Washington, "If they want to refer to a group of terrorists, they may name them, such as al-Qaeda, Jamaah Islamiyah, Islamic Jihad, HAMAS, Hizbollah, etc., instead of using the word Islamic for any ideology emerging from the Muslim tradition and history without a clear definition and full understanding of the characteristics and diversity of Muslim movements."[7] The reaction from Muslim op-ed writers and editorialists was often less polite and frequently not only involved condemnations of Bush for using that phraseology but also threw it back in his face, with enumerations of his own alleged misdeeds. The Saudi and other governments in the region warned against the further use of the term.

As well they might. While some Muslims feel themselves at war with the United States, they form a tiny set of shadowy organizations and are not representative in any way of the some 1.5 billion Muslims in the world. Nor is it clear that they have anything in common with the fascist movements of interwar Europe, which were crafted by persons of Christian heritage but sometimes moved toward pagan or secular emphases. Because of its tendency to express local grievances in nativist language, fascism is notoriously difficult to define. Nonetheless, surely it has to do with a virulent nationalism and the establishment of racial hierarchies, with a celebration of violence and struggle for its own sake and with the idolization of a dominating elite and contempt for the weak. Most Muslim extremists of the al-Qaeda variety, in contrast, reject nationalism, establish multiethnic alliances, and think of themselves as defending the oppressed Muslim masses. Even if one could establish that their ideas had any similarity to European fascism, they should be called Muslim fascists and not Islamic ones since Islam as a religion is universalist in character and therefore antifascist. The neologism "Islamofascist" is particularly inappropriate since it yokes European authoritarianism to Islam as a religion.

The imagining of an implacable Islamic enemy that licenses U.S. aggression is clear in a number of speeches by former U.S. vice president Dick Cheney and by Bush. Bush warned, "The extremists are fighting to take control of Iraq so they can establish it as a base from which to overthrow moderate governments in the region and plan new attacks on the American people. If we fail in Iraq, the enemy will follow us home."[8] Bush thus configured the Sunni Arab population of provinces such as al-Anbar and Diyala as part of a conspiracy to attack the United States and to overthrow the "moderate" Shiite government Bush had installed in Baghdad. Yet, every indication is that the Iraqi Sunni insurgency was simply a nationalist movement fighting for independence from a foreign occupier and its Shiite and Kurdish allies. It was not even apparently very dedicated since many of its members later agreed to take a salary from the United States to form citizen patrols called "awakening councils." Bush's choice of words, however, inevitably configures the Muslim as an inexplicably sinister bogeyman who would "follow us home" unless the United States kept an army boot on his neck.

Dick Cheney, in his March 2007 speech to the American Israel Public Affairs Committee, the powerful coordinator of lobbying for Israel with Congress and other branches of government, used many code words to denigrate Islam. These passages are worth quoting at length:

We are the prime targets of a terror movement that is global in nature and, yes, global in its ambitions. The leaders of this movement speak openly and specifically of building a totalitarian empire covering the Middle East, extending into Europe and reaching across to the islands of Indonesia, one that would impose a narrow, radical vision of Islam that rejects tolerance, suppresses dissent, brutalizes women and has one of its foremost objectives the destruction of Israel. Their creed is extreme and backward looking, yet their methods are modern and sophisticated. The terrorists use the Internet to spread propaganda, to find new recruits, and they're employing every other tool of communication and finance to carry out their plans.

It's odd to think of ideologues out of the Dark Ages having a modern media strategy, but the fact is they do. They take videos of their attacks and put them up on the Internet to get them broadcast on television. They send messages and images by e-mail and tell their followers to spread the word. They wage war by stealth and murder, disregarding the rules of warfare and rejoicing in the death of the innocent.

And not even the instinct of self-preservation is a restraint. The terrorists value death the same way you and I value life. Civilized, decent societies will never fully understand the kind of mindset that drives men to strap on bombs or fly airplanes into buildings, all for the purpose of killing unsuspecting men, women and children who [sic] they have never met and who have done them no wrong. But that is the very kind of blind, prideful hatred we're up against.

And their aim, ultimately, is to acquire the means to match that hatred and to use chemical, biological or nuclear weapons to impose their will by unspeakable violence or blackmail.

An enemy that operates in the shadows and views the entire world as a battlefield is not one we can fight with strategies used in other wars. An enemy with fantasies of martyrdom is not going to sit down at a table for negotiations. Nor can we fight to a standoff—(applause). Nor can we fight to a standoff, hoping that some form of containment or deterrence will protect our people. The only option for our security and survival is to go on the offensive, facing the threat directly, patiently and systematically, until the enemy is destroyed.[9]

Cheney began his speech by identifying the common Israeli and U.S. challenge. In both cases, these societies are called to a "war on terror," and Cheney went on to amalgamate a Shiite regional movement of south Lebanon, a Sunni slum movement of the Israeli-occupied Gaza Strip, and a shadowy

Saudi-Egyptian network that originated in the Reagan administration's covert Islamist war against the Soviets in Afghanistan. That is, Israel and the United States face the same enemy, and it is somehow Islamic, protean, ambitious, grasping, malevolent, and irrational. In the Middle East itself, however, Hamas and Hizbullah would be seen as religious cum nationalist movements against foreign occupation, while al-Qaeda's popularity has plummeted as it has come to be seen as merely a terrorist movement. That is, most Middle Easterners would not accept Cheney's identification of the three.

Cheney unwittingly revealed one conceptual source of his anxiety about the terrorists when he said that "[t]heir creed is extreme and backward looking" but that "their methods are [nevertheless] modern and sophisticated." This configuring of Muslims as somehow out of place in modernity helps him to explain why they are so dangerous. They are medieval (from the Dark Ages) and yet diabolically advanced. Their very fearlessness in the face of superior military might and their unconventional methods, which make it impossible to contain them, leave the United States no option but to go on the offensive (i.e., to wage a series of aggressive wars in the Muslim world). By his choice of words, Cheney arranged for al-Qaeda and other terrorist groups to make the entire Muslim world hostage to U.S. anxieties, such that any Muslim state is at risk of a unilateral, preemptive U.S. attack to deter the shadowy terrorist networks that Cheney perceived as potentially enormously powerful.

Bush and Cheney insisted that they distinguished between proponents of "Islamic fascism" and ordinary Muslims. However, how their rhetoric was received in the Muslim world was revealed in the press commentary on Bush's visit to the Persian Gulf in January of 2008. Columnist Yusuf al-Kuwaylit, writing in the Saudi daily *al-Riyadh*, remarked, "Perhaps President Bush, through his visit to the region, has seen the reality of the people there—that they are not bad, hypocrites or terrorists fighting civilization and development. On the contrary, we are the ones who seek to fill the gaps between developed countries by lighting the paths between us. The USA is the biggest and most important partner, capable of rectifying mistakes and directing them towards constructive and moral actions."[10] Bush's resort to the rhetoric of "Islamic fascism" had been read by local intellectuals as a condemnation of "the people there" in general, as barbarians, medieval romanticists, and terrorists, as just "bad." Even with all this rhetorical excess, al-Kuwaylit was convinced that the United States could still rectify its mistakes.

Not everyone agreed, of course. The Arab nationalist tendency lambasted Bush's visit as a humiliation for the supine Arab regimes. An independent member of parliament in Egypt, Mustafa Bakri, according to Aljazeera, "called on the Egyptian authorities to prevent Bush from entering the country, describing him as 'a war criminal' and holding him responsible for killing more than one million Iraqi citizens and encroaching on the sovereignty of a brother Arab country." The Doha-based satellite television channel added, "In an urgent request to the speaker of the parliament on the visit, Bakri depended on what he termed the US President's interference in internal Egyptian affairs."[11] Bush's invasion and occupation of Iraq deeply damaged the standing of the United States in the eyes of Muslims, and respondents to opinion polls consistently say that a withdrawal of U.S. troops from that country would much improve its image. While Bush configured the Iraq War as a liberation of Muslims, in the Sunni Arab world it has largely been seen as an attack on Islam.

The oddest thing about the Bush administration's (and much of the Republican Party's) attempt to reconfigure swathes of the Muslim world as the successor to the Soviet Union as a threat to the United States is how flagrantly it flew in the face of reality. Arguably, no region of the world outside Europe is so full of regimes friendly to or closely allied with the United States. Turkey is a NATO ally of the United States. The United States has designated Morocco, Egypt, Jordan, Kuwait, Bahrain, and Pakistan as major non-NATO allies, a foreign policy category created in 1989. This status exempts them, as with NATO members, from the restrictions imposed by the Arms Export Control Act. They can conduct cooperative research and development projects with the Department of Defense on a shared-cost basis, participate in counterterrorism projects, enjoy priority shipping of military surplus goods, receive reciprocal training, and have special access to space technology, and their corporations have permission to bid on Department of Defense contracts to keep up and repair U.S. military equipment abroad.[12] Other states in the Muslim world, such as Algeria, Tunisia, Yemen, Indonesia, Malaysia, the Gulf oil states, and most of central Asia, have close diplomatic, economic, and military ties to United States.

Even Sudan and Syria, which have indifferent relations with the United States, were at some points lauded for their help in the "war on terror" by Bush administration officials. Washington's conflicts with Iran are more serious and longstanding, but both countries have at various points in recent history reached out to one another, and they have not been on a war footing. Iran cooperated with the overthrow of the Taliban in Afghanistan in 2001 and with the overthrow of Saddam Hussein in Iraq in early 2007. Iran's public expresses high regard for the United States in polls, so that what conflicts there are appear to be regime driven rather than populist in character. In any case, Iran, a country with a population of 70 million, constitutes less than 5 percent of the Muslim world.

Bush administration aggressiveness deeply damaged the image of the United States in the eyes of Muslims, as well as other people. The invasions and military occupations of Afghanistan and Iraq, the assault on the Iraqi city of Fallujah, and the Abu-Ghraib torture scandal all took their toll. In 2000, some 75 percent of Indonesians had a favorable view of the United States. By 2006, it was only 30 percent, and after the invasion of Iraq it had fallen to 15 percent. In 2000, 56 percent of Turks reported a favorable view of the United States. In 2007, it was 9 percent. In Jordan, positive views of the United States fell from 25 percent in 2002 to 15 percent in 2006.[13]

The Republican field in the 2007–2008 presidential campaign picked up more negative messages in the Bush and Cheney rhetoric about Islam and often took them to new heights.[14] Arizona senator John McCain even attributed his run for the presidency to his concern about "radical Islamic extremism," which he characterized as the transcendent challenge facing the United States in the 21st century.[15] Former Massachusetts governor Mitt Romney actually ran a campaign advertisement warning of a radical Muslim "jihad" that allegedly united the faithful across sectarian lines. He said, "Violent, radical jihadists want to replace all the governments of the moderate Islamic states, replace them with a caliphate." He added, "And to do that, they also want to bring down the West, in particular us. And they've come together as Shia and Sunni and Hezbollah and Hamas and the Muslim Brotherhood and Al Qaeda with that intent."[16] Journalist Matthew Yglesias pointed out that the Muslim Brotherhood is a political party, not a militant militia or terrorist organization, and that Romney's list made no sense.[17] One might also observe that Shiite Muslims do not in fact subscribe to the Sunni conception of a caliphate or popelike figure chosen by community elders. Michigan Republican activist Victor Ghalib Begg complained to the *Detroit Free Press*, "They're all falling over each other to demonize Muslims and Islam . . . They're trying to appeal to the power of prejudice and hate. . . . And it's brainless. Everybody knows we have a problem with terrorism. Let's focus on how to deal with it, instead of focusing on a faith or a people."[18]

Presidential candidate and Congressman Tom Tancredo (R-CO) maintained, without presenting any evidence, that Muslim terrorists in the United States intended to set off a nuclear weapon on U.S. soil. He said, "If it is up to me, we are going to explain that an attack on this homeland of that nature would be followed by an attack on the holy sites in Mecca and Medina. Because that's the only thing I can think of that might deter somebody from doing what they otherwise might do."[19] This sort of inflammatory rhetoric, menacing the holiest cities of Islam, one with a civilian population around the size of Houston, angered Muslims around the world. It impelled the Pakistani newspaper *Nava-i Vaqt* (Rawalpindi) to editorialize that "After the US presidential candidate Tom Tancredo's statement in which he expressed the intention to attack the holy places of Islam, the Organization of Islamic Conference should convene an emergency summit to chalk out a unanimous line of action and decide that Muslim countries should dissociate themselves from the so-called war on terror."[20] The editors urged that the Pakistani parliament immediately dissociate itself from the United States: "Supporting the United States now will be tantamount to betraying Islam." How many hours of desperate fence mending Tancredo's frankly insane nattering cost the U.S. State Department in the Muslim world would be hard to estimate.

Former New York mayor Rudolf Giuliani almost seemed to be running against al-Qaeda in the primaries. Attempting to paint his Democratic opponents as soft on Muslim terrorism, he complained that they "never mentioned the word 'Islamic terrorist,' 'Islamic extremist,' 'Islamic fascist,' 'terrorist,' whatever combination of those words you want to use, [the] words never came up."[21] He added, "I can't imagine who you insult if you say 'Islamic terrorist.' You don't insult anyone who is Islamic who isn't a terrorist." Giuliani had never bothered to learn good English wording on the issue (explained earlier). Individual believers are not properly modified by the adjective "Islamic" but rather are "Muslim." "Islamic" is a term that refers to the ideals, central texts, and practices of a religion or a civilization based on a religious tradition. There cannot be an "Islamic criminal," only a Muslim one.

Giuliani's campaign advertisements showed angry Muslim men and women with a voice-over that said "a people perverted," showing the faces of Muslim leaders as though they were wanted, including Ayatollah Muhammad Baqir al-Hakim, a major ally of the United States against Saddam Hussein in Iraq (albeit an ally of convenience). A key Giuliani adviser, New York congressman Peter King, told Politico.com that 85 percent of American Muslim congregations were dominated by radicals and that there are "too many mosques in this country."[22] (The research of social scientists and pollsters among American Muslims does not bear out the congressman's allegations.[23]) John Deady, a cochair of the New Hampshire Giuliani campaign, said that the mayor could stop "the rise of the Muslims," whom, he said, it was necessary to press until "we defeat them or chase them back to their caves, or, in other words, get rid of them." Reporters demanded to know whether he was denouncing all adherents of the religion. Deady replied, "I don't subscribe to the principle that there are good Muslims and bad Muslims. They're all Muslims."[24] He was forced to resign from the campaign, but it was predictable that Giuliani's overheated rhetoric would attract persons with such views.

Former Arkansas governor Mike Huckabee attempted to appeal to the evangelical voters, his own base, by raising alarms about Muslim immigration. After the assassination of Pakistani politician Benazir Bhutto, he remarked, "I am making the observation that we have more Pakistani illegals coming across our border than all other nationalities except those immediately south of the border." He added, "And in light of what is happening in Pakistan it ought to give us pause as to why are so many illegals coming across these borders."[25] In fact, there are almost no Pakistani illegal aliens to speak of in the United States. Asians make up only about 13 percent of the estimated 12 million illegal immigrants in the United States, but almost all of them are from east Asia. Not only are there few illegal entrants from Pakistan, but south Asian legal immigrants are among the wealthiest in the country. Huckabee was attempting to play on the horror evoked in the American public by the assassination of Bhutto by scaring them on the issue of Muslims coming to the United States—as though Bhutto herself were not Muslim or had not studied and resided in the United States.

The candidate who emerged as the Republican front-runner, John McCain, proclaimed at one campaign stop, "I'm not interested in trading with al-Qaida. All they want to trade is burqas."[26] The senator seemed to be relating the Muslim custom of veiling to terrorism. The *Detroit Free Press*, published in a city that has one of the largest Muslim populations in the United States, reported on January 12, 2008, that McCain's remarks were hurtful to American Muslims. "Local Muslims say that criticizing al-Qaida is legitimate, but wonder why he would make a snide remark about a dress? The remark was especially bothersome, some said, considering that McCain's adopted daughter, Bridget McCain, is from one of the biggest Muslim countries, Bangladesh." One would think that raising a daughter from the Muslim world in the United States today would be difficult enough even without the adoptive father's denigrating the customs of the women of that culture.

On another occasion, asked whether a Muslim candidate for president would be acceptable, McCain replied, "I just have to say in all candor that since this nation was founded primarily on Christian principles . . . personally, I prefer someone who I know who has a solid grounding in my faith. But that doesn't mean that I'm sure that someone who is Muslim would not make a good president. I don't say that we would rule out under any circumstances someone of a different faith. I just would—I just feel that that's an important part of our qualifications to lead."[27] However, according to Article VI of the U.S. Constitution, "no religious Test shall ever be required as a Qualification to any

Office or public Trust under the United States." Jewish Americans and secularists joined American Muslims in denouncing McCain's view that the United States was established on a Christian foundation and that Christianity was a necessary credential for occupying the Oval Office.

McCain, not Giuliani, did set some limits to the theme of Islamophobia in his campaign. McCain initially sought the endorsements of hate-mongering televangelists John Hagee and Rod Parsley. Indeed, he referred to the latter as a "spiritual guide." Parsley called for Christians to make war on Islam and labeled Islam "a false religion." After the endorsements generated controversy and especially after a video emerged of Hagee saying that God had sent Hitler as a hunter of Jews to force them into emigrating to Israel, McCain repudiated both Hagee and Parsley and specifically distanced himself from Parsley's comments on Muslims.[28]

In one of the more memorable moments of the campaign, McCain was confronted by an elderly woman who maintained that Barack Obama is an "Arab" (by which she clearly meant that he is a Muslim, a common error in the United States, where it is not realized that most Muslims are not Arabs and that many Arabs are not Muslims). McCain replied, "No, ma'am. He's a decent family man and citizen." While McCain was widely praised for intervening, some observers felt that he inadvertently cast aspersions on Arab Americans by implying that they are not decent or family oriented.[29] Despite the attempts of the Far Right of the Republican Party to depict Barack Obama himself as a Muslim or a former Muslim, the Islamophobic assault on the Democratic candidate faltered both because the story seemed poorly sourced and because of lack of public interest.[30] Indeed, to demonstrate their contempt for the prejudice implied in the right-wing attack on Obama's middle name, thousands of his supporters began using "Hussein" as their own middle name.[31]

On the Democratic side as well, Islamophobic themes were taken up, though not with the same vigor or, let us say, directness, of a Tancredo or a Giuliani. The tabloid website "Drudge Report" put up a photo of then senator Barack Obama during a visit to Kenya, in which he tried on traditional Kenyan garb, which for some American audiences underlined his paternal line's Muslim origins. Drudge maintained that the photo was provided by the Clinton campaign, which the latter denied.[32] For its part, the Obama campaign seemed to go so far in seeking to distance the candidate from the Muslim side of his heritage that it sometimes insulted Muslims. Veiled Arab American women supporting Obama were made to move from bleachers at a rally where they would have been visible behind the Illinois senator on the television screen.[33] Obama later apologized for the incident, caused by low-level staffers. Obama's campaign let go its liaison to the American Muslim community, Mazen

Asbahi, after political opponents engaged in guilt by association to imply he had shadowy ties to persons and groups that themselves had shadowy ties. The accusations were insubstantial (Bush administration officials had addressed the Islamic Association of North America, which critics had attempted to tie to Asbahi), and the Obama campaign should have stuck by its guns.[34]

The Bush administration's foreign policy toward the states of the Muslim world was characterized by a key contradiction, which limited its effectiveness and profoundly harmed the image of the United States in the region. Washington never stopped pursuing close relations with Muslim-majority states. The U.S. military, then and now, regularly conducts joint exercises with the Egyptian military, for instance. It depends heavily on Turkey, Jordan, Saudi Arabia, Qatar, and Kuwait for logistical support. The Persian Gulf oil monarchies are central to U.S. energy security. It arguably has closer allies and fewer regime critics in the Middle East of 2008 than it does in Latin America. Yet, the Bush administration attempted to depict Islam and the Muslim world as a bogeyman menacing U.S. security. Bush misrepresented a movement of ethnosectarian regionalism like Hezbollah as an international terrorist organization. He demonized Iran, Syria, and the Sudan. Rumsfeld's instinct when under attack for his mismanagement of the Iraq War was to brandish at the American public the tiny Abu Sayyaf group in the Philippines and the petty warlords of Somalia.

Although Bush and his officials maintained that they distinguish between Islamic fascism and the beliefs and practices of ordinary Muslims, a significant proportion of the Muslim public did not believe them. Indeed, even those Muslims who did not view Bush as a "war criminal" generally found the phrase "Islamic fascism" extremely offensive and a sign of bad faith. Still, the 2007 poll of Saudis made it clear that they were eager for better relations with the United States and that many concurred with al-Kuwaylit that the United States can still "rectify" its "mistakes."

If Bush's rhetoric caromed from praising Islam as a religion of peace to depicting "Islamic fascism" as a global behemoth menacing the United States, his would-be successors in the presidential campaign focused on the latter theme. They depicted a monolithic Muslim politics aiming at a new caliphate, supported by moderate political parties, militant militias, and small terrorist groups and by both major branches of Islam. They fretted about Muslim cells in the United States with suitcase nukes and about millions of Pakistani laborers sneaking across the Rio Grande. The Republican nominee for president averred that the menace from radical Muslims was greater than that the United States had faced in Nazi Germany or the Soviet Union and that it would be the "transcendent" challenge for America throughout the coming century.

Ironically, despite the attempt of both Republicans and Democrats to deploy Islamophobia against the Democratic candidate for president, Barack Obama, in the end it turned out that the American public had become impervious to such appeals to its worst instincts. It may be that eight years of heavy-handed use of propaganda techniques and fear mongering about the Muslim world on the part of the Bush administration had made the electorate wary of such bigotry in politics. It is also clear that many in the Muslim world were ready to reconsider their relationship to the United States if Washington adopted new policies. Since the new Obama administration has abandoned the rhetorical excesses and Islamophobic language of the Bush years and of many in the (now much smaller) Republican Party and since Obama seems determined to end the U.S. military presence in Iraq, the prospects for such a rapprochement are good.

NOTES

1. Robin Wright, "From the Desk of Donald Rumsfeld," *Washington Post* (Nov. 1, 2007).

2. Kenneth Ballen, "Look Who's Pro-U.S. Now: Saudi Arabia," *Christian Science Monitor*, Jan. 8, 2008.

3. Tom Raum, "Republicans Target 'Islamic Fascism,'" *Associated Press* (Aug. 30, 2006).

4. Craig Gilbert, "Feingold Decries Creation of Term 'Islamic Fascism': Bush Description Flawed, Insulting, Critics Say," *Milwaukee Journal Sentinel* (Sept. 11, 2006).

5. "Saudi Warns against Accusing Muslims of Fascism," *Agence France Presse* (Aug. 14, 2006).

6. Abdallah al-Jafri, "Ma hiya al-Fashiyah?" *Ukaz* (Aug. 19, 2006).

7. Muhamad Ali, "Why the Epithet 'Islamic Fascism' Is Unhelpful to Search for Peace," *Jakarta Post* (Sept. 12, 2006).

8. "President Bush Discusses Care for America's Returning Wounded Warriors, War on Terror at American Legion," Renaissance Hotel, Washington, D.C., Mar. 6, 2007, http://www.whitehouse.gov/news/releases/2007/03/20070306–1.html.

9. "Vice President's Remarks at the American Israel Public Affairs Committee 2007 Policy Conference," Mar. 12, 2007, http://www.whitehouse.gov/news/re-leases/2007/03/20070312.html.

10. "Mideast Media Doubt Progress of Bush Visit," *BBC Monitoring International Reports* (Jan. 15, 2008).

11. "Egyptian Circles Oppose U.S. President's Visit to Cairo," *BBC Monitoring Middle East—Political,* (Jan. 13, 2008); text of report by Qatari Aljazeera.net website on Jan. 12.

12. "Designation of Major Non-NATO Allies," U.S. Code Collection, Legal Information Institute, Cornell University, http://www.law.cornell.edu/uscode/22/2321k.html.

13. "America's Image Slips, but Allies Share U.S. Concerns over Iran, Hamas; No Global Warming Alarm in the U.S., China," Pew Global Attitudes Project, June 13, 2006, http://pewglobal.org/reports/display.php?ReportID=252.

14. Juan Cole, "Blowback from the GOP's Holy War," *Salon.com* (Feb. 1, 2008), http://www.salon.com/opinion/feature/2008/02/01/islamophobia/.

15. E. J. Dionne Jr., "A 'Challenge' Worth Challenging," *Washington Post* (Feb. 19, 2008), http://www.washingtonpost.com/wp-dyn/content/article/2008/02/18/AR2008021801537.html.

16. "DNC: Romney's 'Jihad' Ad Shows Lack of Foreign Policy Credentials," *PR Newswire* (Oct. 12, 2007).

17. Matthew Yglesias, "Romney versus the Muslim Brotherhood," May 4, 2007, http://matthewyglesias.theatlantic.com/archives/2007/05/romney_versus_the_muslim_broth.php.

18. Niraj Warikoo, "Political Ads Make Muslims Uneasy: Campaigns Sound Bigoted, Some Say," *Detroit Free Press* (Jan. 13, 2008).

19. Chris Dorsey, "Tancredo Says Threat of Attack on Holy Sites Would Deter Terrorism," *IowaPolitics.com*, (July 31, 2007), http://www.iowapolitics.com/index.iml?Article=101389.

20. "Pakistan: Weekly Roundup on Jihad, Terrorism," Aug. 1–7, 2007, Open Source Center.

21. Ken Herman, "Democratic Candidates Avoid Linking Terrorism with Islam, Unlike Republicans," *Cox News Service* (July 1, 2007), http://www.coxwashington.com/hp/content/reporters/stories/2007/07/01/BC_CANDIDATES_ISLAM01_COX.html.

22. "Rep. Peter King: There Are 'Too Many Mosques in This Country,'" *Crypt*, Politico.com (Sept. 19, 2007), (with video), http://www.politico.com/blogs/thecrypt/0907/Rep_King_There_are_too_many_mosques_in_this_country_.html.

23. Pew Research Center, "Muslim Americans: Middle Class and Mostly Mainstream," Pew Research Publications (May 22, 2007), http://pewresearch.org/pubs/483/muslim-americans.

24. James Ridgeway, "Giuliani Campaign's Muslim Fallout: How a Guardian Video Caused the Former New York Mayor Trouble in New Hampshire," *Guardian* (Dec. 31, 2007).

25. Walter Shapiro and Michael Scherer, "Mike Huckabee on 'Violence and Terror' at Home," *Salon.com* (Dec. 28, 2007), http://www.salon.com/politics/roadies/2007/12/28/huckabee/.

26. Perry Bacon Jr. and Michael D. Shear, "Hopefuls Clash in Debate as 1st Southern Primary Nears," *Washington Post* (Jan. 11, 2008).

27. Dan Gilgoff, "*John McCain: Constitution Established a 'Christian Nation,'*" June 2007, *Beliefnet.com*, http://www.beliefnet.com/News/Politics/2007/06/John-Mccain-Constitution-Established-A-Christian-Nation.aspx.

28. Juan Cole, "John McCain's Arab-American Problem," *Salon.com* (May 28, 2008), http://www.salon.com/opinion/feature/2008/05/28/mccain/.

29. James Zogby, "John McCain: I Am an Arab and a Decent Man," *Huffington Post* (Nov. 2, 2008), http://www.huffingtonpost.com/james-zogby/john-mccain-i-am-an-arab_b_133884.html.

30. Eric Boehlert and Jamison Foser, "Daniel Pipes Relied on Disputed LA Times Article to Revive Obama-Muslim Falsehood," *County Fair*, Media Matters for America (Jan. 2, 2008), http://mediamatters.org/items/200801020004.

31. Jodi Kantor, "Obama Supporters Take His Name as Their Own," *New York Times* (June 29, 2008).

32. "Robed Obama Picture Ignites Row," *BBC News*, (Feb. 26, 2008), http://news.bbc.co.uk/2/hi/americas/7263783.stm.

33. "Veiled Muslims Banned from Obama Photo Op," *Agence France Presse* (June 19, 2008).

34. Jake Tapper, "Help Wanted: Muslim Outreach Adviser for Obama Campaign," *Political Punch*, *ABC News* (Aug. 6, 2008), http://blogs.abcnews.com/political-punch/2008/08/help-wanted-mus.html.

9

Islamophobic Discourse Masquerading as Art and Literature: Combating Myth through Progressive Education

Anas Al-Shaikh-Ali

For the great enemy of truth is very often not the lie—deliberate, contrived, and dishonest—but the myth—persistent, persuasive, and unrealistic. Too often we hold fast to the clichés of our forebears. We subject all facts to a prefabricated set of interpretations. We enjoy the comfort of opinion without the discomfort of thought.

—President John F. Kennedy,
Commencement Address at Yale
University, June 11, 1962

An American president once sent a poem by a well-known English poet to a fellow politician with a note saying, "I send you an advance copy of a poem . . . which is rather poor poetry, but good sense from the expansionist standpoint."[1] It is a revealing comment. The poet was Rudyard Kipling, and the imperialist theme and title of the poem, "The White Man's Burden," were directed largely at America's foray into the Philippines in the aftermath of the Spanish-American war. The stirring lines excite great controversy today, although they capture well the sentiments of the time:

Take up the White Man's burden–
Send forth the best ye breed–
Go, bind your sons to exile
To serve your captives' need;
To wait, in heavy harness,
On fluttered folk and wild–
Your new-caught sullen peoples,
Half devil and half child.

What relevance does a hundred-year-old poem have to issues of social cohesion, security, citizenship, and democracy today? In terms of Islamophobia, the answer is, surprisingly, a great deal if one understands the power of popular culture to form public opinion and to perpetuate historically widely held false beliefs and myths concerning peoples, faiths, and cultures whose right to self-identity we fail—or perhaps fear—to comprehend.

Real multiculturalism is an ideal that is yet to be realized, although societies can congratulate themselves on having managed to become conscious of the existence and validity of the "Other," mainly on a purely humanitarian level, which, though at times protected by national legislation, does not percolate down to the national consciousness or collective unconscious. Movement of communities through migrant labor forces has brought that Other to our front door and severely tested our own conflicting values. Unfortunately for us, however, although the language of Kipling may have appreciably changed, those deeply held ideas, underscored by nationalism and xenophobia, still motivate societal systems—no matter how insidiously—and therefore continue to be exploited in wider elements of popular culture today. This includes TV and radio talk shows, comics, cartoons, science fiction, almost all genres of popular fiction, movies, computer games, magazines, and so on.

My primary interest in this chapter is to examine, through key samples, the existence of a particular type of Islamophobia predominantly found in popular culture and, for the purposes of this chapter, the world of art and literature. It is a trend that has its roots in the realm of empire and imperialism, when hostility was justified under the pretext of bringing civilization to the uncivilized and when moral standpoints were reasoned away under the guise of "burden," responsibility, and mission, Kipling style. So, Islamophobia did not start in the wake of 9/11 but long before. In recent years, however, the phenomenon has substantially increased and, more disturbingly, evolved to become an explicit, almost anti-Semitic-style criticism of Islam and Muslims without in fact being acknowledged as such.[2] Moreover, it is widely tolerated, if not even encouraged, by knee-jerk reactions and irresponsible pronouncements by parliamentarians, politicians, prime ministers, presidents, and even the upper echelons of the Vatican. We now have a rapidly deteriorating situation whereby a representation of Islam and Muslims is taking place wholly at variance with reality and often legitimized by masquerading as intellectual, objective, and justifiable discourse.

The fact is that security, citizenship, and democracy will work only if racism and radicalized notions of imperialism are rooted out and not given moral credence as legitimate responses to world events. The spread of Islamophobia (generally understood to be the fear of Islam and Muslims, as well as the dissemination of such fear whether by material produced, pronouncements made, or action taken), is not only injecting layers of fear and distrust into all levels of society but also playing into the hands of right-wing elements, creating an undercurrent of volatile hostility that threatens the general well-being of minority groups and ultimately society. We are in fact increasingly jeopardizing meaningful dialogue and interaction, hallmarks of a functioning democracy.

Although Islamophobia is a relatively new word in the English language, the realities it refers to have historically been circulating in Europe and European cultures for many centuries. A report by the Commission on British Muslims and Islamophobia stresses that "hostility towards Islam and Muslims" has for centuries "taken different forms at different times" and goes on to conclude that, as a result, "it may be more apt to speak of 'Islamophobias' rather than of a single phenomenon. Each version of Islamophobia has its own features as well as similarities with, and borrowings from, other versions."[3] This being the case, to understand Islamophobia, its process, objectives, and rationale, we need to go back in time and examine a number of classical examples that illustrate the hypothesis that art has often been used as a vehicle to project propaganda.[4] Todd Porter Field illustrates how even prior to the conquest of Algiers by France, "French artists and governments provided a rationale for the imperial project" and "produced an imperial culture that preceded France's imperial expansion":[5]

> It is no marvel that the Empire's arts administrators would cultivate public art that ballyhooed (and concocted) heroic exploits of its leaders . . . what is of particular interest . . . is how the artists and political strategies of the battle paintings were, unexpectedly, employed . . . making of them a renewable legacy and the basis of a truly national culture.[6]

During the age of empire, art and literature were extensively used to paint a derogatory image of Islam and Muslims. One of the strategies employed was that of "moral contrasts," which pitted "French science, morality, masculinity, and intellectual rigor against supposedly representative traits of Easterners: fanaticism, cruelty, idleness, vice, irrationality, deviance, and degeneracy."[7] The author also notes that one hundred years after the Algerian conquest, exhibitions in Paris "celebrated the role art had played not only in depicting imperial expansion but also as active agent in the quest."[8]

In *Turks, Moors, and Englishmen in the Age of Discovery* Nabil Matar points out the following:

> In a frenzy of racism and bigotry that dominated the late Elizabethan, Jacobean, and Caroline periods, dramatists and travelers, theologians, and polemicists created the representations that would define early modern Britains' image of the Muslims. They established in their popular and widely read books the stereotypes of the Muslim—a stereotype that was presented and represented in numerous plays and pageants . . . The "Turk" was cruel and tyrannical, deviant, and deceiving; the "Moor" was sexually overdriven and emotionally uncontrollable, vengeful, and religiously superstitious.[9]

It seems that the "Muslim was the Other with whom there could only be holy war." This sentiment was not limited to England but was being entrenched in Spain, Portugal, France, and Italy, where stereotypes, developed in art and literature, began playing an extraordinarily influential role in shaping anti-Muslim hostility and fear. Matar further notes:

> The great national literature of Europe sustained the idea of the Otherness of Muslims from the Renaissance into the early modern age: as long as Tasso, Camoes, Ariosto, Cervantes, Marlowe, and Shakespeare, along with *El Cid* and *Roland*, were viewed, rightly, as the supreme icons of European imagination, the polarization with Islam and Muslims could only continue. While the national consciousness of many European countries was being forged in the late medieval and Renaissance periods, the foremost enemy was identified as the Muslim, and the foremost hero was the 'ancestral' fighter against the 'infidels.'[10]

At issue here is the idea that art and literature are in essence an exercise in intellectual achievement and impression, to be judged primarily on artistic merit alone and not political furtherance or historical distortion. Yet, art has always intended far more than that. It is, therefore, of far greater interest to pose the questions, of what influence were they, and in whose service were they created.

Conventionally, the term "the Classics" refers to literature and arts that, over a significant period of time, are considered to be of the highest quality and examples of their kind. This chapter, however, uses the phrase to refer to typical examples that have little or no literary value or high artistic standards in themselves, yet have exerted and continue to exert influence beyond their time and space, due in part to the pragmatic utility of the racist and xenophobic content of their message. Thus, works of art and literature are not necessarily gospels of love and peace or espousers of the highest and noblest virtues but rather have been used to spread prejudice, falsehoods, stereotypes, and myths that incite people to conflict. Many examples can be given of works of art and literature that have encompassed and assimilated earlier influences and presented them in a form and style that at the time gave their message an impetus and impact far beyond their life span. They continue in one way or another to shape either events on the ground or the psyches and attitudes of generations by passing the same message through other written or visual forms and helping to generate negative values that continue to endure.

It is hence clear that historical Islamophobia is informing contemporary Islamophobia, which, in turn, is affecting individuals, communities, and nations by sowing the seeds of future conflict and instability. Moving into our own time, this form of "classical Islamophobia" has taken on a new dimension, a contemporary twist, crossing borders to represent a far more formidable cultural, educational, and political challenge. Indeed, it has taken on a form of "cultural terrorist offensive" that seeks to undermine an entire religious community. Add to this the global reach of the media, and we have a potentially serious and explosive mix.

Many people underestimate the impact of literary works and works of art in shaping not only popular consciousness or psyches but also policies. On October 4, 2004, the *Washington Times* published an article titled "Reliving Fears from Fiction," by Arnaud Borchgrave, who commented on the developments and pronouncements by politicians and the media regarding the accession of Turkey into the EU. The article referred to a best-selling French novel by a prize-winning French author, titled *Le Camp des Saints* (1973),[11] translated into English as *The Camp of the Saints* in 1975 and since then into other European languages.[12] Borchgrave remarked that the "novel/parable keeps selling thousands of copies a year, presumably because of fears Europe has of being slowly 'Islamized' by its estimated 20 million Muslims from North Africa, sub-Saharan Africa, the Middle East, South and Southeast Asia." He felt that "many Europeans are opposed to Turkey's entry to the European Union, convinced it would allow 71 million Muslim Turks to settle anywhere and overrun Europe's Christian civilization." He referred to a speech given by EU commissioner Fritz

Bolkestein, who believed that "Europe will implode if Turkey is admitted . . . [the] EU would be like the late Austrian-Hungarian Empire, which became ungovernable after taking on too many different ethnic groups."

The newspaper's linking of a work of fiction to something as momentous as Turkey's bid to membership in the EU is significant. It proves that fiction does have an impact. Fear of Muslim Turks swamping Europe is a form of Turkophobia that has its roots largely in the art and literature of the period, with French popular fiction, as well as contemporary European popular fiction titles, simply echoing the success of bygone authors. Turkey's situation is interesting since, despite its loss of power, the dismemberment of the Ottoman Empire and the introduction of an extreme form of secularism by Kemal Ataturk, it is still very much seen as a "Muslim specter" that haunts Europe. Attitudes that crystallized centuries ago continue to hold sway. While earlier literary works have shaped the sentiments and carried them on through the centuries, contemporary popular fiction is ensuring a wider dissemination of old views with added twists and turns.

Returning to Rudyard Kipling's redoubtable poem, although not strictly Islamophobic, it well illustrates the point that racist and xenophobic literature has helped shape and influence events, ideology, and policies. The poem, which used racially prejudiced language to develop the idea of a divine mission of the white colonists' work, was aimed at influencing political decision makers and public opinion in the United States. Kipling wrote the poem, intending it to "echo around the world for decades." Actually, it has been echoing for more than a century and continues to do so in Afghanistan, Iraq, and elsewhere. Kipling claimed that the Caucasian people were the protectors of democracy under God, and it was their duty to lead others toward the light of democracy. Little, it seems, has changed. The poem appealed to the American people to extend "the law" far beyond their shores to countries where people are "half devil and half child." The United States at the time had just emerged from a "crusading" Spanish campaign that had the impact of turning the country into a naval and colonial power. The poem was published on February 4, 1899, in the *London Times* and the next day in the *New York Sun* and the *New York Tribune*. For several years, Congress had voted against the involvement of the United States in the Philippines. However, after the publication of the poem and the publicity it received, including the reading of parts in Congress, the U.S. Senate voted on February 6 by a sufficient majority to send armed forces into the Philippines and take over its administration.[13] This act marked the beginning of the expansionist and imperial policies of the United States as it went on to control Puerto Rico, Guam, Cuba, and the Philippines.

An advance copy of the poem was sent a month before its publication to Theodore Roosevelt, who had just been elected governor of New York. He in turn sent it to H. Cabot Lodge with the words already quoted: "I send you an advance copy of a poem by Kipling which is rather poor poetry, but good sense from *the expansionist standpoint.*"[14] Five years later, now president, Theodore Roosevelt wrote to Kipling about the impact the poem had upon him and of his "attempt to take the White Man's burden." It was "on this record" that he "stood, and was elected, for a second term."[15] All in all, the literary impact of the work helped transform U.S. policy, and the repercussions of that transformation are still felt around the world today.

As for the literary quality of the poem, it was not only President Roosevelt who was critical of its standards but also a host of other specialists and literary critics, among them the well-known novelist and critic George Orwell, who could scarcely disguise his disgust: "Kipling *is* jingo imperialist, he *is* morally insensitive and aesthetically disgusting. It is better to start by admitting that, and then to try to find out why it is that he survives."[16] He further describes Kipling's poetry as "almost a shameful pleasure, like the taste for cheap sweets that some people secretly carry into middle life."[17]

Kipling's shadow haunts the French novel *The Camp of the Saints*, which in fact echoes the internal racism of "The White Man's Burden," albeit in a modern setting. While Kipling states that "Oh, East is East and West is West, and never the twain shall meet," the French novel stresses that "black would be black, and white would be white. There is no changing that except by total mix, a blend into tan. They would be enemies on sight, their hatred and scorn could only grow as they come to know each other."[18] One of its messages calculatingly proclaims that "cultures and races develop to their ultimate perfection through necessary segregation." There is no hope of integration whatsoever: "Now they both felt the same utter loathing . . . 'No hope, Dr. Haller?' 'No hope, Mr. Mayor. Unless you kill them all, that is, because you'll never change them.'"[19]

Kipling's upbeat anthem, however, is in stark contrast to the despondent conclusions of *The Camp of the Saints*. The novel relates the story of the downfall and collapse of Europe as a bastion of civilization when an armada of ships carrying almost one million Ganges Indian immigrants arrives on the coast of France. These form only the tip of an iceberg, and when thousands of others follow them, France collapses, and so does Europe: "The mixture of races, and cultures, and life-styles. The different levels of ability, different standards of education. Why, it would mean the end of France as we know it, the end of the French as a nation."[20]

This is the new face of fear: terrorism on one side and immigration on the other. Though admittedly placed in a fantastic, even ludicrous, scenario, this xenophobia as expressed in the novel does not even wish to "civilize people" Kipling style but rather to simply get rid of them. Are we to infer from the word "Saint" that Europe's benevolence is a form of martyrdom, a holy suicide? Let us not forget that words are powerful and evoke our deepest emotions and fears.[21]

Interestingly, the novel showcases Muslims as an advance team that has already arrived in Europe. And the old familiar Orientalists' oversexualization of the Easterners is revived to blame the coming defeat or rape of Europe on young immigrants, whose high fertility rates are being used as a "form of calculated revenge for colonialism and debt burden." Triumphantly, one of the characters warns: "This country of mine is a roaring river. A river of sperm. Now, all of a sudden, it's shifting course, my friend, and heading west."[22] Although the character in the novel is not a Muslim, the Muslims would eventually be blamed. On October 26, 1985, *Figaro* magazine published a feature article written jointly by Raspail, the author of the novel, and François Dumont, the then president of the Institute of Political Demography, below a photograph of a veiled Muslim woman. The scaremongering headline ran, "Will we still be French in 30 years?"[23] Jean-Paul Gourevitch stated that publishing the picture of the veiled Muslim woman "changes the source of the invasion it is no longer Indian but North African . . . Let us be clear. It was politically incorrect and legally dangerous to allude to North African and Moslem immigration at a time when militant anti-racism held the high ground."[24]

Another illustrative example is that of an early American book written by Captain John Smith, a British American settler, titled *The True Travels, Adventures, and Observations of Captain John Smith.*[25] The work is considered to be the first American book written, and it had people "gripped with excitement" after its publication. It purports to relate the true adventures of a British American sailor and adventurer by the name of John Smith, whose thrilling accounts include the Pocahontas story brought to life by Disney. One part of his travels records a sensational encounter with "barbaric Muslim Turks," a stereotype that Smith had brought with him from Europe to America. However, in the story, the narrator claims that while fighting against the Turks in Hungary in 1602, he was wounded in battle, captured, and sold as a slave to a Turkish pasha. The pasha then sent Smith to Istanbul as a gift to his sweetheart, who, according to Smith, fell in love with him and sent him to her brother to be trained for the Turkish imperial service. Smith escaped after murdering the brother.

Modern readers and audiences will be amused to see in Smith a seventeenth-century precursor of Ian Fleming's redoubtable agent 007 since Smith, like James Bond, happens to be irresistible to women and routinely escapes his savage enemies by killing them. He is also a "resplendent and invincible hero,"[26] though the sequence of his adventure stories "read[s] like a bit of oriental fairy tales."[27] He encounters enemies so villainous, barbaric, and godless that they have to be fought and killed at all costs. The manner of their killing and beheading is surpassed only by the following illustrations, which are taken from the book (figures 9.1–9.3).

John Smith's big claims that the account of his travels and adventures was true have been debated, discussed, and dismissed by many historians and writers as figments of his fertile imagination.[28] One could, therefore, argue that the work may be considered the first American Islamophobic popular fiction title, whose legacy stalks hundreds of contemporary Islamophobic but popular American works of fiction. The book, as many literary critics assert, carries no literary value whatsoever. Its only importance stems from the fact that Captain Smith was (and still is) seen as one of the first American heroes who takes a full measure of credit in the founding of the nation and its settlements. His Pocahontas tale is a staple of American folklore. In this sense, his fiction, literary shortcomings aside, carries weight.

FIGURE 9.1. Captain Smith killing the Turkish pasha. Reproduced by permission of The Huntington Library, San Marino, California.

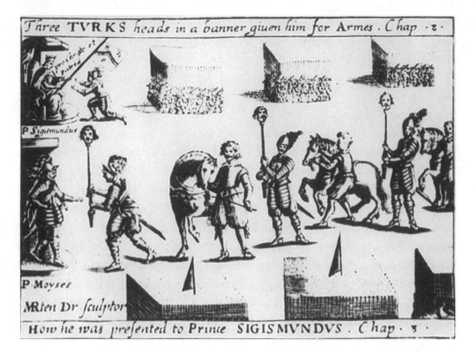

FIGURE 9.2. The severed heads of three Turks being presented to Captain Smith. Reproduced by permission of The Huntington Library, San Marino, California.

Historical reality undermined by fiction is also a feature of Cervantes's *Don Quixote*, where murderous Turks appear in full force. Published in 1605, the novel quickly became (and still is) one of the most beloved in European literature, and John Smith, born in 1580, could well have been exposed to it as a young man. Passionate, vengeful, violent, yet easily led by the nose, infidel Moors and Turks appear in many other works of fiction, as well as plays of the period. The list is extensive, but suffice it to say that layers of mistrust, hostility, and Islamophobia historically crafted into such classical works are still with us in the guise of contemporary popular fiction. Here also we find the relentless pitting of one set of people against another, with millions of readers compelled (some would say trained) to identify with the moral standpoint of authors who are determined to undermine any efforts to build a climate of trust and peaceful coexistence.

I do not wish to imply that all literary talent has been cannibalized by racist propaganda. Quite the opposite. Great writers like George Orwell and Charles Dickens have expounded upon the injustices of social conditions and championed the lot of the poor and the downtrodden. *Uncle Tom's Cabin* broke all sales records of the period and bravely flew in the face of prevailing racism. Regrettably, it is also true that many of those who seemingly did advocate some level

FIGURE 9.3. Captain Smith being led captive to the Muslim bashaw. Reproduced by permission of The Huntington Library, San Marino, California.

of truth often gave with one hand and took with the other. In *Uncle Tom's Cabin*, Harriet Beecher Stowe very nobly championed the freeing of slaves and portrayed them as human beings at a time when they were seen as little more than cattle. However, toward the end of the novel she undermines her own generosity by concluding that they should all be packed off to a mythical country in Africa rather than live side by side on an equal footing with their white "masters." Furthermore, Christianity is made to play a fundamental role in their "redemption." Did they need redeeming?

Works of art, including sculptures and paintings, have been no less averse to manipulating reality and emotions for vested interests. A fine example of this is Hiram Powers's famous statue, *The Greek Slave*, considered to be one of the most popular works of art of nineteenth-century America. Indeed, Powers was lauded as one of the "most gifted artists of all time."[29] The statue was the first case of "moral nudity" that America had ever seen and an "adaptation" of the famous Venus de Medici (Medici Venus), a Hellenistic marble sculpture depicting Aphrodite, created in the first century BC. In fact, the statue's exhibition in London in 1846 was "a triumph," and it became "the sensation" of the

Crystal Palace Exhibition in 1851.[30] Why was it so successful? To a great extent the interest it aroused was due as much to its "literary and philosophical" content as to Powers's "artistic merits."[31] Carl Bode notes that "the crusading like struggle" between the Greeks and the Turks at the time triggered great public interest and brought about the success of the tour in the United States.[32] Tens of thousands paid to see it during its tour in 1847–1849 in the United States and Europe. Six replicas were made for this tour, and miniature copies became immensely popular for homeowners (figure 9.4).

In fact, the real secret of its popularity lay in the underlying story of its subject matter (carefully supplied by the artist and tour organizers): The statue depicts a young *Christian* virgin taken captive by "cruel and *heathen Muslim Turks*," who kidnap her after killing her family. They put her up for

FIGURE 9.4. The *Greek Slave*, an image of the statue during one of its tours.

sale as a sexual object, the point at which the artist sculpts her. She stands, head slightly bowed, completely naked, with hands chained to a post and exposed to the gaze of "barbaric Muslims," people she hates and abhors. Her suffering and anxiety are tempered by the support of her reliance upon the goodness of God. Therefore, "her Christian fortitude and resignation leave no room for shame."

The statue was received with extraordinary fanfare and was accorded both critical acclaim and public praise. It helped greatly in generating the now-familiar Islamophobic sentiments and hatred that had already manifested in many earlier literary works dealing with Orientals, roughly falling under the banner of Turks, Moors, and "Mohamedans." Writers have recorded the great impact that *The Greek Slave* and its traveling circus had on the psyche of the people who witnessed it. Some have surmised that the Turkish dimension of the statue could have "subconsciously evoked the stereotypes of the Middle East's exoticism, Turkish harem imagery, and sexual provocativeness"[33] of the Muslims and Turks. Additionally:

> [A]s Powers needed a reason to depict his subject in the nude, and just as in his narrative his *Slave* is protected by her piety, America's need to actively seek out and deal with the evil in the world was justified by the condemnation of the foreign "Other" who did not adhere to Christian traditions, a "truth" which could be spread by the expansion and conversion of people to Christianity.[34]

The devotional reaction of mid-nineteenth-century America to the statue is very interesting. It allowed nudity to be viewed without guilt at a time when religious sentiment dominated views concerning matters of the flesh. Hence, like the Victorians, contemporary Americans were expected to react with moral horror to a traveler's account of belly dancers, to reject sensuality in art and literature, and to loathe nudity in any shape or form. Yet, the same people stood speechless in front of *The Greek Slave*, admiring its naked form with a religious devotion that brushed aside any thought of visual sin. Why? Because the coming rape of *The Greek Slave* represented a possible rape of the West, and religious sentiment was drowned by religious hatred. Spectators convinced themselves that this type of explicit nudity was not for the sake of sensuality but for a noble cause and therefore well worth viewing.[35]

Given its lack of real artistic merit, one would imagine that having played its part, the statue would have disappeared from memory long ago, but this is not the case. So enduring has its message been that even a cursory search on the Internet comes up with posters, bookmarks, miniatures, and so on, giving new life to a fabrication that should have died decades ago.

Hiram Powers lived in Italy in the 1830s and 1840s and must have been familiar with a well-known classic novel of Victorian erotica titled *The Lustful Turk*,[36] first published in 1828, when the traffic in pornography was growing at an enormous rate and had shifted from France to England.[37] There is no doubt that in producing *The Greek Slave*, Powers was influenced by the sexual fantasy of *The Lustful Turk*. This adult novel forms a crucial juncture of literature and is credited for setting the stage for many other so-called great pornographic classics. Since 1828, it has gone through a large number of reprints and is still available in many bookstores in the United States and Europe, not necessarily from porn outlets only. It has also appeared in a number of adult magazines. Advertised as a "faithful and vivid" depiction of life in an eighteenth-century Turkish harem, the plot relates the story of a beautiful European Christian girl who is kidnapped and sold to a Turkish bey, who uses her as a sex slave and beats and abuses her. In addition, whenever she is raped and sodomized, the Muslim bey thanks the Almighty and the Prophet Muhammad for the gift they have bestowed on him.[38] In 1968 David Friedman directed and produced a film version that at the time became the most expensive adult feature film ever made. The sound bites advertising the film are illustrative of racist hype in a particularly aggressive form:

> When you see *The Lustful Turk*, a motion picture in the magnitude
> and tradition of *Lawrence of Arabia* but with girls, you will recoil with
> horror when you witness the barbaric Turks, unrestrained,
> uncivilized, disrobe their fragile yet nonetheless proud captives and
> force them into unimaginable positions completely heedless of the
> wall-busting shrieks of the hapless young women. You will wince
> with pain when you behold savage heathen tortures inflicted on the
> unsullied white bodies of the innocents who vainly seek to preserve
> their virtues.[39]

There are two types of nudes in the Western artistic tradition, those that are considered an expression of high artistic endeavor (e.g., Michelangelo's *David*), which symbolize a reverence for the human form and underscore Western understanding of Renaissance man, and those that speak a different language, one of sexual degradation. *The Lustful Turk* is a good example of a work that uses the Muslim world to display in form what the title conveys in words. More than simply a graphic portrayal of Western female nudity succumbing to the Muslim man, it is a full frontal assault on the cultural norms that define the Islamic world. Its more lauded counterpart is often found in Orientalist paintings that excite the senses in a not too dissimilar way. We may snigger in private at *The Lustful Turk*'s outlandishly poor taste, but, reading between the lines, it is apparent that we are not simply to view these violently sensual images but also to experience them and by doing so impress upon ourselves the false validity of the idea that, yes, the Muslim world is characterized by a savage, dark emotionalism whose most perverse form is cruel sexuality.

The legacy of *The Adventures of Captain John Smith*, *The Lustful Turk*, *The Greek Slave*, and "The White Man's Burden" continues today in the shape of xenophobic and Islamophobic imagery that inundates the contents and covers of many modern, mass-produced titles of popular fiction. These include thrillers, techno-thrillers, spy fiction (sometimes labeled "political thrillers"), romances, historical romances, historical fiction, nuclear (alternatively chemical and biological) holocaust fiction, missionary fiction, evangelical fiction, graphic fiction, young people's fiction, children's fiction, and, of course, adult and pornographic fiction. The power of images is such that one need not actually read the contents; by simply glancing at a cover, one perceives the entire message in one fell stroke. Thus, images influence people's thinking without their real consent.

Covers of mass-produced titles have usurped visual propaganda techniques and given them global reach. It is the logic of *The Greek Slave* in twenty-first-century packaging. Where *The Greek Slave* relied on its background story, contemporary writers, artists, and graphic designers rely on coded messages conveyed through the visual form. They simplify reality and link it to fear, associating the very real with the potentially dangerous. This coded language therefore uses minarets, *hijabs*, daggers, mosques, and so on (elements of the Muslim world) and then superimposes guns, nukes, masked riders, and scantily clad women on top. Circulating globally, this undisguised propaganda is then read as some sort of trademark of truth, often taken at face value.[40] Filling contemporary society with constant negative images absorbed by billions will have consequences. There is always an emotional, intellectual link between readers and their subject matter, and to say that one cannot influence the other is analogous to stating that violence on television has no effect on the young. The mind can and will absorb an idea or an image, with everything that it entails, in a fraction of a second. In that short amount of time, the word "terrorist" can conjure up an image and a whole body of ideas that a thousand words could not convey, manipulating a desired reaction. Indoctrinating while they entertain, many popular novels are painting a deeply disturbing picture of the Muslim world, making the lives of those living in non-Muslim communities (particularly in the West) extremely precarious.

While in the earlier popular fiction of the 1950s and 1960s fictional and potential perpetrators of nuclear holocaust and terrorism were depicted as mad scientists, deranged generals, and frustrated Nazis (Germans, Chinese, or

Russians), since the 1970s, Muslims have gradually replaced them as the new face of the enemy. Popular fiction, largely ignored as harmless entertainment, has phenomenal power and a tremendous part to play in shaping public imagination.

Grant Hugo is one of those writers who have addressed the political influence of the thriller and who believes that novels not only project but also shape attitudes by appealing to "emotions, prejudices and potent cravings." Hugo was surprised to find that, even as late as 1972, the political influence of the thriller had received "little notice" since, as a means of communication, the thriller (and conversely other subgenres of popular fiction) offer greater opportunities than any of the conventional methods: "[O]vertly political ideas do not always attract attention even among the minority actively interested in politics . . . exceptional talents or opportunities are needed if explicitly political propaganda is to exercise much impact beyond the narrow circle of party workers and others already committed."[41] Hugo further notes that the thrillers have been very popular not only with the general reader but with leaders and politicians as well.[42]

It may not be very difficult to discover why contemporary popular fiction goes down so well with the public. As with other forms of modern entertainment (e.g., films, songs), it is largely light, racy, topical, gossipy, casual, and morally and dramatically simplistic. It is packed not only with action but also with a dose of violence and gore, exotica, and sex, the last ranging from the titillating to the explicit. It is also cheap to buy, especially in paperback.

Popular fiction readership in the West is not limited to one age group. It is extremely popular with various age groups and strata of society. Readership includes young people, housewives, businessmen and women, civil servants, politicians, decision makers, ministers, prime ministers, and presidents. "Many illustrious people have publicly confessed their addiction to so innocent and popular a form of relaxation."[43] For example, former prime minster Stanley Baldwin was an avid reader of the works of John Buchan. President John F. Kennedy was one of Ian Fleming's faithful readers. It is also a known fact that president Ronald Reagan was an admirer of Tom Clancy, who, we are told, lectured Pentagon, CIA, and White House staff. Former president Bill Clinton is an avid reader of popular fiction, and during the 1992 presidential campaign (when he was a candidate), he expressed his admiration for Walter Mosley's novels.[44] Moreover, some of the authors of recent popular fiction titles include former presidents, leaders of political parties, former diplomats, and former members of the armed forces and the intelligence services and agencies. Among them in the UK are Douglas Hurd, former foreign secretary; Edwina Curry, former member of Parliament and minister; Ian Smith, former leader of the Conservative Party; Lord Jeffery Archer, former deputy chairman of the Conservative Party; and, most recently, the former head of MI5, Stella Rimington, whose first novel, *At Risk*, was published in 2004. In the United States, former president Jimmy Carter published his first novel, *The Hornet's Nest*, on the Civil War, in 2003. In 2003 congressman Peter T. King published his *Vale of Tears*, on Muslim terrorism. Former vice president Dick Cheney's chief of staff, Lewis Scooter Libby, published *The Apprentice*, and after his indictment its sales soared. Richard Clarke, special assistant to president Clinton for eight years and special security advisor to president Bush, published his first novel in 2005, titled *The Scorpion's Gate* (figures 9.5–9.6).[45]

FIGURE 9.5. Translated from the Italian edition. Many Islamophobic British and American fiction titles have been translated into European and other languages. Used by permission of The Random House Group, Ltd.

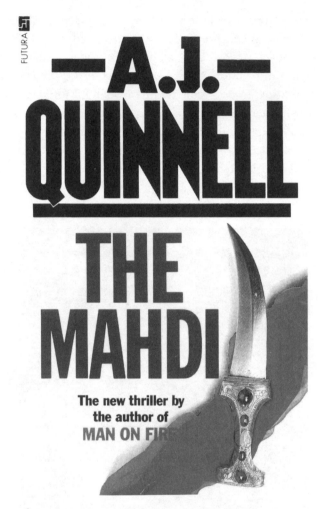

FIGURE 9.6. Both the first edition of *The Mahdi*, as well as this 1983 edition, carried the following blurb: "A spectacular espionage story of international secret agencies who plan to control the emerging power of Islam by creating an artificial miracle—before the eyes of millions of faithful in Mecca . . . to provide a new Mahdi . . . provided, of course, that the prophet remains a puppet."

Islamophobia, the hallmark of present-day mass fiction, is designed not so much to sow the seeds of misunderstanding as to sow the seeds of willful hostility and nonacceptance. As old and new fiction continues to portray Islam and Muslims in negative terms and to present Muslim communities in the West as the enemy within, it also is training citizens of Europe to see their Turkish neighbors and 71 million Turkish citizens as potential adversaries, a situation that can only be exacerbated if Turkey's borders with Europe disappear and Turkey becomes part of the EU. To sum up, in the words of Richard Bulliet:

> Thus it appears that we do not include Islam in our civilization club mainly because we are heirs to a Christian construction of history that is deliberately exclusive. Western Christendom has regarded Islam as a malevolent Other for many centuries and has invented any number of reasons for holding this view . . . Shifting Western portrayals of Islam over the centuries make it clear that reasons for disliking Islam have been constructed as rationales for a preexisting and ongoing animosity and not vice versa. This pattern persists to the present day.[46]

So, what is the solution to a fear that sees the clash of civilizations as a very possible, if not inevitable, future? I do not advocate the banning of books, the burning of literature, or the implementation of censorship. Fortunately, we have within our capability and our societal structure frameworks that can be harnessed to diffuse the level and nature of this onslaught. Progressive education espousing the values of real multiculturalism, coexistence, and human development is the way forward. People need to be intelligent and discerning when interpreting and analyzing what they see around them, not allowing themselves to become mental doormats and easy prey for those who know the art of manipulation.

Since 9/11, I have been invited to more than thirty workshops, conferences, and roundtables on the issues of dialogue, engagement, media, stereotyping, racism, and xenophobia in relation to Islam and Muslims. Although commendable in themselves and held with great sincerity and much fervor, the practical results seem, I am afraid, a little thin on the ground. The validity of analysis is often lost in debate, with discussions, on the whole, generating some short-term theoretical "fixes" rather than long-term effective strategies. And, by effective, I mean carefully thought-out policies or programs of action that have a meaningful, long-term positive impact.

We live and work in multicultural societies, and it is this very idea of a global vision and an understanding of others that gives society and community relations stability, peace, and a broad social policy agenda, which, by promoting equality and cross-cultural understanding, works to eliminate racism and discrimination. The European Muslim community is an acid test of this cherished ideal, and we must work hard to move much faster beyond dialogue to halt the polarization that is being promoted by vested interests that are encouraging and fanning the flames of radicalization on both sides.

What is the situation facing us today? No matter how we try to gloss over reality, the fact remains that levels of mistrust, fear, and instability are rising as societies are held hostage by events and a hostile media with global reach. Prejudice, bigotry, racism, and discrimination are generating extremism and violent radicalism on both sides. On one side, such attitudes dehumanize the "Other," thus making extreme action and violence against that Other legitimate and acceptable. On the other side, they generate feelings of isolation, resentment, and hatred, which—when manipulated by unscrupulous characters—lead to violence and destructive extremism. This will put serious obstacles in the way of engagement, confidence, and trust building, thereby increasing alienation and exclusion. Exclusion such as this can only be counterproductive. People, when isolated from each other in this way, only cling more desperately to their worldviews and in this case see reality couched in a conflict between Muslims and non-Muslims or simply "us" and "them." A "secular and democratic" society is constantly being pitted against an "oppressive and backward" religious identity, and this theme is played out repeatedly by the press to foster a sense of legitimized racism. The anti-*hijab* movement, for instance, is a good example of how the news media have widened the debate from focusing on violent extremism and terrorism to singling out Islam as a whole (that is, a way of life) and Muslims as a race to exclude and criticize openly.

Inclusion and participation and the efforts to confront extremism and violent radicalization are being jeopardized as Islamophobia becomes the acceptable face of xenophobia. To engage in effective dialogue and to build real bridges, this phenomenon has to be recognized and challenged at all levels, and the scapegoating of Muslims stopped. We have to appreciate and realize that the relentless media assault is having alarming effects. Unfortunately, whatever positive steps are taken by various authorities and Muslim and non-Muslim NGOs and community leaders, they are made almost immediately impotent by sensational and negative coverage by the media, which have played a considerable part in reinforcing and indeed erecting barriers between the Muslim community and other members of society.

Given the magnitude of what is out there, short-term measures and quick fixes are unfortunately reeds against a storm, reaching a limited number of people and needing to be updated and repeated again and again, probably endlessly. It is also important to remember that when people have already formed their ideas and developed their prejudices, it is difficult to change them easily. Such change needs considerable energy, time, and mental discipline.

What can be done to address all of these challenges and produce multidimensional, lasting change? I believe with absolute conviction that one of the most effective strategies to defeat extremism, xenophobia, and Islamophobia is education. Educational systems produce the future teachers, policymakers, politicians, artists, writers, and media experts. So what is more effective than tackling the issue at its core? There is widespread criticism that the national curricula in Europe are currently too Eurocentric inasmuch as they fail to value wider cultural and ethnic diversity. In the United States, education is seen as responsible for the largely negative and stereotyped image of Islam and Muslims.[47] Therefore, the values of morality, citizenship, peaceful coexistence, revulsion of racism and discrimination, and acceptance of the Other should be married to actively taught skills of critical thinking and awareness, forming part of all national curricula not only in the West but also in Muslim countries.

It is true that, in an effort to stem radicalization, alienation, and discrimination through education, some action may have been taken. However, none to my knowledge has focused exclusively on education as the *prime force* for long-term change despite the fact that there have been repeated calls through conferences, papers, reports, and research recommendations to tackle racism, radicalization, and xenophobia strategically through education. One notable example has been the report *Pathways to Tolerance: Student Diversity*, published in 1998 by the National Association of School Psychologists in the UK. Ideas to help schools learn to support tolerance and celebrate student diversity are presented in a series of articles such as "The Tolerance-in-Action Campaign" and "An Anti-bias Approach to Early Childhood Education." A document titled the *1999 Berlin Declaration: An Agenda for Future Action*, which grew out of a conference held in that city outlined, among other things, concrete proposals to improve intercultural education; transmission of a differentiated view of other cultures; elimination of stereotypes from schoolbooks; and the need for interreligious and ethical education in state and private schools.[48]

In addition, under the title *The International Basis for Intercultural Education including Anti-racist and Human Rights Education*, Pieter Batelmaan and Fons Coomans compiled and published, also in 1999, a selection of articles from relevant documents adopted by the governments of member states of the United Nations, UNESCO, the Organization for Security and Cooperation (OSCE), and the Council of Europe (CE). In the preface to this publication, aimed at policymakers, teachers, and educators, Professor Theo van Boven stressed the crucial role of intercultural education in the comprehensive elimination of all forms of racism and racial discrimination, xenophobia, and related intolerance, which is seen as a priority by governments and international organizations such as the UN and the CE. The various documents and declarations stress in different terms the need to "encourage the creation in schools, from the primary level upwards, of a climate of active understanding of, and respect for, the qualities and cultures of others."[49]

The vision of the *Curriculum Review: Diversity and Citizenship*, another important document, published by Sir Keith Ajegbo and colleagues in 2007, proposes that "in five years . . . all schools . . . [should] be actively engaged in nurturing in pupils the skills to participate in an active and inclusive democracy, appreciating and understanding difference."[50] The report makes important and relevant recommendations, especially in developing citizenship education, but stresses that "education for diversity is key to preparing children and young people for the 21st-century world, where borders are becoming more porous and global citizenship is an increasing imperative."[51] The report also recommends that the Department for Education and Skills (DfES) commission a review of existing resources covering issues that explicitly relate to linking identity, diversity, and political and historical contexts.[52]

A key proponent of this vision is a fourth report published in June 2006 by a UK think tank, the Focus Institute on Rights and Social Transformation (FIRST). The report underlines the need to address racist attitudes and behavior from an early age in nurseries, children's centers, and schools, stressing the positive impact of such an approach in combating racism throughout society. The report, titled *Right from the Start*, calls for the adoption of "a national strategic approach" in all levels of the government to foster racial equality in the early years through services and settings:

> These early years are a period of intense learning for children and also a time when family members are most involved in their care and education . . . It is therefore a critical opportunity for children to begin the process of learning to appreciate each other equally and to be positive about people who are different from themselves as well as those who are similar to them.[53]

Right from the Start stresses that only by tackling racism in early education will there be a long-term impact in combating racism in society as a whole.

Other recent reports and studies on this issue include the *Alliance of Civilizations Report of the High-level Group*, launched in November 2006. *The Alliance of Civilizations'* project mandate is to "bridge divides and overcome prejudice, misconceptions, misperceptions, and polarization which potentially threaten world peace." One of the recommendations of this project targets education as an effective and viable avenue toward realizing a paradigm of mutual respect among nations. Among its main fields of action the project strongly recognizes that "mutual fear, suspicion, and ignorance across cultures has spread beyond the level of political leadership into the hearts and minds of populations—so much so that the notion that there are essential and irreconcilable differences between cultures and religions now arises regularly as an explanation for a range of cultural and political conflicts."[54]

In order to address this, the report emphasizes that "education systems today face the challenge of preparing young people for an interdependent world that is unsettling to individual and collective identities. Education about one's own history fosters a sense of community and solidarity, but it must be balanced by knowledge of global issues and an understanding and appreciation of other cultures and societies . . . through understanding of shared values and ideals."[55]

Some of these and other reports and studies underline the need to train pupils in critical thinking right from the beginning. Thinking critically or being intellectually aware is a skill; it therefore needs to be learned, nurtured, developed, and strengthened through training and practice. In short, it must be part of an educational system and should be integrated into the school curriculum. Thinking critically cannot be left to happen naturally, especially given the barrage of information and misinformation out there. It takes early training and nurturing on how to read outside the box, knowing that one should find alternative sources and then learning how to find them, how to evaluate opposing opinions before deciding on the correct version of things. Not only do people not have the time, inclination, or experience to do so these days, but they are also becoming accustomed to having premises worked out for them. They expect the truth to appear in short sound bites—three-word slogans, which are the fast-food version of truth. This very strange logic underscores the fact that we do not live in an age of intelligent discrimination but one of confusion.

In conclusion, the concepts of citizenship, coexistence plurality, and shared values will be better taught, better understood, and better realized once trust is built, and there is no other area where a long-term solution can be successful at all levels other than that of education. We need to educate the younger generation to understand the importance of other cultures and to instill in these young people a respect for humanity in general. This global vision will allow future generations to fight all forms of intolerance and seek real, stable solutions to complex problems. The ethos of a society based on equality, respect, and trust for everyone is today an unrealized ideal, and what we have in its place is a climate of fear and, at best, tolerance. We must go beyond creating a culture of tolerance, for toleration is dangerous and fickle, a thin crust that separates reason from violence and can easily crack under the slightest pressure, and neither community will fully live at ease with the Other unless we understand how to stop the anger that is being deliberately provoked and spread on both sides, as well as how to deal with it:

The thesis is that our identity is partly shaped by recognition or its absence, often by the misrecognition of others, and so a person or group of people can suffer real damage, real distortion, if the people or society around them mirror back to them a confining or demeaning or contemptible picture of themselves. Non-recognition or misrecognition can inflict harm, can be a form of oppression, imprisoning someone in a false, distorted mode of being.[56]

To illustrate these issues and underline the importance of focusing on a long-term educational strategy, I conclude by looking at a twelve-part series of evangelical novels titled *Left Behind*. The series is presented as "novels of the earth's last days." A kids' series and a military series have also been produced. These works are sold on CD-ROM, as graphic-novel editions, and as videos. The series has been spectacularly successful; by 2005 more than 62 million copies had been sold, thus "outstripp[ing] the popular *Da Vinci Code*."[57] The twelfth and final title, *Glorious Appearing*, sold two million copies prior to publication in March 2004 and reached the number 2 spot on the *New York Times'* bestseller list.

The series relates the story of Jesus' return to Earth to fulfill God's will by wiping out from the planet all those who do not believe in Jesus, a form of en masse religious cleansing. I do not present a detailed analysis of the series or of *Glorious Appearing*, but I would like the reader to imagine the uproar that would result if a novel predicting the return of Prophet Muhammad to wipe out all nonbelievers, that is, an en masse cleansing of Christians and other non-Muslims, were to hit the market, especially the best-seller list. The author would not only be roundly attacked by the media and political and religious leaders but also be accused of being a Muslim extremist following the "extreme message" of the "wicked Qur'an," promoting and encouraging violence and hatred. The author would most probably end up in a European court charged with inciting hatred and terrorism or put on a ghost plane to Guantanamo. Although the authors of *Glorious Appearing* have received mild and "civilized" criticism, they have escaped accusations of inciting mass murder and terrorism.

For instance, Nicholas D. Kristof in "Jesus and Jihad" states that "we should be embarrassed when our best-selling books gleefully celebrate religious intolerance and violence against infidels."[58] In his analytical article on the popularity and impact of the *Left Behind* series, Elliot Colla points to a dangerous phenomenon:

Those who doubt whether Christian Millenarianism is related to US foreign policy owe it to themselves to read the Left Behind novels, especially since there is much to suggest that American evangelicals are reading these works not as fiction, but as the faithful rendering of real-life prophecies in which Americans figure as righteous mujahideen. While it is unclear whether President Bush is a reader of the Left Behind series, he has often decried his appreciation for evangelism. And when he speaks of "evildoers," or warns that "you're either with us or against us," he is consciously citing the same language that provides vocabulary for the Left Behind series.[59]

Colla also noted that a spokesperson for the U.S. Armed Forces admitted that numerous copies of the Military Series of Left Behind were given away to soldiers in Iraq and Afghanistan.[60] He further states that the novels of the Military Series relate the story of Army Rangers' and Marine Special Forces' involvement in aspects of Armageddon. He believes that "any resemblance [sic] to current US interventions in the Middle East *are not accidental*."[61] The popularity of these works "suggest [sic] that many American audiences are viewing contemporary events in the Middle East through an extremist evangelical lens."[62] On May 24, 2004, *Newsweek* magazine published a picture of a GI in Iraq reading a hard copy of *Glorious Appearing* (figure 9.7). Elliot Colla wonders in a letter published by *ISIM Newsletter* whether "some soldiers in Iraq reading these novels aren't thinking that they're involved in the first stages of Armageddon."[63] He adds that although "we cannot say with any empirical exactness the degree to which evangelical theology . . . is shaping the Middle East foreign policy of the Bush administration . . . such theology is 'informing' (rather than commanding) the thought, and probably even some aspects of policy."[64]

In this context it is important to note that Sarah Palin, the Republican vice presidential nominee in 2008, who has attended an evangelical church since she was a teenager, told "the graduating class of commission students at her one-time church, Wasilla Assembly of God," in June 2008 that the Iraq war is "a task that is from God." She added: "[T]hat's what we have to make sure that we're praying for, that there is a plan and that plan is God's plan."[65] Compressing the war in Iraq to such reductionist terminology not only signals willful mental closure at the highest levels of American leadership but also legitimizes ideology under the flag of religion. David Gates feels that "it's not coincidence that the [*Left Behind*] books are a favorite with American soldiers in Iraq."[66] In fact, "many critics of the series see a resonance between its apocalyptic scenario and the born-again President Bush's apocalyptic rhetoric and confrontational Mideast policies."[67] Colla warns:

> Currently, the idea of Holy War against Islam would be abhorrent to most mainstream Christians and secular liberals, even those whose

ideas about the use of geopolitical force against Islam are not radically divergent from those of the evangelicals. But if the Left Behind series is any indication, millions of Americans are reading about, and perhaps even praying for, just such a Holy War.[68]

Needless to say, these novels, which echo the standards of the "White Man's Burden," *The Lustful Turk*, and *The True Travels and Adventures of Captain John Smith*, are badly written, underwhelming, pedestrian, dull, prosaic, and humdrum, yet they continue to be overwhelmingly popular.

Manipulators love easy targets and short-cut methods of indoctrination, banking on little or no mental resistance. They agitate emotions, exploit insecurities, take advantage of the ambiguity of language, and bend the rules of logic. Fiction, media, and other forms of popular culture allow them to do just that. It is about time that we brought the ball back into our court and educate our children not only *how to read the lines* but, more important, *how to read between them*. Bulliet cautions:

> Today's anti-Muslim rants are concerned less with recycling Islamophobic canards from centuries past, such as Muhammad being a lying demagogue, than with finding new ways of articulating old hatreds. Under current circumstances, however, the emotional satisfaction some audiences derive from this updating and repackaging of traditional Islamophobia is not worth plunging the world into a series of wars.[69]

FIGURE 9.7. A U.S. soldier in Iraq resting while reading a hard copy of *Glorious Appearing. Newsweek* magazine (May 24, 2004).

Bulliet's words are no mere exaggeration. The real threat facing humanity is not Islam but ignorance, myths, and stereotypes, and, as such, it is only through progressive education that effective change, stimulating debate, intelligent discussion, and critical thinking can be attained to ultimately define truly free societies based on an ethos of respect and trust.

NOTES

This is a revised edition of a paper delivered at the international conference on Citizenship, Security, and Democracy, organized by the Association of Muslim Social Scientists (AMSS) (UK) and the Foundation for Political, Economic and Social Research (SETA) (Turkey) in Istanbul, September 1–3, 2006.

1. Charles Carrington, *Rudyard Kipling: His Life and Work* (London: Macmillan, 1978), 337.

2. My own particular research comparing anti-Semitic Nazi propaganda in the form of literature, pamphlets, cartoons, children's books, and illustrations has yielded remarkable similarity to much that appears in print today concerning Muslims.

3. Commission on British Muslims and Islamophobia, *Islamophobia: Issues, Challenges, and Action*, ed. Robin Richardson (Stoke on Trent: Trentham, 2004), 7.

4. See, for example, Todd Porter Field, *The Allure of Empire: Art in the Service of French Imperialism, 1798–1836* (Princeton: Princeton University Press, 1998).

5. Ibid., 4.

6. Ibid., 7.

7. Ibid.

8. Ibid., 11.

9. Nabil Matar, *Turks, Moors, and Englishmen in the Age of Discovery* (New York: Columbia University Press, 1999), 12–13.

10. Ibid., 13.

11. Jean Raspail, *The Camp of the Saints*, trans. Norman Shapiro (Petoskey: Social Contract Press, 2007); first published 1975 by Scribner's.

12. Interestingly, the third English edition (1982) was published by the Institute for Western Values, and the fourth edition (1987) was published by the Immigration Control Foundation.

13. Carrington, *Rudyard Kipling*, 337.

14. Ibid., 337; emphasis mine.

15. Ibid., 338.

16. George Orwell, *Essays* (London: Penguin Classics, 2000), 204.

17. Ibid., 213.

18. Raspail, *The Camp of Saints*, 18.

19. Ibid.

20. Ibid., 87.

21. When, on February 17, 2001, a ship loaded with a thousand Iraqis beached near the French resort of Nice, Paul Craig Roberts wrote, "Truth Follows Fiction: *The Camp of the Saints* begins in France." He noted the prophetic message of the novel,

written twenty-eight years earlier. He also noted the media's positive appraisal of the novel when it first appeared. The *Wall Street Journal's* Edmond Fuller described it as "sensational," and Linell Smith in the *Baltimore Sun* predicted that "no reader will remain unaffected by the questions [the novel] raises."

22. Raspail, *The Camp of the Saints*, 43.

23. The subtitle reads: "Here, revealed for the first time, you will find the hidden numbers which will endanger national identities and shape the destiny of our civilization in the thirty years ahead"; translated in Jean-Paul Gourevitch, "Parable or Reality—Thirty Years after 'The Camp of Saints,'" *Social Contract* 14, no. 2 (Winter 2003–2004), http://www.thesocialcontract.com/artman2/publish/tsc1402/article_1192.shtml.

24. Ibid.

25. *The True Travels, Adventures, and Observations of Captain John Smith, in Europe, Asia, Africa, and America from Anno Domini 1593–1629* (London: 1630).

26. Moses Tyler, *History of American Literature 1607–1765* (Ithaca: 1949), 17.

27. Ibid., 32.

28. Benjamin Woolley describes it as an "incoherent and unreliable autobiography" in *Savage Kingdom: Virginia and the Founding of English America* (London: HarperPress, 2007), 26.

29. Wayne Craven, *Sculpture in America from the Colonial Period to the Present* (New York: Thomas Y. Crowell and Co., 1968), 116.

30. Samuel M. Green, *American Art: A Historical Survey* (New York: Ronald Press, 1966), 290.

31. Ibid., 117.

32. Carl Bode, *The Anatomy of American Popular Culture 1840–1861* (Berkley: University of California Press, 1959), 98.

33. "The Greek Slave of American Orientalism," http://homepage.mac.com/kmcspadden/AmericanOrientalism.htm#.

34. Ibid.

35. It is suggested that the man behind the success of the American tour was the American painter Miner Kellogg (1814–1889), who escorted the statue from one city to another, circulating pamphlets containing "the favorable critiques" from England and "brainwashing" those of Puritan heritage to a degree that "they saw chastity, piety, and holiness triumphant" in the statue rather than a nude girl. See Craven, *Sculpture in America*, 118. Also see Miner Kellogg, *Justice to Hiram Powers: Addressed to the Citizens of New Orleans* (Cincinnati: 1848), 145.

36. Anonymous, *The Lustful Turk: The Infamous Account of a Victorian Lady's Life in a Harem* (London: Allen, 1988).

37. "The Roots of Western Pornography," http://www.libidomag.com/nakedbrunch/archive/europorno6.html.

38. See, for example, pages 21, 26, and 42 in Anonymous, *Lustful Turk*.

39. The audio clips are available on "Tall Armenian Tale: The Other Side of the Falsified Genocide," http://www.tallarmeniantale.com/Wheatcroft-TerribleTurk.htm.

40. To illustrate the point and taking just one example of many, Pastor John Hagee's knowledge of "Islamic law" does not come from scholarly research and books

written by Muslim and non-Muslim scholars and academics but from a novel titled *The Last of Days* (1983). In his book *Final Dawn over Jerusalem: The World's Future Hangs in the Balance with the Battle for the Holy City* (Nashville: Nelson, 1998), he quotes from the popular fiction title and writes on page 141: "Islamic law stipulates that to fulfill Muhammad's task, every 'infidel domain' must be considered a territory of war. According to Moris Farhi, author of *The Last of Days*, Muslims believe there can be no peace with the Jew or the Christian or any other non-Islamic people." It may be interesting to note that Hagee is president of Global Evangelism Television, whose daily and weekly programs on radio and television reach people in the United States and around the world.

41. Grant Hugo, "The Political Influence of the Thriller," *Contemporary Review* (December 1972): 284–85.

42. Ibid., 285. This is further detailed in my chapter "Public Opinion and Political Influence: Issues in Contemporary Popular Fiction," in *Citizenship, Security, and Democracy: Muslim Engagement with the West*, ed. Wanda Krause, 47-75 (UK: AMSS and TURKEY: SETA, 2009).

43. "The Political Influence of the Thriller," 285.

44. See "Ten Things You Didn't Know about Clinton," *Guardian* (Nov. 5, 1992); Sean O'Hagan, "Time for a New Black Power Movement," *Observer* (Aug. 18, 2002).

45. Richard Clarke, *The Scorpion's Gate* (New York: Putnam's, 2005). The cover carries the following sentence: "Sometimes you can tell more truth through fiction." The novel, it is believed, was used to settle his differences and disagreements with the administration on the war on terror.

46. Richard W. Bulliet, *The Case for Islamo-Christian Civilization* (New York: Columbia University Press, 2004), 14–15.

47. See Joe L. Kincheloe and Shirley R. Steinberg, eds., *The Miseducation of the West: How Schools and the Media Distort Our Understanding of the Islamic World* (Westport: Praeger, 2004). See also Michael Hamilton Morgan, *Lost History: The Enduring Legacy of Muslim Scientists, Thinkers, and Artists* (Washington, D.C.: National Geographic, 2007), and Barry van Driel, ed., *Confronting Islamophobia in Educational Practice* (Stoke on Trent: Trentham, 2004).

48. The conference was the initiative of the then president of the Federal Republic of Germany, Roman Herzog, and under the patronage of the heads of state or government of twelve European and Muslim countries.

49. Compilation and introduction by Pieter Batelmaan and Fons Cooms, with a preface by Professor Dr. Theo van Boven, 2d ed., published by the International Association for Intercultural Education (IAIE) in cooperation with UNESCO, the International Bureau of Education (IBE), and the Council of Europe.

50. Sir Keith Ajegbo, *Curriculum Review: Diversity and Citizenship* (London: Department of Education and Skills, 2007), 1.

51. Ibid., 21.

52. Ibid.

53. Jane Lane, *Right from the Start* (London: Focus Institute on Rights and Social Transformation, 2006).

54. *Alliance of Civilizations: Report of the High-level Group* (New York: United Nations, 2006), 25.

55. Ibid.

56. Charles Taylor, *Multiculturalism: Examining the Politics of Recognition*; quoted in Ajegbo, *Curriculum Review*, 29.

57. Elliot Colla, "A Culture of Righteousness and Martyrdom," *ISIM Newsletter* (June 14, 2004), 6.

58. Published in the *New York Times* (July 17, 2004).

59. Colla, "Culture of Righteousness," 7.

60. See Elliot Colla's response, in Letters to the Editor, *ISIM Newsletter* 15 (Spring 2005), 5.

61. Colla, "Culture of Righteousness," 6. Emphasis author's.

62. Ibid.

63. Colla's response (see note 60).

64. Ibid.

65. See "Palin's Church May Have Shaped Controversial Worldview," *Huffington Post* (September 2008), http://www.huffingtonpost.com/2008/09/02/palins-church-may-have-sh_n_123205.html.

66. David Gates, "Religion: The Pop Prophets," *Newsweek* (May 24, 2004), 46.

67. Ibid, 47.

68. Colla, "Culture of Righteousness," 7.

69. Bulliet, *Case for Islamo-Christian Civilization*, 15.

10

Orientalist Themes in Contemporary British Islamophobia

Kate Zebiri

Is contemporary Islamophobia merely the most recent manifestation of an age-old hostility to Islam on the part of Christendom and the West, an antagonism that has existed since the very beginning? This chapter challenges this claim and illustrates ways in which the discursive content of selected themes has evolved according to the nature of the societies in which the discourse circulates.

While the term *Orientalist* has primarily applied to academic scholarship, art, and literature, the term *Islamophobia* generally applies more to popular culture, including the media and grassroots prejudice. For various reasons, including the declining importance of the nation-state and the rise of postmodernism, academics are now far less likely to represent particular national interests than they were in the colonial period or even in the 1970s, when Edward Said wrote his seminal book.[1] The atmosphere in the academy is now one of greater uncertainty and an unwillingness to subscribe to metanarratives.[2] Therefore, continuities with classical anti-Muslim themes are more likely to be found in popular culture, the focus of this chapter.

Three main themes—namely gender, violence, and foreignness—have been selected for analysis because they were the main ones that emerged from my field research; I found that even the nonverbal hostility my interviewees encountered seemed to fall under one of these three headings. The focus on specific themes (together with their accompanying *topoi* and motifs) makes it possible to observe the various ways in which they are constructed, their relative and shifting importance, and their interrelationship. The extent to which the treatment of these themes echoes or departs from traditional Orientalist approaches is analyzed, as are ways in which they reflect contemporary British and/or European concerns and anxieties, for example about national identity.

This chapter is based mainly on interviews with British Muslim converts who were asked about their experiences of hostility or discrimination,[3] but it also includes some reference to the media, which will provide useful contextualization. Since converts are usually targeted as Muslims (rather than specifically as converts), this will shed light on contemporary British Islamophobia in general. Furthermore, the experiences of white converts (who made up approximately two-thirds of my sample) provide an opportunity to observe anti-Muslim hostility in its purest form, excluding (in theory at least) the ethnic/racial dimension.

Gender, Violence, and Foreignness as Perennial Themes in Anti-Muslim Discourse

Orientalist discourse up until the Enlightenment was predominantly Christian led, primarily religious and theological, and Muhammad, the Quran, and Islamic theology were the main areas of discussion. The primary concerns were the alleged falseness of the revelations, Muhammad's deliberate manipulation of these, and his failure to perform miracles on a par with those of Jesus. Norman Daniel's magisterial study of late medieval Christian anti-Islamic polemic demonstrates the perennial nature of the preoccupation with violence and sensuality. In a medieval society in which Christianity formed the central element of individual, social, and communal identity, distortions of Islam reached the point where "nonsense was accepted . . . because whatever seemed useful to faith was thought likely to be true."[4]

The rise of secular humanism in the Enlightenment period and beyond gave rise to a reassessment of Islam, sometimes resulting in more positive views, for example secular-oriented admiration of Muhammad as a robust and effective leader, in contrast to Jesus' lack of worldly success. However, it also led to a view of religion in general as irrational—a view that still often finds favor in the secular-dominated media. In the Romantic period, symbols and images of foreignness, sensuality (usually gender related), and even violence were exoticized in ways that attracted the European imagination.[5]

The colonial period gave rise to more geographically and politically oriented forms of Orientalism. Anti-Muslim discourse now embraced a new function that has been amply documented in Said's *Orientalism*: the justification of the imperial project, with a corresponding need to show the irrationality, barbarity, obscurantism, and backwardness of Muslims and Islam (and therefore their need to be "civilized" and "enlightened"). Ernest Renan's famous lecture, "Islam and Science" (delivered at the Sorbonne in 1883), which depicted Islam as antithetical to reason, progress, creativity, and reform, was an early example of such attitudes.[6] In the postcolonial period, postmodernism has had conflicting and contradictory results, its championing of the "underdog" having a leveling effect with regard to genders, sexualities, and races and (in theory at least) giving a voice to oppressed and disadvantaged minorities. In light of global inequalities, Muslims may be seen as such minorities, both internationally and in Western nation-states. The dominance of human rights discourse offers hope to dispossessed Muslims but can also give rise to the construction of Islam as politically repressive and intolerant (continuing the colonialist theme of the Oriental despotic ruler), as well as oppressive of women and minorities.

Issues of gender and sexuality have a high profile in both Muslim and non-Muslim discourse on Islam. The subject of women in Islam is highly sensitized due to the long history of polemic and apologetic between Muslims and non-Muslims on this issue, and it is not without political implications. In the colonial period, claims that Islam's teachings on women were evidence of its "backwardness" provided justification for political intervention in Muslim countries, and the construction of Islam as "oppressive" of women continues to serve specific Western political interests; an example is the invocation of women's rights issues in connection with U.S. military intervention in Afghanistan in recent years.[7] The gender-related discourse has changed markedly over time. In the early centuries of Muslim-Christian encounter, Islam was attacked for its alleged moral laxity and sensuality, and accusations focused on Muhammad's alleged "lustfulness" (with reference to his multiple marriages and in particular his marriage to Zaynab), the Quran's sensual depiction of paradise, and the licitness of concubinage, divorce, and polygyny. In the Romantic period, by contrast, the harem and the *seraglio* became objects of nostalgia, fascination and desire.

The theme of violence has been no less persistent than gender-related themes in anti-Muslim discourse, though the reasons for its prominence have changed. For early Christians, the idea that Islam was "spread by the sword" (and the accompanying idea of Muhammad and Muslims as "bloodthirsty") was significant because it contrasted markedly with the Christian ideal model of Jesus, who did not engage in military activity. At certain points of the history of Muslim-Christian relations, various parts of Europe were in fact under threat of Muslim military expansion, fueling violence-related discourse. In recent decades, the alleged violence of Islam is related to the rise of political Islam and, latterly, Jihadist activism and so-called Islamic terrorism.

Foreignness, in a sense, stands for otherness in general—the perception of an alien culture, values, way of life, and so on. Inevitably, it is constructed differently in a world of nation-states than it was in former times. In the early centuries of Muslim-Christian/European encounter, foreignness/otherness was usually constructed in religious terms, and Islam was viewed as heretical or as a harbinger of the apocalypse, for example.[8] If nineteenth-century Romanticism, inspired by the tales of travelers such as Richard Burton and Charles Doughty, constructed an exotic and alluring vision of the Orient (which has not wholly died out), twenty-first-century nations in the West are more concerned with issues of national identity, immigration, and social cohesion.

Islamophobia in the British Context

Unlike other parts of the world, Europe has a long history of conflict with Islamic polities, and this has clearly influenced the development and evolution of its views of Islam. While not denying the impact of distant events on shaping the discourse, I suggest as a general rule that the more recent the event, the greater its impact on contemporary views. To risk stating the obvious, imperialism is rather more important in the scheme of things than the Crusades. Halliday points out that British imperial history differs from that of France both in terms of its general impact on national identity (imperialism is more formative in the case of France) and in terms of the role played by Muslims (again, it is rather more significant in the case of France). Britain's most difficult encounters were with non-Muslim groups such as Hindu mutineers and Irish Catholic republicans rather than with Muslims.[9] Events of the past few decades such as the 1973 OPEC oil price hikes, the Iranian hostage crisis, the ongoing Israeli-Palestinian conflict, and more recently 9/11, while important globally and having some influence on British views, have been relatively more significant for Americans' perceptions of Islam.[10] The July 2005 London bombings notwithstanding, these considerations, taken together with Britain's recent history of multiculturalism, may mean that a less contentious view of Islam prevails in Britain, as compared to France and the United States.

One incident that has had particular resonance in Britain occurred at the end of the 1980s; the Rushdie affair gave a new impetus to anti-Muslim hostility in Britain. The events surrounding this affair marked a shift from race and ethnicity to religion as the core element not just in British Muslim identity but also in anti-Muslim hostility, which was now increasingly expressed in religious rather than racial terms. Widely circulated (and sometimes staged) images of bearded, robed, foreign-looking Muslims demonstrating and burning books contributed to a view of Islam and Muslims as anti-modern, repressive, intolerant, and obscurantist. The protestors appeared to be challenging one of the most cherished values of contemporary Western societies: freedom of speech. Equally important, by bringing religion into the public sphere they were going against the model of European modernity, whose trajectory over the past two or three centuries had been in the opposite direction.

One of the most powerful driving forces of anti-Muslimism in Britain is arguably the news media, the primary source of information about Islam and Muslims for most non-Muslim Britons; Poole's research shows a close correspondence between representations of Islam in the press and public opinion.[11] The 2007 report commissioned by the then mayor of London, Ken Livingstone, *The Search for Common Ground: Muslims, Non-Muslims, and the UK Media*, found the prevailing view to be that "there is no common ground between the West and Islam, and that conflict between them is accordingly inevitable."[12] The overall picture in the media is that, globally, Islam is "profoundly different from, and a serious threat to, the West, and that within Britain Muslims are different from and a threat to 'Us.'"[13] Muslims are depicted as "challenging 'our' culture, values, institutions and way of life."[14] The report, which examined press material from the year 2006, identifies several components of the dominant narrative. These include the failure of Muslims to integrate, their unreasonable demands, their mixed loyalties and support for extremism, their obscurantism, and the incompatibility of their values and interests with those of mainstream society.[15] Other studies, notably those by Poole and Richardson,[16] which focus on material from the mid- to late 1990s, confirm the overriding impression of the otherization of Muslims in the British press, which constructs non-Muslims and Muslims as "us" and "them," respectively. Both studies found strong, consensual interpretive frameworks operating in the representation of Muslims, with coverage mostly confined to a limited range of themes and stories selected on the basis of how well they fit in with those themes.

The Experience of British Muslim Converts

On beginning my research, conducted in 2005–2006, I anticipated that the nature of the hostility encountered by converts would be broadly similar to that encountered by born Muslims, with the possible added dimension of "betrayal"—whether cultural, political, or racial—when they are targeted *as converts to Islam*. While discourse related to foreignness (e.g., "Why don't you go back where you came from?") could be expected to be less prominent, at least in the case of white converts, I expected that there could be an element of "racism by proxy," as described by Franks.[17] She found that some of her white Muslim respondents experienced racial abuse; she explains this with reference to the fact that these Muslims are "linked by association" with Pakistani or South Asian Muslims.[18] Franks suggests that converts are of particular interest in this context: "As *white* Muslims in Britain, located at the intersection of religious and 'racial' boundaries, their experience of wearing the *ḥijāb* in a liberal democracy draws attention to the issues of religious tolerance and discrimination."[19]

Methodology

In all, thirty in-depth, semistructured interviews were conducted between August 2005 and July 2006.[20] Potential interviewees were contacted mainly via snowballing and convenience sampling, and some effort was made to ensure a spread that reflected the makeup of British converts as a whole (insofar as this is known) in terms of gender, age, ethnic background, and Islamic orientation. The interviewees consisted of twenty women and ten men (possibly corresponding to the male-female ratio among British converts generally, though this is not known for sure) between the ages of 19 and 59, with an average age of 34. The length of time that they had been Muslim varied from 4 months to 28 years, with an average of 10.5 years. With one exception, the interviewees were brought up in the UK and (in one case) southern Ireland.[21] Twenty-four of them were living within the greater London area, while six lived in small towns or rural areas in the Midlands and Home Counties.[22] Twenty of the interviewees were white (eleven English, four Irish, two Scottish, one Welsh, and two mixed European), six were Black African or Afro-Caribbean, one was mixed race (Afro-Caribbean and white English), and three were Asian. This tallies reasonably well with the probable national profile of converts (approximately one-third black, a tenth Asian, and the rest white).[23] The educational level of the sample was above average, with just over half being educated to first-degree level or higher (including one PhD). As far as professional qualifications are concerned, the sample included three teachers, a doctor, a chartered accountant, a psychologist, an engineer, and a social worker, although not all of these were currently employed. With regard to employment status, seventeen people were in salaried employment (including five who worked in an Islamic context), two were self-employed, and three were students; in addition, five women were at home with young children, and three people were unemployed.

Experiences of Hostility and Discrimination

The interviewees reported varying types of experience ranging from verbal abuse to more subtle forms of discrimination such as difficulty in getting a job or in being promoted at work. Most people felt that things had gotten worse since 9/11 and that they had deteriorated at least temporarily in the immediate aftermath of 7/7; however, sometimes the interviewees were describing a general impression rather than a direct personal experience of hostility. Not surprisingly, men reported far fewer problems than women, whose religious identity tends to be much more visible. In fact, a relatively small minority of male converts dress in a way that is identifiably Muslim;[24] while many have beards, the beard is usually not unambiguously Islamic. Of the ten men in my sample, nine wore a beard, but only three of these regarded their beard as distinctively or recognizably Islamic. Only one man habitually dressed in "Islamic" style, wearing a robe, but because his ethnic origin was black African, he found that people often took his attire to be African rather than Islamic (and his "African" appearance did not seem to evoke hostile reactions).[25]

Due to this low profile, most of the men were unsure as to whether they had encountered prejudice or whether any negative experience could be attributed to their religious affiliation. The black African male convert mentioned earlier, whose appearance was perhaps more "African" than "Islamic," felt that he had definitely suffered racially motivated discrimination but was not sure whether religious prejudice had also been a factor. In addition to the visibility factor, it emerged that men were less likely to be verbally abused than women because the latter were a softer target. One male convert's wife, who was present during the interview, said that she was sometimes verbally abused when she was on her own but never when she was with her husband. The types of experiences the men reported had largely to do with getting job interviews or jobs (in the case of those who used their Muslim names in that situation) or being promoted at work. One man who felt he had been "left out of the loop" at work, commented that he never went to the pub when invited: "I may have inadvertently excluded myself." As Modood points out, cultural racism can affect groups that do not accept mainstream norms, including, as in this case, those who abstain from drinking alcohol in a social context, as well as those who choose to dress in distinctive ways.[26]

The women's experience differed markedly from that of the men. For example, almost half of them reported definite incidents of verbal abuse. None of the women had actually been physically assaulted, though some knew of women who had. Probably the most traumatic-sounding experience was reported by someone who had been attacked by a woman in the street, seemingly out of the blue and without provocation: "She was going with her fists as though she was gonna punch me in the face . . . and then she made the sound of a bomb." At the time this convert had been pregnant and accompanied by her toddler, so she had felt particularly vulnerable and unable to challenge the attacker as she normally would have. She said that she had been reluctant to go out with her children for some time following that incident.

Women also described more subtle forms of prejudice. Several had noticed whispering or funny looks or felt they were stared at when they took on the hijab.[27] One woman said that she often had people look her up and down from head to toe; sometimes she would smile at them, at which point they would usually look away or get embarrassed. She compared this to the experience of people with visible disabilities: "People forget that you're not just an object." The women who did not wear hijab, of whom there were three, tended to experience the same kinds of discrimination as the men (i.e., work related). One of these described a form of social exclusion similar to that of the man quoted earlier, who had refrained from going to the pub with his coworkers. She had previously worked in the city and said that she had experienced "bullying" in the form of pressure to go to the pub and drink at lunchtime. She had found that there was "a very heavy pub culture, and if you don't comply you do get the sense that you're not being considered one of the gang . . . You lose chances." Another woman who did not wear hijab spoke of "sarcastic comments" at work but ironically perhaps felt that people would not dare to make them if she *did* wear the hijab (possibly an implicit reference to new legislation against religious discrimination in the workplace).[28]

Gender, Violence, and Foreignness

Gender and Hijab

Gender and hijab provide the richest set of motifs, arguments, and images both in media coverage and the popular imagination. Islamic gender norms are represented in much of the discourse as challenging or negating some of the most cherished and recently won "Western" values of human rights, female emancipation, and sexual liberation. While it is not surprising that press coverage is mainly devoted to politics, violence, and terrorism, gender themes are given an airing whenever current events (such as the Jack Straw *niqab* affair) provide an opportunity.[29] Issues such as female circumcision, arranged/forced marriages (the two are sometimes conflated), and honor killings have periodically become prominent in the news, and certain relationships—particularly those involving a glamorous/rich/famous white female and a Muslim male—received extensive coverage in the 1990s.[30] The Runnymede Trust's seminal report on Islamophobia, published in 1997, found a recurring theme in the media representation of Islam to be "the claim that Islam oppresses women, in ways significantly different from and worse than the ways in which women are treated in other religions and cultures."[31]

The "veil" (a term that can incorporate both hijab and niqab and is often ambiguous) provides a rich and endlessly versatile symbol, perhaps the most powerful symbol of Muslims' otherness and alien values. Often portrayed in the media as "restrictive and burdensome," it is closely related to the theme of women's subjugation and is seen as something imposed rather than chosen.[32] In the wake of the Jack Straw affair, the word "niqab" was added to the existing repertoire of "burqa," "veil," and "hijab," enabling columnists to make finer distinctions between the different types of covering. Excerpts reproduced in *The Search for Common Ground* show the variety of themes that come into play. Joan Smith of the *Independent*, in an emotive piece in which she declares that she "loathes" the niqab and the burqa, sees the phenomenon of female covering as "a human rights issue": "I can't think of a more dramatic visual symbol of oppression, the vast majority of women who cover their hair, faces and bodies do so because they have no choice." Melanie Phillips sees "the Muslim veil" in even more explicitly political terms, pronouncing it "unacceptable" on the grounds that it is associated with "the most extreme version of Islam . . . It's inherently separatist and perceived by some as intimidatory."[33] For Suzanne Moore of the *Observer*, issues of sexuality are uppermost: "If the female body is so sinful it must be completely covered, or if its exhibition shows the whorishness of all women, we make all sexuality something which is women's fault. The idea that men can't control sexual impulses while women must does nothing to liberate women—or men—from the horrific round of repression, guilt, blame and shame."[34]

The hijab clearly played a significant part in the hostility encountered by the female interviewees. When women converts adopt the hijab, they usually experience some kind of adverse reaction from family, friends, and/or work colleagues. In many female testimonies, the family is reasonably accepting of their conversion until they take on the hijab, at which point the attitude changes. Because female converts are aware of this, the decision to take on the hijab is often preceded by much trepidation and hesitation. Several of the women had felt extremely self-conscious when they started wearing hijab, like the one who commented: "I found it hard at first. Everyone's staring at you. You become completely paranoid."

The theme of Muslim women's supposed oppression came up fairly regularly in the interviews in the context of female covering. The only woman in my sample who wore niqab full time in public said that she had received a lot of sympathetic smiles and comments such as "You all right, love?" She added: "They think you're oppressed." Another said of the hijab that "A lot of people think you must have been forced to wear it because you're married to an Arab." A third woman said that her friends had asked her why she had gone into "a religion that treats women so badly."

Women who convert to Islam sometimes find themselves on the receiving end of a particular type of hostility—they are accused of having betrayed the cause of feminism, for which women in the West fought so hard. Katherine Bullock, a Canadian convert and author of an academic study on perceptions of the hijab, reports that she was told that she "didn't belong" at an International Women's Day gathering as it was felt that she represented the subjugation of women.[35] One interviewee related that her mother (who was not particularly feminist and in fact held quite traditional values) had told her that her (the mother's) friends felt that the interviewee had "betrayed everything they'd fought for" in terms of women's rights.

While women who wear the hijab sometimes encounter anger from non-Muslim women as a result of their alleged betrayal of the feminist cause, they may encounter anger from non-Muslim men, and sometimes women as well, for an entirely different reason. One woman had had a man comment: "Look at the state of that, must be boiling" (a reference to wearing full covering during the summer months). Another had heard a woman in the street remark: "Look at that for a pig's ear." These comments are likely to be a reaction to the sexual nonavailability of Muslim women (if not literally, then at least symbolically—they are not even playing the game and making a pretense of such availability); Franks points out that women, as well as men, can find it hard to forgive those who "disrupt" the "pattern of the masculine gaze."[36] Several interviewees volunteered the view that it was mostly *men* who expressed hostility toward women who wear the hijab in the street.

Violence

Both Poole and Richardson found that, in the mid- to late 1990s, conflict and violence were central to reporting on Islam and Muslims and that "Muslim" or

"Islamic" terrorism was a central theme; Poole's follow-up article, coming into the 2000s, found that this theme predominated over all others relating to Muslims.[37] Muslims in general are routinely portrayed as a threat to security, with the motifs of "the enemy within" or "fifth column" implicating British Muslims in particular.

It is not difficult to find references to violence in the media that chime in with age-old anti-Muslim themes. The first Runnymede Trust report reproduced a particularly crude example from an article by Robert Kilroy-Silk, published in the *Daily Express* in 1995. After referring to the public cutting off of ears and hands in Iraq, the article continues: "Moslems [*sic*] everywhere behave with equal savagery. They behead criminals, stone to death female—only female—adulterers, throw acid in the faces of women who refuse to wear the chadar [*sic*], mutilate the genitals of young girls and ritually abuse animals."[38] Kilroy-Silk's infamous article, titled "We Owe Arabs Nothing," published several years later in the *Sunday Express*, did not explicitly refer to "Moslems." However, the reference to "suicide bombers, limb-amputators, women repressors" was clearly intended to invoke Islam, and not just the Arabs of the title.[39] *Evening Standard* columnist Brian Sewell argues that "Islam has always been militant; the urge to conquer and convert began with the great imperial thrust of Mohammed himself." Asking rhetorically what "Islam" will gain from a clash with the West, Sewell replies: "It will secure the old certainties of poverty, disease, the suffocating conformism compelled by the beatings, amputations and hideous executions of sharia law—'the will of Allah,' as they say when children die, and 'God is great,' they shout when men and women, hanged for what we see as mere misdemeanor, choke slowly in the noose."[40] Thus, we find a potent mix of old and new themes combined in mutually reinforcing ways: the initial Islamic conquests, harsh Islamic punishments, and "Islamic terrorism."

Given the timing of my interviews, which began the month after the July 2005 bombings, it is perhaps not surprising that the interviewees felt that the theme of terrorism was somehow present even if it was not verbally expressed; several commented that their families expected them to explain or defend so-called Islamic terrorism or political extremism. One woman said that, since 7/7, "People look at you like you are a terrorist. As soon as they see your head covering, they think you're going to blow them up." Another commented on an experience of being stared at by both customers and staff in a bank: "I was so scared . . . I actually felt that they were feeling I was a terrorist or something." Such experiences were more common immediately following the July 2005 London subway bombings, but most said that the sense of hostility had subsided somewhat fairly soon afterward. One woman said that, after the bombings, she had felt uncomfortable at work when her colleagues were discussing the event. When a non-Muslim colleague had mentioned that she was scared to take the subway, this convert had said that she, too, was scared: "They looked at me in surprise—to see that I felt the same way that they did."[41]

At times, the theme of violence is linked to the hijab. As Farhia Thomas of the Muslim Women's Resource Centre in Glasgow points out, describing reactions that she and her hijab-wearing friends encounter: "We're either oppressed, or we've got Kalashnikovs under our coats."[42] Interestingly, a male interviewee who was himself very discreet about his Muslim identity, preferring a culturally minimalist and theologically oriented version of Islam, echoed the view expressed earlier by Melanie Phillips: "Niqab is the uniform of an al-Qaeda sympathizer . . . When I see women in niqab, I just think they're the sympathizers of the terrorists of today and the breeders and nurturers of the terrorists of tomorrow. You don't wear that unless you're committed to a hard-line version of Islam, which is anathema to me."

Foreignness

Quantitative and qualitative studies of the British press show that although at times British Muslims are seen in a slightly more favorable light and in less stereotypical ways, the lines between British Muslims and Muslims globally are blurred and direct links are frequently made between them.[43] While global Islam outweighs British Islam in terms of quantity of coverage, there is a good deal of osmosis between the two, for example, when British Muslims are seen as "the enemy within" or as a conduit for the penetration of "foreign" values into Britain.[44] The permeability of the boundaries between domestic and foreign Islam/Muslims contributes to the sense of the Muslim presence in and immigration to the UK as threatening. Indeed, both Richardson and Poole found that British Muslims, like other Muslims, are strongly otherized, to the extent that they are excluded from Britishness either because of values or characteristics they are perceived as lacking or because of those that they are perceived as having (namely "Islamicness").[45]

Both the Honeyford and the Rushdie affairs in the 1980s had a strong foreign dimension (pertaining to pupils' extended visits to Pakistan and Khomeini's so-called *fatwa*, respectively), and with the rising specter of "Islamic fundamentalism" and then "Islamic terrorism" in the 1990s, specific connections were made between events abroad and the infiltration of Islamists into Britain (bringing right-wing criticism of Britain's relatively liberal immigration and asylum policies). The link between foreignness and violence is made even more explicit in stock images of cartoonists who, in recent years, have depicted an enemy who resembles bin Laden—complete with beard, turban, robes, Kalashnikov, and hooked nose.[46] Bin Laden is of course just one of a number of obligingly foreign-seeming and bellicose "folk devils," including Abu Hamza and Omar Bakri Mohammed.

As indicated earlier, a major motif in Muslims' perceived foreignness is their allegedly alien culture and values. A certain emphasis on education in press coverage of Muslims, especially in the 1990s, arose from the recognition of the key role that education plays in transmitting cultural values and social norms to the younger generation.[47] This strand of discourse resonates with Huntington's famous "clash of civilizations" thesis. In much anti-Muslim rhetoric, exclusion of Muslims goes beyond the national context; as Miles and Brown observe, "the difference which is imputed to Muslims is not just cultural but civilizational."[48] Poole reports that Islamic cultural practices are seen as "restrictive and abhorrent to a modern liberal society," while Richardson observes the centrality and dominance of the idea that Muslims are "barbarians in need of (Our) civilisation."[49] Cultural difference is predominantly seen as "cultural deviance" and increasingly as a cultural threat.[50] Thus, Samuel Brittain of the *Financial Times* contends that "Islamist militancy is a self-confessed threat to the values, not merely of the United States, but of the European Enlightenment: to the preference for life over death, to peace, rationality, science and the humane treatment of our fellow men, not to mention fellow women. It is a reassertion of blind, cruel faith over reason."[51] As seen earlier, attitudes about gender are framed as a particularly prominent part of Muslims' alternative cultural values.

Like violence, foreignness is often linked with the hijab. Franks observes that the wearing of the headscarf can be seen as "very unBritish"; when one white Muslim woman wearing a headscarf was asked by a friendly older woman on a train where she was from, she "felt almost obliged to claim to be foreign." As Franks points out, white Muslims (the most visible of whom are hijab-wearing women) are sometimes seen as "race-traitors" by white supremacists.[52] For my interviewees, family reaction was sometimes exacerbated by the sense that the son or, more likely, the daughter was adopting a "foreign" culture. Some of the comments received by the female interviewees indicated that they were being perceived as foreigners; one white English woman was told to "go back to [her] tent" and referred to as a "bloody Arab," while a mixed-race woman was told to "go back to [her] own country." An Afro-Caribbean woman said that other Afro-Caribbean people did not see her as "one of them" but "just as a refugee or someone who's just come over; she's 'other.'"

The assumption of foreignness was not always accompanied by hostility. A rather less pernicious experience of women wearing hijab was that of being spoken to slowly as if they did not speak or understand English very well (and subsequently of encountering a shocked reaction when they answered in an English/Welsh/Irish/Scottish accent). One female interviewee said this on the subject of adopting the hijab: "You became an ethnic minority . . . not that many comments but odd looks and also people treating you like you're stupid," adding: "I kind of miss those days because now you get treated like you're evil."

Conclusions

What emerged from the grassroots interview material (as opposed to newspaper coverage, which places more emphasis on politics and, correspondingly, violence) was the predominance of issues related to gender. For non-Muslims in contemporary Britain and no doubt elsewhere, it seems to be issues related to gender and sexuality rather than religious concerns in the narrower sense that epitomize Islam's otherness; no doubt this is because Islamic teachings on male-female relations are highly distinctive when set against the norms of contemporary mainstream Western society. The hijab provides a visual stimulus and seems to act as a lightning rod for feelings of hostility, to the extent that it even becomes associated in some cases with violence and terrorism, as indicated earlier. While at certain times and places the veil has been constructed as exotic and sensual, in contemporary, highly sexualized Western societies, it may be resented for its perceived repression of sexuality.

The various issues that are commonly raised by the discourse around the veil in contemporary Britain—the subjugation of women, the insertion of religion into the public sphere, together with the removal of sexuality from that same public sphere (in both cases going against the grain of mainstream society)—all relate to a broader theme, that of the alleged dichotomy between the veil and modernity. Blatant religiosity itself is seen as offensive, the more so when the religion in question espouses values that are seen as belonging to a bygone age (as seen in the accusations of betrayal of the feminist cause). This is particularly highlighted in the case of converts, who cannot simply be dismissed as having an "exotic" or a foreign culture.

Repeated references to the violence, barbarity, and cruelty of the other clearly fulfils the function of distancing these undesirable traits from the self, which can then be seen as decent, peace loving, just, humane, and promoting human rights. The treatment of the theme of violence is quite closely linked to contemporary global political events; while the Iraq War did not have the same kind of impact as 9/11 or 7/7, it nevertheless raised questions about Muslims' loyalty (notwithstanding widespread opposition to the war among non-Muslim British people). Werbner suggests that the Muslim as "religious fanatic" or as "violent terrorist" is "the folk devil *par excellence* of a post-modern age."[53]

The theme of foreignness fulfils the overriding function of otherization, polarizing categories of humanity into "us" and "them." As Poole observes, "to exoticise and render the internal Other inherently different, if not foreign, allows the Other to be managed, and promotes a sense of national identity at the Other's expense."[54] She concludes that such representations are used to justify social and aggressive policies to manage Muslims worldwide.[55] Given that Islamophobia can be seen as a form of cultural racism, it is perhaps ironic that while in previous decades media images were of Arabs (especially in the 1970s) or Iranian mullahs and ayatollahs (especially in the 1980s), the "Islamic terrorist" of the past decade or two is comparatively less racialized.

In conclusion, a significant factor in understanding Islamophobia is the seemingly unusual capacity of Muslims/Islam to resist—in terms of culture, moral values, and religiosity—Western universalistic aspirations; Islam appears to challenge prevailing intellectual trends of relativism and pluralism. The rapid changes brought about by globalization, including increasing pluralization and shifts in the international political order, contribute to a feeling of insecurity. For Britain in particular, the end of empire, the nation's gradual diminution as a world power, its involvement in Europe, migration, and regional devolution have all added to the sense of uncertainty.[56] At such times, the creation of "folk devils" onto which one can project one's own "shadow side" (unwanted or unacknowledged traits) is especially appealing. The representation of Muslims as barbaric, cruel, irrational, backward, repressive of women, irredeemably alien, and other goes hand in hand with a view of the self—whether it be the West, Europe, or Britain—which is modern, progressive, rational, civilized, humane, and liberal. The shadow side may also include the past self. Referring to Western civilization's prolonged struggle to overturn the domination of the church, Werbner observes that, in facing Islam, Europe in some sense faces its own past: "Islam evokes the specter of puritanical Christianity, a moral crusade, an attack on permissive society."[57] Reactions to the hijab bring this out particularly clearly: the subjugation of women, the covering of women's bodies, and the restrictions on sexuality or maybe just old-fashioned "family values," whereby the wife takes care of home and husband, all conjure up a past that for some people is still a living memory. The "threat" of Islam is perhaps all the greater because it conjures up such a recent past.[58]

NOTES

An expanded version of this chapter appears in *Studies in Contemporary Islam* 10 (2008): 4–44. That article includes critical discussion of Islamophobia as both a term and a concept, which space does not permit here.

1. Edward Said, *Orientalism* (New York: Pantheon, 1978).

2. Bryan Turner, "Orientalism, or the Politics of the Text," in Hastings Donnan, ed., *Interpreting Islam* (London: Sage, 2002), 27–29.

3. While the general findings of that research were written up in my book *British Muslim Converts: Choosing Alternative Lives* (Oxford: Oneworld, 2008), the issue of discrimination was touched on only briefly.

4. Norman Daniel, *Islam and the West: The Making of an Image*, rev. ed. (Oxford: Oneworld, 1997), 302.

5. See, for example, Maxime Rodinson, *Europe and the Mystique of Islam*, new ed., trans. Roger Veinus (New York: Tauris, 2002), 59.

6. Albert Hourani, *Arabic Thought in the Liberal Age: 1798–1939* (New York: Cambridge University Press, 1983), 120–21.

7. Lila Abu-Lughod, "Do Muslim Women Really Need Saving? Anthropological Reflections on Cultural Relativism and Its Others," *American Anthropologist* 104 (2002): 783–90.

8. Kate Zebiri, *Muslims and Christians Face to Face* (Oxford: Oneworld, 1997), 188.

9. Fred Halliday, *Islam and the Myth of Confrontation: Religion and Politics in the Middle East*, 2d ed. (New York: Tauris, 2003), 180.

10. Ibid., 182.

11. Elizabeth Poole, *Reporting Islam: Media Representations of British Muslims* (New York: Tauris, 2002), 240, 250.

12. *The Search for Common Ground: Muslims, Non-Muslims, and the UK Media* (London: Greater London Authority, 2007), xiii.

13. Ibid., 18.

14. Ibid., 30.

15. Ibid., 103.

16. John E. Richardson, *(Mis)representing Islam: The Racism and Rhetoric of British Broadsheet Newspapers* (Philadelphia: Benjamins, 2004). Poole has also published a follow-up article dealing with more recent developments: "The Effects of September 11 and the War in Iraq on British Newspaper Coverage," in *Muslims and the News Media*, ed. Elizabeth Poole and John E. Richardson, 89–102 (New York: Tauris, 2006).

17. Myfanwy Franks, "Crossing the Borders of Whiteness? White Muslim Women Who Wear the *Hijab* in Britain Today," *Ethnic and Racial Studies* 23 (2000): 926.

18. Ibid., 922.

19. Ibid., 918.

20. Seven out of the thirty interviews were conducted by my research assistant, Aisha Masterton.

21. The exception was a woman who was brought up in an English-speaking country and had spent nearly all of her adult life in Britain.

22. Interviewee numbers were too small to enable me to discern any significant regional differences in experiences of hostility; however, several of the London-based interviewees expressed a positive appreciation of London's diversity and multicultural ethos.

23. See Yahya Birt, "Lies, Damn Lies, Statistics, and Conversion!" *Q-News*, no. 350 (October 2002).

24. Maha al-Qwidi's doctoral thesis found that all twenty men in her sample dressed in European style: "Understanding the Stages of Conversion to Islam: The Voice of British Converts" (University of Leeds, 2002), 210; similarly, in Ali Köse's study of conversion to Islam in Britain, only three out of fifty men radically changed their dress: *Conversion to Islam: A Study of Native British Converts* (London: Kegan Paul International, 1996), 131.

25. In addition, three of the men wore Islamic dress on an occasional basis, for example at the mosque or Islamic events or when in a Muslim country.

26. Tariq Modood, *Multicultural Politics: Racism, Ethnicity, and Muslims in Britain* (Edinburgh: Edinburgh University Press, 2005), 41–42.

27. In a broad sense hijab is used (among other things) to denote the female dress code prescribed in classical Islamic law, usually understood as covering everything except the face and hands. The word is also often used to mean "headscarf."

28. In December 2003 the European Directive on Employment outlawed religious discrimination in the workplace.

29. In late 2006, heated public debate followed comments by Jack Straw (then leader of the House of Commons) and then prime minister Tony Blair that strongly implied that the *niqab* (face veil) represented an obstacle to the integration of British Muslims.

30. Poole, *Reporting Islam*, 255.

31. Runnymede Trust, *Islamophobia: A Challenge to Us All* (London: Runnymede Trust, 1997), 28.

32. Richardson, *(Mis)Representing Islam*, 91.

33. *Search for Common Ground*, 13.

34. Ibid., 14. Ironically, she hereby reproduces the male-dominated Islamic discourse on woman as *fitna* (temptation), ignoring the female-dominated discourse on hijab as liberation.

35. Katherine Bullock, *Rethinking Muslim Women and the Veil: Challenging Historical and Modern Stereotypes* (Herndon: International Institute of Islamic Thought, 2002), xv.

36. Franks, "Crossing the Borders of Whiteness?" 920.

37. Poole, "Effects of September 11," 102.

38. Runnymede Trust, *Islamophobia: A Challenge to Us All*, 26.

39. See http://www.bintjbeil.com/E/news/040104_kilroysilk.html (accessed June 6, 2009).

40. Brian Sewell, "A Noose around the Globe," *Evening Standard* (Oct. 22, 2002).

41. A few weeks after the bombings, a female English convert who assisted me in my research on British converts was accosted in the street by a man shouting

"Muslims are murderers!" This confrontation was actually shown on *Newsnight* on Aug. 3, 2005. Aisha Masterton had been walking along the road talking to the *Newsnight* interviewer with the cameras rolling when the incident took place.

42. See http://www.nujglasgow.org.uk/understandingislam.html (accessed Nov. 11, 2006).

43. See, for example, Poole, *Reporting Islam*, 98.

44. Poole, "Effects of September 11," 96.

45. See Richardson, *(Mis)Representing Islam*, 152, and Poole, *Reporting Islam*, 249, 259.

46. Runnymede Trust, *Islamophobia: Issues, Challenges, and Action* (London: Runnymede Trust, 2004), 17. The report explains that this enemy is depicted not just as evil and threatening but also as "stupid, naïve, unsophisticated, unscientific, primitive, a figure of fun."

47. Richardson, *(Mis)Representing Islam*, 137.

48. Robert Miles and Malcolm D. Brown, *Racism*, 2d ed. (New York: Routledge, 2003), 164.

49. Poole, "Effects of September 11," 99; Richardson, *(Mis)Representing Islam*, 230.

50. Richardson, *(Mis)Representing Islam*, 232.

51. Cited in Runnymede Trust, *Islamophobia: Issues, Challenges, and Action*, 11.

52. Franks, "Crossing the Borders of Whiteness?" 923–24.

53. Pnina Werbner, "Islamophobia: Incitement to Religious Hatred—Legislating for a New Fear?" *Anthropology Today* 21 (February 2005): 8. Werbner explains this with reference to the fact that this particular folk devil negates the impulses of "consumption and individual self-gratification," which are celebrated in Western societies today.

54. Poole, *Reporting Islam*, 251.

55. Poole, "Effects of September 11," 101.

56. For further details, see Commission on the Future of Multi-Ethnic Britain, *The Future of Multi-Ethnic Britain* (London: Profile, 2000).

57. Werbner, "Islamophobia," 8.

58. As Werbner comments, it is not only *difference* that is threatening in the other but also *resemblance*. Werbner quotes Julia Kristeva: "[T]he Other, the alien producing animosity and irritation, is in fact my own unconscious, the return of the repressed" ("Islamophobia," 8).

II

From Muhammad to Obama: Caricatures, Cartoons, and Stereotypes of Muslims

Peter Gottschalk and Gabriel Greenberg

"It wasn't meant to insult or hurt anybody's feelings," said the editor in light of the uproar about his publication's cartoon caricatures. Although the comment could as likely have been spoken by David Remnick of the *New Yorker*, referring to his magazine's cover cartoon depicting Barack and Michelle Obama as terrorists, the words are those of Fleming Rose of *Jyllands-Posten* as he responded to the outrage stirred up by caricatures of the Prophet Muhammad, published in his newspaper. While in each case the images in question relied on the notoriously contentious art of political cartooning to describe both an individual and his supposed relation to an imagined Islam, the controversies each caricature elicited differed in ways that pointedly demonstrate how Islamophobic stereotypes inform Americans' interpretations of Muslim behavior. A brief comparison of the two controversies offers an insight into the dynamics of both Islamophobia and editorial cartoons. A lengthier reflection on the history and themes of Islamophobic sentiment in the United States will demonstrate how these dynamics have both changed and persisted over the past half century.

Judging by Two Standards

In 2006, Muslims around the world decried the satirical cartoons of Muhammad that Rose had commissioned for his newspaper in the previous year, most of which maligned the Muslim prophet. American news organizations focused on the response of a violent minority, preferring to broadcast images of the few occasions of unwarranted violence rather than the more numerous instances of peaceful protest in various corners of the world. In the United States, as in Europe, many commentators declared that the controversy (not just the destruction) was further evidence that Muslims—if not Islam itself—sought to stifle "freedom of expression," in this case because of prohibitions against depicting the religion's founder. Indeed, Rose originally commissioned the images in response to what he recognized as selective self-censorship after hearing about a comedian who dared to urinate on a Bible but not a Quran in his performance, as well as the disinclination of artists to portray Muhammad for a forthcoming children's book.[1] The controversy originated, then, in a provocative act meant to highlight the presumably exceptional sensitivity of Muslims, which in turn seemed to manifest during the subsequent destructive demonstrations upon which much of the news media exclusively focused. Yet, only two years later, the same news agencies offered very different interpretations of protests against a more recent Muslim caricature.

The cover of the July 21, 2008, edition of the *New Yorker* displayed a cartoon lampooning the persistent rumors and allegations that presidential hopeful Barack Obama and his wife, Michelle, were closet terrorists, with Islamic ties to boot. The cover depicts the two bumping fists, he dressed in turban, sandals, and long gown and she in fatigues, rifle, and gun belt. Above the fireplace, in which a U.S. flag burns, a portrait of Osama bin Laden gazes upon them enthusiastically. Many in the intended audience mistook artist Barry Blitt's attempted *satirization* of the slander as an *endorsement* of the slander, and a storm of complaint ensued. Some *New Yorker* readers threatened to cancel their subscriptions, while various Obama supporters cried foul. Meanwhile, numerous journalists and columnists criticized the image, and even John McCain, engaged in his own efforts to cast shadows of suspicion on his competitor, felt compelled by the public protest to deem it "totally inappropriate." Once again a publication had provoked an outcry (albeit entirely peaceful) through a depiction of Islam and a prominent personality. Yet, in contrast to the anxious interpretations by Americans and Europeans that the Muslim protests in 2006 sought to squelch free speech, no one in 2008 appeared concerned that condemnations of the Obama cartoon would imperil freedoms of expression. Why? Two issues stand at the heart of the different responses to these two incidents: the delicacy of satire and the pervasiveness of Islamophobia.

Political cartoons have both delighted and infuriated viewers since their inception. A political cartoon works only by successfully managing a meager economy of words and images. This thrift in content allows for a forceful simplicity in expression; this, however, increases the possibility of misinterpretation. Some students at George Washington University had an unwitting education in the dynamics of satiric art when, in 2007, they attempted to lampoon a campus program on "Islamofascism." They used posters that depicted a stereotypical Muslim man and various Islamophobic sentiments under the declaration "Hate Muslims? So do we!!!" Unfortunately, the posters failed to provide a clear enough signal of their satirical intent, and, thus, some campus members confused this mockery of stereotyping as hate speech. To their credit, the responsible students immediately owned up to the act.

A similar failure occurred in crafting the *New Yorker* cover. Although most readers understood that the cartoon *intended* to be satire, its failure to adequately declare itself allowed it to be confused for something else: a reiteration of the very slurs it sought to criticize. The magazine's editor recognized this failure as he defended the image in an interview, when he explained that "the title tries to make sure" of the clarity of the image.[2] Indeed, this title, "The Politics of Fear," does neatly frame the artist's intention. However, the editor put the cartoon on the cover without it and included the title only inside the magazine, where few readers saw it. Subsequently, many were left without enough information to confidently understand the artist's message.

No such misunderstanding accompanied the reception of the caricatures of Muhammad in *Jyllands-Posten*. Although much of the U.S. news coverage claimed—and continues to claim—that the outrage was due to Islamic prohibitions against visual depictions of the Prophet, in fact most Muslims protested the intentional derision of Muhammad found among most of the twelve images commissioned by Rose. Globally, Muslims read the satiric messages quite clearly. The image that garnered particular infamy, drawn by Kurt Westergaard, depicted the Prophet with a bomb for a turban on which is inscribed the *shahada*, or Islamic proclamation of faith. Another portrayed Muhammad aggressively posturing with a scimitar while guarding two *burqa*-clad women. The direct simplicity of these portrayals allowed for a seemingly universal intelligibility of this political art.

Nonetheless, foibles of editorial cartooning explain only part of the difference between mainstream Americans' perceptions of the *New Yorker* and *Jyllands-Posten* controversies. The other concerned who did the protesting. When Obama supporters denounced the cover art, American audiences could view them as rising to the defense of a candidate who had endured slander based on his race and religion. This made sense relative to the narrative of Obama the underdog, facing down centuries-old racism in his bid for the nation's highest office. However, when Muslims defended Muhammad, Americans tended to view them as acting according to their inherent reactionary and intolerant nature. Of course, some Muslims responded to the Danish cartoon controversy with unjustifiable violence, but the fact that the media focused on these isolated cases despite the overwhelmingly peaceful nature of most demonstrations evidences how firmly a narrative of violence among stereotypically intolerant Muslims is lodged in the collective American psyche. Few commentators, if any, offered to draw parallels between the 2006 Muslim outcry and earlier Christian protests against depictions of Jesus by director Martin Scorsese in *Last Temptation of Christ* and by artist Andres Sarrano in his "Piss Christ." Moreover, no one seemed to protest the decision of *Jyllans-Posten* senior editors to censure Rose's efforts to publish Iranian cartoons about the Holocaust. Instead, the Muslims' declamations were depicted as examples of an overall Islamic intolerance, in this case driven by an ancient proscription against portraiture, which in turn seemed to threaten artistic and editorial expression.

In the United States, whereas responses to the Danish cartoon controversy reflected Americans' Islamophobia by misinterpreting Muslim behavior, the larger issues surrounding the *New Yorker* cover debate revealed it in another manner. "The politics of fear" that the image attempted to criticize revolved around the allegation that Obama was Muslim. The artist of the cover recognized that being labeled "Muslim" in America amounts to slander because of its attendant associations with terrorism, anti-Americanism, and essential otherness. Indeed, neither the Obama election camp in its strenuous effort to refute allegations of the candidate's Muslim upbringing nor any prominent public personality sought to respond to these allegations by reminding the public of the legal right of an elected representative to practice any or no religion, including Islam. General Colin Powell's October 2008 declaration of support for Obama endorsed not only the candidate but also American Muslims. His comments offered the exception that proved the rule: that being identified as Muslim in the United States runs the strong risk of being stereotyped in a manner quite removed from any notion of the American norm. Through a brief investigation of political cartoons spanning the past five decades, we can better understand how they manifest and reassert antithetic stereotypes of Muslims.

From Caricature to Stereotype

In February 2007 political cartoonist Paul Conrad drew an image of a man wearing a *gutra* (a cotton headscarf), holding a poppy, and saying "Allah Akbar" (figure 11.1). He apparently intended to lampoon the dubious religiosity of the

Taliban for its support in the cultivation of Afghan opium. However, Afghans do not wear *gutras*. By confusing (and conflating) Afghans with Arabs and underscoring the alleged Islamic justification of poppy cultivation, Conrad neatly demonstrated how Islamophobia leads to a simplification among Americans in their view of the world's more than one billion Muslims to a single generalization characterized by Arabs, the Middle East, and—most prominently of all—threats to the West. When confronted by those who criticize their depictions of Muslims, many political cartoonists respond that they expose Muslims to the same method of critique they level against all whom they draw—American and foreign, Muslim and non-Muslim. Indeed, editorial cartoons work by combining humor, criticism, and caricature, and no one, they argue, should be beyond their attention. Yet, such arguments miss what this cartoon demonstrates: Due to Islamophobia, caricatures of Muslims too often slip into stereotypes of Islam.

FIGURE 11.1. "Allah Akbar" © Tribune Media Services, Inc. All Rights Reserved. Reprinted with permission.

TABLE II.I.

	Extreme of Too Little	Norm of the Middle Ground	Extreme of Too Much
religion	atheism	secularism	political religion
men	effeminate passivity	properly masculine	masculine rage
women	scantily clothed object of desire	clothed according to choice	entirely covered object of oppression
morality	hedonistic	balanced	puritanical

Islamophobia is particularly pernicious because, like sexism, racism, and homophobia, the fear of Islam has become normalized within American and other Western cultures. In other words, news organizations, entertainment businesses, political discourse, and everyday conversations of individuals express anxiety about Islam by using conclusions so taken for granted that they become truisms—neither needing substantiation nor likely to be challenged. Political cartoons, in particular, demonstrate quite vividly the Islamophobia that has been alternately latent and manifest in the United States for more than two centuries. By distinguishing between caricatures and stereotypes in political cartoons one can better understand the negative and unwitting role Muslims play in defining the American norm.

Americans often attempt to characterize their behavior, beliefs, and values as the "norm" by defining these as the middle ground between the extremes of too little and too much. So, in terms of religion and the state, most Americans tend to see the secularism of the United States as normal relative to, on one hand, the purported atheism of communists and, on the other, the political agenda of some Islamists. (Of course, many American Christians would prefer another norm, one that rescinds the supposed godlessness of secular humanism and establishes the Christian nation that they claim the country's founders intended.) In any case, over the past five decades Americans have viewed Muslims as variously typifying one and then the other extreme that negatively defines their conception of what is normal.

As table II.I shows, this normalcy involves expectations of the masculinity of men, the clothing of women, and the morality of society. The descriptions of the cartoons that follow demonstrate that, despite the shifts in how Muslims have been portrayed since the 1950s, they have tended to be marginalized on one extreme or the other of the American norm.

Men: Between Effeminateness and Rage

In the 1950s and 1960s, the only predominantly Muslim area of the world that garnered much attention from American editorial cartoonists was the Middle East. However, cartoonists of this period tended not to depict Middle Easterners qua Muslims but rather as primarily Arabs. Nevertheless, historical evidence attests to the long association Americans have made between Arabs and Islam. It remained only a matter of time before shifting circumstances provoked them to emphasize the Muslim identity of certain Middle Easterners rather than their Arabness. The following images, therefore, focus on portrayals of Arabs with the understanding that the conclusions Americans drew about Arabs implicitly inhered to their identification as Muslims as well.

Arabs were often personified in the body of a woman. In one contemporary cartoon, a Soviet officer posing as a vacuum cleaner salesman bangs on a house door labeled "Middle East." A scantily clad woman answers innocently and is soon sucked into the machine (figure 11.2). The femininity of this Arab woman, familiar to Americans from Orientalist representations of diaphanously clad harem inmates, contrasts with the gruff masculinity of the devious officer serving as a symbol of the Soviet Union.

DEMONSTRATION ON FILLING A VACUUM

STAMPONE, *THE ARMY TIMES*

FIGURE 11.2. "Demonstration on Filling a Vacuum." John R. Stampone. *Army Times.* 1956.

Another cartoon from this period again uses a vulnerable woman to signify all Arabs, though this time the woman makes the best of her helpless position. As the masculine figures labeled "France" and "USSR" molest her, she picks the pockets of these Cold War antagonists. Here we see the distinction between caricature and symbol. The cartoonist had systematically exaggerated the facial features of former prime minister Pompidou of France and former premier Brezhnev of the Soviet Union so as to make them immediately recognizable to the reader. In contrast, Arab men and women are symbolized by a hapless female. Also, the cartoon's title, "Arms for the Love of Allah," casually associates Arabs with Islam—an association the cartoonist must have expected his audience to share—although the political situation to which the cartoon alludes appears devoid of Islamic connotations.

The representation of Muslim men as effeminate takes a more strident turn in a 1959 image in which president Nasser of Egypt becomes Cleopatra, who receives the fawning attention of the United States and the Soviet Union (figure 11.3). Here the distinction between symbol and caricature becomes more pronounced as Uncle Sam symbolizes the United States, a caricature of

Cleopatra

Warren King. *Daily News* (New York). 1959.

FIGURE 11.3. "Cleopatra" © New York Daily News, L.P. Used with permission.

premier Khrushchev represents the Soviets, and a caricature of Nasser's face is married to a body intending to represent his political seductiveness.

An important shift in representations of Arabs occurred beginning with OPEC's 1973 oil embargo of the United States and some of its allies. Abruptly, cartoon Arabs shed their effeminateness for an angry masculinity. Cartoonists now used male figures to represent groups of Arabs, commonly arming them with knives, guns, cannon (figure 11.4), or that pervasive symbol of Arab/

BIG GUN

FIGURE 11.4. "Big Gun." Copyright by Bill Mauldin, 1973. Courtesy of Bill Mauldin Estate LLC.

Muslim militancy, the scimitar (figure 11.5). Scimitar sizes became outlandish in proportion to the claims made as to the Arabs' purported ambitions to control or bleed the world. One cartoon from the period depicts a stereotypical Arab man in beard and *gutra*, wielding in one hand an enormous scimitar with which he has stuck a bleeding globe held in the other.

Yet some cartoons—however few—resisted marginalizing Arabs. In notable contrast to the previous two examples, which emphasized the distinctive violence of Arabs who used their so-called oil weapon, another cartoon argued the similarity of capitalism shared among Americans and OPEC members (including the non-Arab Venezuela). It depicted an agitated Uncle Sam complaining to an Arab and a Venezuelan that, in light of their reduction of oil production to inflate prices, "You're like a bunch of . . . of . . . of . . . CAPITALISTS!" In sharp contrast to most of the cartoons discussed so far, this one included Arabs within the norm—in this case, the norm of capitalism—instead of using them as a negative example to define the norm from which they seemingly excluded themselves.

Neal von Hedemann, 1974.

FIGURE 11.5. "Touché . . . and Touché again!" Neal Von Hedemann © King Features Syndicate

Several years later, cartoonists commenting on the Iranian Revolution and the subsequent hostage situation perpetuated the images of male rage, though this time—for obvious reasons—with a certain shift in noting the Islamic character of those critiqued. One image placed a caricature of the Ayatollah Khomeini abreast the four horsemen of the Apocalypse, sharing the wide-eyed aggressiveness of his fellow warrior-like scourges while lofting a scimitar.

Of course, we would not expect anything but the most negative depiction of those men responsible for the 9/11 hijackings. That a cartoonist represented one in hell unpersuasively pleading his case before a bemused devil does not surprise us (figure 11.6). However, his visage should. The turban and raggedy beard of the cartoon hijacker hardly matched the images of the alleged terrorists in the photographs run by newspapers, showing each as bare headed well kempt and with trimmed facial hair on those few who had any. Clearly, the cartoonist portrayed the qualities he anticipated his audience would have in their mind's eye of a Muslim's appearance. Because he did not systematically exaggerate the physical features of any specific individual— as we saw in the caricatures of Nasser and Khrushchev—the cartoonist clearly drew on the

FIGURE 11.6. "There's been some sort of mix-up . . ." Glenn McCoy © Belleville News-Democrat. Dist. By Universal Uclick. Reprinted with permission. All rights reserved.

stereotype of the hypermasculine, violent Muslim man. His pronounced nose—a racialized feature of Arabs that occurs repeatedly in cartoons—demonstrated how cartoonists often conflate Arabs and Muslims.

In light of the 1950s' representations of Arabs as a woman, one 2001 cartoon that personified Islam as a group of identically dressed men, most with large beards, indicated how cartoonists shifted their depiction of embodied Muslims from female to male once Muslims changed from being seemingly passive objects of American interest to an active threat to those U.S. concerns. The image showed four similar men, labeled "Islam," mesmerized by the theatrical head of bin Laden, controlled by a hidden devil who declares, "PAY NO ATTENTION TO THE MAN BEHIND THE CURTAIN." Although the cartoonist attempted to differentiate Islam from the phantom bin Laden manipulated by the devil, he nevertheless enforced a stereotyped image of Muslims in his representations of the Muslim masses.

Before turning to the representations of Muslim women, it is useful to mention that previously menacing Muslim men occasionally appear to lapse back into effeminate-ness in moments of defeat, such as those that beleaguered the Taliban in 2001. A variety of cartoons portray Taliban fighters dressed in burqas in a cowardly effort to avoid Coalition forces. This demonstrates that depictions of Muslims are not stagnant and may flip from one extreme to another if circumstances change. However, they seldom suggest that Muslims can be "normal" by American standards.

Women: Between Titillation and Oppression

The depiction of the harem-dwelling victim of the Soviet salesman in the cartoon described earlier demonstrates how Americans have long been exposed to such titillating images of Arab and Muslim women. Popular Orientalist productions, such as Rudolph Valentino's The Sheikh (1921) and the use of harem girls in advertising, all propagated this image, which would be televised weekly with the advent of I Dream of Jeannie in 1965. Yet this would be the zenith of the depiction of Muslim women as objects of Western desire as they would soon slide to the other extreme as objects of Muslim oppression.

While aggressive masculine figures replaced the passive feminine personifications of Arabs and Muslims when OPEC began flexing its economic muscle, the feminine figures that did appear tended no longer to imply sexuality but to become symbolic of oppression. One 1973 cartoon titled "Harem" showed an obese, scheming Arab man grinning lecherously and labeled "OPEC" sitting in front of a dozen identically veiled women identified as "importing nations."

This representation of the captive women of an avaricious Arab man abandons the earlier, sexually appealing overtones of harem life for the oppressive sameness of veiled oppression. It seems that American condemnations of perceived Muslim sexual mores could no longer accommodate the titillations that had previously accompanied them, before changes in the U.S. put into question the position of women there (figure 11.7).

Another cartoon, drawn during the Iranian Revolution, takes this theme even further by depicting an international fashion show in which glamorous women personifying Rome, Paris, and New York stand next to a veiled woman representing Tehran (figure 11.8). Not only does the latter remain faceless under her burqa and hobbled by a ball and chain, but inexplicably she is hunchbacked and obese as well: the very opposite not only of the personifications of Western cities for whom she stands but also of her harem-dwelling sisters in earlier representations. Seemingly, the forbidden beauties of Western male fantasy have turned into an ugly stepsister in the context of an American political nightmare.

Of course, the women's liberation movement of the 1970s in part helped spur these changes. One might expect that along with the long overdue and rising consciousness of the lack of parity between men and women in the United States came a heightened awareness of women in other societies. However, the fact that the shift of cartoon portrayals of Muslim women from objects of fancy to objects of oppression parallels the shift from passivity to

FIGURE 11.7. "Harem." Oliphant © Universal Uclick. Reprinted with permission. All rights reserved.

FIGURE 11.8. "International Fashion." Mike Keefe, The Denver Post & InToon.com.

aggression in depictions of Muslim men can hardly be unconnected to the increasing challenge of Middle Easterners and Iranians to U.S. political and economic interests.

A more recent cartoon attempted a critique of what the cartoonist perceived as the current juxtaposition of women and men in Muslim societies. It depicted a stereotypical Arab man sitting in a chair with his feet across his prostrate wife's back (figure 11.9). While he reads a newspaper with the well-publicized image of an American female soldier holding a leash connected to a prone Iraqi man, she imagines that she holds a leash with her husband at its end. The cartoonist juxtaposed the revelations of torture and degradation at Baghdad's Abu-Ghraib prison with the oppression and denigration of the stereotypical Iraqi wife wearing a facial veil. Indeed, she fantasizes that the mistreatment of the prisoners will be visited upon her similarly stereotyped husband with his turban, scraggly beard, and long nose. Through this fantasy turnabout, the cartoonist suggested that the humiliations practiced by U.S. soldiers paled in comparison with those supposedly meted out by all Iraqi (or perhaps all Arab) husbands.

Again, counterexamples have occasionally appeared and have been increasingly visible as the wars in Afghanistan and especially Iraq have dragged on and lost the certainty of their justifications in the minds of growing

FIGURE 11.9. "Husband-wife imagined role reversal." Glenn McCoy © Belleville News-Democrat. Dist. By Universal Uclick. Reprinted with permission. All rights reserved.

numbers of Americans. Following the 2004 elections, one cartoonist depicted a group, including a woman in hijab, commenting on a Kerry poster (figure 11.10). Each of the three appeared dissimilar, dressed differently, yet shared in the same conversation without distinction. This cartoon successfully portrayed a Muslim participating in political discourse without saying anything that identified her as a Muslim. As we noted in the cartoon about OPEC and capitalism, the depiction of marginalized people as acting like or sharing the values of those purportedly representing the norm undermines stereotypes of difference.

Morality: Between Hedonism and Puritanism

Finally, we consider the delineation of an American norm of morality between the extremes of "too much" and "too little." In one image from the 1950s titled "Reading the Arab Mind," a cartoonist uses a caricature of Nasser to argue for a stereotype of all Arabs. Using a microscope and magnifying glass, scientists examine Nasser's brain, which apparently lacks an adequate morality as it is divided into sections labeled "vengeance," "fanaticism," and "no peace with

FIGURE 11.10. [Kerry] "I'm not sure about his message . . ." By permission of Chip Bok and Creators, Syndicate, Inc.

Israel." The same stereotypical attributes are often ascribed to all Muslims today. Although the caricatured head is Nasser's, the caption leaves no doubt that the conclusion applies to all Arabs. Shockingly, this cartoon bore a near perfect resemblance to an anti-Jewish image from 1950s' France, which also attempted to relate the inherent qualities of a stereotyped people.

The oil crisis of the 1970s and the concomitant rise of Arab purchases of American real estate and business interests compelled many cartoonists to portray Arabs as omnivorous gluttons who threatened to consume the United States. In one caricature of King Faisal of Saudi Arabia that replaces his nose with a gas pump nozzle, we see the implicit racism of Arab stereotyping merge with the definition of Arabs as businessmen. Notably, Faisal also kneels in prayer, demonstrating again that Islam has remained implicit in Americans' stereotypes of Arabs, even in contexts not involving religion.

However, the cartoon that perhaps best depicts how Americans imagine Muslims to inhabit two extremes in their role as America's foil is one situated in a Taliban school. A Taliban schoolteacher expresses his surprise that his young student would hesitate to be aroused by the martyr's reward of seventy beautiful women. The child explains that he has never seen a woman (figure 11.11).

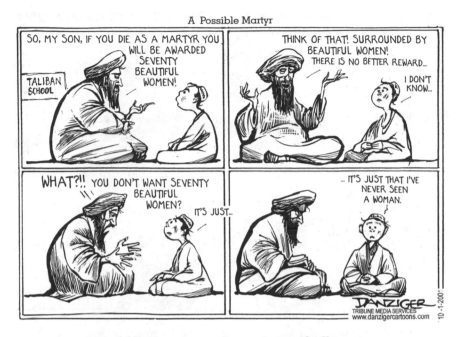

FIGURE 11.11. "A Possible Martyr." 2001. By permission of Jeff Danziger.

According to the cartoonist, the Taliban are both puritanical (in their segregation from women) *and* hedonistic (in their deferred lust for them in the afterlife). Although the cartoonist intended to signify that his critique was aimed at the Taliban, the stereotypical image of the teacher in his long beard, large turban, and robes might prompt some audiences to infer that this is so for all Muslim men.

Our final cartoon demonstrates again the efforts of some cartoonists to challenge stereotypes. Two nearly identical couples (one labeled "U.S.A." and the other "Muslim world") point to images of the crimes committed by members of their community (the electrocuted Abu-Ghraib prisoner and the burning twin towers) and fearfully plead with one another to understand that they are the work of a small minority of extremists (figure 11.12). Although one might argue that the Muslim woman's hijab reflects a stereotype, her husband has a short mustache and beard, which would hardly be out of place on any non-Muslim American man. Most significantly, the cartoonist portrays Americans and Muslims sharing a common ground defined by a mutual fear of those in their communities who practice extreme behaviors.

The trends and dynamics demonstrated in political cartoons have parallels in other American media as well. Motion pictures, television shows, and radio programs all reflect the dynamics described here. However,

FIGURE 11.12. "Remember, it was just a handful of extremists!"

editorial cartoons effectively illustrate how caricatures of individual Muslims have slipped into stereotypes of all Muslims, often in the service of perpetuating a particular image of the purported American norm. That well-publicized controversies about satirical images continue to erupt following the Danish cartoon controversy demonstrates that these portrayals represent more than "just cartoons." Certainly the Dutch government acted on this conclusion when it detained artist Gregorious Nekschot in May 2008 after an investigation of his web-published cartoons mocking Muhammad. Political caricaturing operates as a serious vehicle of expression in the United States—as elsewhere—and is made particularly potent by its simple economy of images and words. As a genre of editorial comment and pictorial art, these cartoons achieve their creators' intentions according to how well they meet their audience's expectations, which are shaped by norms and narratives. For most Americans, Muslims serve as foils of a presumed set of American norms—situated on the extreme of either too little or too much—and popularly prevalent stories about Muslim zealotry, intolerance, and violence serve to illustrate how Muslims supposedly abjure acceptance of U.S. mainstream values while reinforcing the "normality" of non-Muslim Americans.

NOTES

Portions of this chapter draw on material previously published by the authors in *Islamophobia: Making Muslims the Enemy* (2007) and appear with the permission of the publisher, Rowman and Littlefield. The authors wish to acknowledge the inspiration of John Woods in their work.

1. Fleming Rose, "Why I Published Those Cartoons," *Washington Post* (Feb. 19, 2006).

2. Rachel Sklar, "David Remnick on That *New Yorker* Cover: It's Satire, Meant to Target 'Distortions and Misconceptions and Prejudices' about Obama," *Huffington Post* (July 13, 2008), http://www.huffingtonpost.com/2008/07/13/david-remnick-on-emnew-yo_n_112456.html?page=22&show_comment_id=14148595#comment_14148595 (accessed Dec. 6, 2008).

Bibliography

Abbas, Tahir. "After 9/11: British South Asian Muslims, Islamophobia, Multiculturalism, and the State." *American Journal of Islamic Social Sciences* 21, no. 3 (Summer 2004): 26–38.

———. *British Islam: The Road to Radicalism.* New York: Cambridge University Press, 2009.

———. "Images of Islam." *Index on Censorship* 29, no. 5 (2000): 64–68.

———. *Islamic Radicalism and Multicultural Politics: The British Experience.* New York: Routledge, 2010.

———. "Media Capital and the Representation of South Asian Muslims in the British Press: An Ideological Analysis." *Journal of Muslim Minority Affairs* 21, no. 2 (2001): 245–57.

Abraham, Nabeel. "Anti-Arab Racism and Violence in the United States." In *The Development of Arab-American Identity*, ed. Ernest McCarus, 155–214. Ann Arbor: University of Michigan Press, 1994.

AbuKhalil, As'ad. *Bin Laden, Islam, and America's New "War on Terrorism."* New York: Seven Stories, 2002.

Afshar, H. "Can I See Your Hair? Choice, Agency, and Attitudes: The Dilemma of Faith and Feminism for Muslim Women Who Cover." *Ethnic and Racial Studies* 31, no. 2 (2008): 411–27.

———, R. Aitken, and M. Franks. "Feminisms, Islamophobia, and Identities." *Political Studies* 53, no. 2 (2005): 262–83.

Agamben, Giorgio. *State of Exception*, trans Kevin Attell. Chicago: University of Chicago Press, 2005.

Ahmed, Leila. *Women and Gender in Islam: Historical Roots of a Modern Debate.* New Haven: Yale University Press, 1992.

Ajegbo, Keith. *Curriculum Review: Diversity and Citizenship.* London: Department of Education and Skills, 2007.

Akhtar, Shabbir. *Be Careful with Muhammad: Salman Rushdie Affair.* London: Bellew, 1989.

Alexander, Jeffrey C. "Theorizing the 'Modes of Incorporation': Assimilation, Hyphenation, and Multiculturalism as Varieties of Civil Participation." *Sociological Theory* 19, no. 3: 237–49.

Ali, Tariq. *The Clash of Fundamentalisms: Crusades, Jihads, and Modernity.* London: Verso, 2002.

———. "Islamophobia and Its Consequences." In *European Islam: Challenges for Society and Public Policy,* ed. Samir Amghar, Amel Boubekeur, and Michael Emerson, 144-168. Brussels: Center for European Policy Studies, 2007.

Allen, Chris. "Justifying Islamophobia: A Post-9/11 Consideration of the European Union and British Contexts." *American Journal of Islamic Social Sciences* 21, no. 3 (Summer 2004): 1–25.

———, and Jorgen Nielsen. *Summary Report on Islamophobia in the EU after 9/11.* Prepared on behalf of the European Monitoring Centre on Racism and Xenophobia (EUMC). Vienna, 2002.

Alliance of Civilizations. *Report of the High-level Group.* New York: United Nations, 2006.

Allievi, Stefano. "Muslim Minorities in Italy and Their Image in Italian Media." In *Islam in Europe: The Politics of Religion and Community,* ed. S. Vertovec and C. Peach, 211–23. London: Macmillan, 1997.

Almond, Phillip. *Heretic and Hero: Muhammad and the Victorians.* Wiesbaden: Harrassowitz, 1989.

Alsultany, Evelyn. "Selling American Diversity and Muslim American Identity through Nonprofit Advertising Post-9/11." *American Quarterly* 59, no. 3 (2007): 593–622.

Ameli, Saied R., Manzur Elahi, and Arzu Merali. *Social Discrimination: Across the Muslim Divide.* London: Islamic Human Rights Commission, 2004.

Anonymous. *The Lustful Turk.* Reading, UK: A Star Book, 1985.

"Austrian Politician Calls Prophet Muhammad a 'Child Molester'." January 14, 2008. http://www.spiegel.de/international/europe/0,1518,528549,00.html (accessed June 2010).

Asad, Talal. "Multiculturalism and British Identity in the Wake of the Rushdie Affair." *Politics and Society* 18, no. 4 (1990): 455–80.

BBC News. "Oslo's Rooftop Religious Rivalry." (Mar. 30, 2002).

Bauer, Robert A., ed. *The Austrian Solution: International Conflict and Cooperation.* Charlottesville: University Press of Virginia, 1982.

Behdad, Ali. "Critical Historicism." *American Literary History* 20, nos. 1–2 (Summer 2007): 286–99.

Bennett, Clinton. *In Search of Muhammad.* New York: Cassell, 1998.

———. *Victorian Images of Islam.* London: Grey Seal, 1992.

Bennett, W. Lance. *News: The Politics of Illusion,* 4th ed. New York: Addison-Wesley Longman, 2001.

Berthou, Katell. "The Issue of the Voile in the Workplace in France: Unveiling Discrimination." *International Journal of Comparative Labour Law and Industrial Relations* 21, no. 2 (2005): 281–320.

Bischof, Güter, and Pelinka, Anton, eds. *Austria in the New Europe*. London: Transaction, 1993.

Blackledge, Adrian. "The Racialization of Language in British Political Discourse." *Critical Discourse Studies* 3, no. 1 (2006): 61–79.

Bloul, Rachel. "Islamophobia and Anti-discrimination Laws: Ethno-religion as a Legal Category in the UK and Australia." Sidney, 2003. http://www.anu.edu.au/NEC/Archive/bloul_paper.pdf.

Bovenkerk, Frank. "Integratie is niet de oplossing." NRC Handelsblad. June 25, 2007. http://www.nrc.nl/nieuwsthema/marokkanen_in_nederland/article1810954.ece/Integratie_is_niet_de_oplossing?service=Print.

———. "Islamophibia in Anne Frank's House: Monitor Racism and Extremism (7th Report)." December 13, 2006. http://www.annefrank.org/content.asp?PID=756&LID=2.

Bowen, John. *Why the French Don't Like Headscarves: Islam, the State, and Public Service*. Princeton: Princeton University Press, 2006.

Bronner, Stephen E. *A Rumor about the Jews: Reflections on Antisemitism and the Protocols of the Learned Elders of Zion*. New York: St. Martin's, 2000.

Buaben, Jabal. *Image of the Prophet Muhammad in the West: A Study of Muir, Margoliouth, and Watt*. Leicester: Islamic Foundation, 1996.

Bulliet, Richard W. *The Case for Islamo-Christian Civilization*. New York: Columbia University Press, 2004.

Bunzl, Matti. *Anti-Semitism and Islamophobia: Hatreds Old and New in Europe*. Chicago: Prickly Paradigm, 2007.

———. "Between Anti-Semitism and Islamophobia: Some Thoughts on the New Europe." *American Ethnologist* 32, no. 4 (November 2005): 499–508.

Bureau of Democracy, Human Rights, and Labor. *2005 Country Report on Human Rights Practices: France* (March 2006).

Byman, Daniel L. "Al-Qaeda as an Adversary: Do We Understand Our Enemy?" *World Politics* 56, no. 1 (2003): 139–63.

Cainkar, Louise. *Homeland Insecurity: The Arab American and Muslim Experience after 9/11*. New York: Russell Sage Foundation, 2009.

———, and Maira Sunaina. "Crossing the Boundaries of Asian and Arab American Studies: Criminalization and Cultural Citizenship of Arab/Muslim/South Asian Americans." *Amerasia Journal* 31, no. 3 (2006): 1–27.

Cesari, Jocelyne. *When Islam and Democracy Meet: Muslims in Europe and in the United States*. New York: Palgrave Macmillan, 2004.

Cesari, Jocelyne, ed. *Muslims in the West after 9/11: Religion, Law, and Politics*. New York: Routledge, 2009.

Choudhury, Tufyal. "Muslims and Discrimination." In *European Islam: Challenges for Society and Public Policy*, ed. Samir Amghar, Amel Boubekeur, and Michael Emerson, 77–106. Brussels: Center for European Policy Studies, 2007.

Cole, David. *Enemy Aliens: Double Standards and Constitutional Freedoms in the War on Terrorism*. New York: New Press, 2003.

Cooke, Miriam. "Islamic Feminism before and after September 11." *Duke Journal of Gender Law and Policy* 227, no. 9 (Summer 2002). http://www.law.duke.

edu/shell/cite.pl?9+Duke+J.+Gender+L.+&+Pol'y+227. Accessed
June 20, 2010.

Council on American-Islamic Relations (CAIR). *American Public Opinion about Islam and Muslims*. Washington, D.C.: Author, 2006.

———. *The Status of Muslim Civil Rights in the United States*, 2007. http://www.cair.com/Portals/0/pdf/2007-Civil-Rights-Report.pdf.

Dabashi, Hamid. "Native Informers and the Making of the American Empire." *Al-Ahram Weekly*, 2006. http://weekly.ahram.org.eg/print/2006/797/special.htm. Accessed Nov. 16, 2006.

Damon, George, Jr. "A Survey of Political Cartoons Dealing with the Middle East." In *Split Vision*, ed. Edmund Ghareeb. Washington, D.C.: American-Arab Affairs Council, 1983.

Daniel, Norman. *Islam and the West: The Making of an Image*. Oxford: Oneworld, 1997. First published 1960 by Edinburgh University Press.

Department of Work and Pensions. Household Below Average Income Series, 2003.

Dinet, Étienne. "L'Orient vu de l'Occident." *Journal of the Royal African Society* 21, no. 84 (July 1922): 347–48.

Driel, Barry van. *Confronting Islamophobia in Educational Practice*. London: Trentham, 2004.

Dunbar-Ortiz, Roxanne. "The Grid of History: Cowboys and Indians." In *Pox Americana: Exposing the American Empire*, ed. John Bellamy Foster and Robert W. McChesney, 31-40. New York: Monthly Review Press, 2004.

Dwyer, Claire, Bindi Shah, and Gurchathen Sanghera. "'From Cricket Lover to Terror Suspect'—Challenging Representations of Young British Muslim Men." *Gender, Place, and Culture* 15, no. 2 (2008): 117–36.

Edwards, Holly. "A Million and One Nights: Orientalism in America, 1870–1930." In *Noble Dreams, Wicked Pleasures: Orientalism in America, 1870–1930*, ed. Holly Edwards, 11–57. Princeton: Princeton University Press, 2000.

Edwards, Holly, ed. *Noble Dreams, Wicked Pleasures: Orientalism in America, 1870–1930*. Princeton: Princeton University Press, 2000.

Elorza, Antonio. "Terrorismo islámico: Las raíces doctrinales." In *El nuevo terrorismo islamista*, ed. Antonio Elorza and Fernando Reinares Nestares. Madrid: Temas de Hoy, 2004.

Erner, Guillaume. *Expliquer l'antisémitisme*. Paris: Presses Universitaires de France, 2005.

Esposito, John. *The Islamic Threat: Myth or Reality?* New York: Oxford University Press, 1999.

European Commission against Racism and Intolerance (ECRI). http://www.coe.int/t/e/human_rights/ecri/1-ecri/2-country-by-country_approach/netherlands/Netherlands%20third%20report%20-%20cri08-3.pdf.

European Monitoring Centre on Racism and Xenophobia (EUMC). *Anti-Islamic Reactions in the EU after the Terrorist Acts against the USA: A Collection of Country Reports from RAXEN National Focal Points*. Vienna, 2001.

———. *Comparative Report on Housing*. 2006.

————. *Muslims in the European Union: Discrimination and Islamophobia*. Vienna, 2006.

————. *Perceptions of Discrimination and Islamophobia: Voices from Members of Muslim Communities in the European Union*. Vienna, 2006.

————. *Reports on Anti-Islamic Reactions within the European Union after the Acts of Terror against the USA*. Vienna, 2002.

————. *The Fight against Antisemitism and Islamophobia: Bringing Communities Together*. Vienna, 2006.

————. *The Impact of 7 July 2005 London Bomb Attacks on Muslim Communities in the EU*. Vienna, 2005.

European Network against Racism (ENAR). Shadow Report. 2007. *Racism in the Netherlands*. http://cms.horus.be/files/99935/mediaarchive/pdf/en/netherlands%20-%20sr%202007.pdf.

European Union Agency for Fundamental Rights (FRA). "Community Cohesion at Local Level: Addressing the Needs of Muslim Communities." 2008. For examples of local initiatives, see http://194.30.12.221/fraWebsite/research/publications/publications_per_year/2008/pub_tr_communitycohesion_08_en.htm.

European Union Monitoring and Advocacy Program (EUMAP). *Muslims in the UK: Policies for Engaged Citizens*. London: Author, 2005.

Ewing, Katherine. *Being and Belonging: Muslims in the United States since 9/11*. New York: Russell Sage Foundation, 2008.

Feichtlbauer, Hubert. *The Austrian Dilemma: An Inquiry into National Socialism and Racism in Austria*, trans. Andrea Smith and Penny Senften. Vienna: Holzhausen, 2001.

Fekete, Liz. *A Suitable Enemy: Racism, Migration, and Islamophobia in Europe*. New York: Palgrave Macmillan, 2009.

Fetzer, Joel S., and J. Christopher Soper. "The Roots of Public Attitudes toward State Accommodation of European Muslims' Religious Practices before and after September 11." *Journal for the Scientific Study of Religion* 42, no. 2 (June 2003): 247–58.

Field, Todd Porter. *The Allure of Empire: Art in the Service of French Imperialism 1798–1836*. Princeton: Princeton University Press, 1998.

Fitzmaurice, John. *Austrian Politics and Society Today: In Defence of Austria*. London: Macmillan, 1991.

Foxman, Abraham H. *Never Again?: The Threat of the New Anti-Semitism*. San Francisco: Harper SanFrancisco, 2003.

Fraser, Nancy. *Justice Interruptus: Critical Reflections on the Postsocialist Condition*. New York: Routledge, 1997.

Furedi, F. *Invitation to Terror: The Expanding Empire of the Unknown*. London: Continuum, 2006.

Gaede, S. D. *When Tolerance Is No Virtue: Political Correctness, Multiculturalism, and the Future of Truth and Justice*. Downers Grove: InterVarsity, 1994.

Gallis, Paul, Kristin Archick, Francis Miko, and Steven Woehrel. *Muslims in Europe: Integration Policies in Selected Countries*. Washington, D.C.: Congressional Research Service, 2005.

Gallup World Poll. "Beyond Multiculturalism and Assimilation." Prepared by Dalia Mogahed. http://media.gallup.com/muslimwestfacts/PDF/londonbrief-full041307.pdf. 2007.

Galster, Ingrid. *Sartre et les juifs: Actes du collique international.* Paris: La Découverte, 2005.

Ganguly, Keya. *States of Exception: Everyday Life and Postcolonial Identity.* Minneapolis: University of Minnesota Press, 2001.

Gereluk, Dianne. "Should Muslim Headscarves Be Banned in French Schools?" *Theory and Research in Education* 3, no. 3 (2005): 259–71.

Gerstenfeld, Manfred, and Shmuel Trigano. *Les habits neufs de l'antisémitisme en Europe.* Paris: Editions Café Noir, 2004.

Gingrich, Andre. "Anthropological Analyses of Islamophobia and Anti-Semitism in Europe." *American Ethnologist* 32, no. 4 (November 2005): 513–15.

Goodrick-Clarke, Nicholas. *The Occult Roots of Nazism: The Ariosophists of Austria and Germany 1890–1935.* Wellingborough, Northamptonshire: Aquarian, 1985.

Gottschalk, Peter, and Gabriel Greenberg. *Islamophobia: Making Muslims the Enemy.* New York: Rowman and Littlefield, 2008.

Goujon, Anne, Vegard Skirbekk, Katrin Fliegenschnee, and Pawel Strzelecki. "New Times, Old Beliefs: Projecting the Future Size of Religions in Austria." In *Vienna Yearbook of Population Research,* 237–70. Vienna: Vienna Institute of Demography, Austrian Academy of Sciences, 2007.

Greene, Molly. *A Shared World: Christians and Muslims in the Early Modern Mediterranean.* Princeton: Princeton University Press, 2000.

Gregory, Derek. *The Colonial Present.* Malden: Blackwell, 2004.

Grosfoguel, Ramon, and Eric Mielants. "The Long-Durée: Entanglement between Islamophobia and Racism in the Modern/Colonial Capitalist/Patriarchal World System." *Human Architecture: Journal of the Sociology of Self-knowledge* 5, no. 1 (Fall 2006): 1–12.

Grunenberg, Sara, and Jaap van Donselaar. "Deradicalisation: Lessons from Germany, Options for the Netherlands?" http://www.annefrank.org/upload/Downloads/Mon7-UK-Ch8.pdf. 2006.

Gunny, Ahmed. *Images of Islam in Eighteenth-century Writings.* London: Grey Seal, 1996.

———. *Perceptions of Islam in European Writings.* Leicester: Islamic Foundation, 2004.

Haddad, Yvonne Yazbek, ed. *Muslims in the West: From Sojourners to Citizens.* New York: Oxford University Press, 2002.

———, and Jane Smith, eds. *Muslim Minorities in the West: Visible and Invisible.* Lanham: Altamira, 2002.

Hafez, Kai, ed. "Images of Islam and the West in German Media: A Reappraisal." In *Mutual Misunderstandings: Muslims and Islam in the European Media, Europe in the Media of Muslim-majority Countries,* ed. Kerem Öktem and Reem Abou-el-Fadl, 28–50. Oxford: European Studies Center, 2009.

———. *Islam and the West in the Mass Media: Fragmented Images in a Globalizing World.* Cresskill: Hampton, 1999.

Halliday, Fred. *Islam and the Myth of Confrontation*. London: Tauris, 1995.

———. "Islamophobia Reconsidered." *Ethnic and Racial Studies* 22, no. 5 (September 1999): 892–902.

Harrison, Malcolm, and Deborah Phillips. *Housing and Black and Minority Ethnic Communities: Review of the Evidence Base*. London: Office of the Deputy Prime Minister, 2003.

Hasan, Asma G. *American Muslims: The New Generation*. New York: Continuum, 2000.

Hastings, Donnan, and Pnina Werbner, eds. *Economy and Culture in Pakistan: Migrants and Cities in a Muslim Society*. London: Macmillan, 1991.

Hewer, Chris. "Schools for Muslims." *Oxford Review of Education* 27, no. 4 (December 2001): 515–27.

Hillenbrand, Carole. *The Crusades: Islamic Perspectives*. London: Routledge, 2000.

Hippler, Jochen, and Andrea Lueg, and Laila Friese, eds. *The Next Threat: Western Perceptions of Islam*. London: Pluto Press with Transnational Institute, 1995.

Hofbauer, Sophie, ed. "The Impact of Immigration on Austria's Society: A Survey of Recent Austrian Migration Research." Austrian contribution to the European pilot study "The Impact of Immigration on Europe's Societies," Vienna, 2008.

Hourani, Albert. *Europe and the Middle East*. London: Macmillan, 1980.

———. *Islam in European Thought*. New York: Cambridge University Press, 1991.

———. *Western Attitudes towards Islam*. Southampton: Southampton University Press, 1974.

Howell, Sally, and Andrew Shryock. "Cracking Down on Diaspora: Arab Detroit and America's 'War on Terror.' " *Anthropological Quarterly* 76, no. 3 (2003): 443–62.

Huntington, Samuel P. *The Clash of Civilizations and the Remaking of World Order*. New York: Simon and Schuster, 1996.

Husain, Ed. *The Islamist*. London: Penguin, 2007.

Hutton, Christopher M. *Race and the Third Reich*. Malden: Polity, 2005.

International Helsinki Federation. *Intolerance and Discrimination against Muslims in the EU: Developments since September 11, 2005*.

International Helsinki Federation. *Report on Intolerance, 2005*.

Irwin, Robert. *For Lust of Knowing: The Orientalists and Their Enemies*. New York: Lane, 2006.

IslamOnline.Net and News Agencies. "Seven German States Back Hijab Ban, Eight Refuse." http://www.islamonline.net/English/News/2003–10/11/article08.shtml.

Jonker, Gerdien, and Valérie Amiraux, eds. *Politics of Visibility: Young Muslims in European Public Spaces*. Bielefeld: Transcript Verlag, 2006.

Kabbani, Rana. *Imperial Fictions: Europe's Myths of Orient*. London, 1994.

Kalin, Ibrahim. "Islam and the West: Deciphering a Contested History," http://www.oxfordislamicstudies.com/Public/focus.html (April 2009).

———. "Roots of Misconception: Euro-American Perceptions of Islam before and after September 11th." In *Islam, Fundamentalism, and the Betrayal of Tradition*, ed. Joseph Lumbard, 143–87. Bloomington, IN.: World Wisdom, 2004.

Kaplan, Amy. "Left Alone with America": The Absence of Empire in the Study of American Culture." In *Cultures of United States Imperialism*, ed. Amy Kaplan and Donald Pease, 3–21. Durham: Duke University Press, 1993.

Keen, Sam. *Faces of the Enemy*. San Francisco: Harper Collins, 1986.

Khattak, Shahin Kuli Khan Khattak. *Islam and the Victorians: Nineteenth-century Perceptions of Muslim Practices and Beliefs*. New York: Tauris, 2008.

Kidd, Thomas S. *American Christians and Islam: Evangelical Culture and Muslims from the Colonial Period to the Age of Terrorism*. Princeton: Princeton University Press, 2009.

Kincheloe, Joe L., and Shirley R. Steinberg, eds. *The Miseducation of the West: How Schools and the Media Distort Our Understanding of the Islamic World*. London: Praeger, 2004.

Klausen, Jytte. *The Cartoons That Shook the World*. Yale: Yale University Press, 2009.

Kohut, Andrew. *America's Image in the World: Findings from the Pew Global Attitudes Project: Testimony to Subcommittee on International Organizations, Human Rights, and Oversight Committee on Foreign Affairs, U.S. House of Representatives*. March 14, 2007. http://pewglobal.org/commentary/display.php?AnalysisID=1019 (October 28, 2009).

———. *Arab and Muslim Perceptions of the United States: Testimony to U.S. House International Relations Committee, Subcommittee on Oversight and Investigations*, November 10, 2005. http://pewresearch.org/pubs/6/arab-and-muslim-percep-tions-of-the-united-states (October 28, 2009).

Krause, Wanda, ed. *Citizenship, Security, and Democracy; Muslim Engagement in the West*. London: Association of Muslim Social Scientists UK and SETA, 2009.

Küçükcan, Talip, and Veyis Güngör, eds. *Turks in Europe: Culture, Identity, Integration*. Amsterdam: Turkevi Research Center, 2009.

Kumar, Deepa. "Islam and Islamophobia." *International Socialist Review* (March–April 2007): 36–45.

Kundnani, Arun. "Islamism and the Roots of Liberal Rage." *Race and Class* 50, no. 2 (2008): 40–68.

———. "Stop and Search: Police Step Up Targeting of Blacks and Asians." Institute of Race Relations (Mar. 26, 2003).

———. *The End of Tolerance: Racism in 21st-century Britain*. London: Pluto, 2007.

Laurence, Jonathan, and Justin Vaisse. *Integrating Islam: Political and Religious Challenges in Contemporary France*. Washington, D.C.: Brookings Institution Press, 2006.

Lechner, Frank J. *The Netherlands: Globalization and National Identity*. New York: Routledge, 2008.

Leonard, Karen. "American Muslims, before and after September 11, 2001." *Economic and Political Weekly* 37, no. 24 (June 15–21, 2002): 2293–97, 2299–2302.

Lindemann, Albert S. *Anti-Semitism before the Holocaust*. New York: Longman, 2000.

Little, Douglas. *American Orientalism: The United States and the Middle East since 1945*. Chapel Hill: University of North Carolina Press, 2002.

Loewenstein, Rudolph. *Psychanalyse de l'antisémitisme*. Paris: Presses Universitaires de France, 2001. First published 1952.

MacCabe, Colin. "Multiculturalism after 7/7." Roundtable convened by Colin MacCabe with Monica Ali et al. *Critical Quarterly* 48, no. 2 (2006): 1–44.

MacDonald, Myra. *Exploring Media Discourse*. London: Hodder Arnold, 2003.

Magdoff, Harry. *Imperialism without Colonies*. New York: Monthly Review Press, 2003.

Maira, Sunaina. *Missing: Youth, Citizenship, and Empire after 9/11*. Durham: Duke University Press, 2009.

Malik, Kenan. "The Islamophobia Myth." *Prospect* 107 (February 2005).

Mamdani, Mahmood. *Good Muslim, Bad Muslim: America, the Cold War, and the Roots of Terror*. New York: Pantheon, 2004.

Manji, Irshad. *The Trouble with Islam: A Muslim's Call for Reform in Her Faith*. Toronto: Random House Canada, 2003.

Maréchal, Brigitte, Felice Dassetto, Jorgen Nielsen, and Stefano Allievi, eds. *Muslims in the Enlarged Europe: Religion and Society*. Leiden: Brill, 2003.

Marranci, Gabriele. "Multiculturalism, Islam, and the Clash of Civilisations Theory: Rethinking Islamophobia." *Culture and Religion* 5, no. 1 (2004): 105–17.

Matar, Nabil. *Turks, Moors, and Englishmen in the Age of Discovery*. New York: Columbia University Press, 1999.

Mazrui, Ali. "Between the Crescent and the Star-spangled Banner: American Muslims and U.S. Foreign Policy." *International Affairs (Royal Institute of International Affairs 1944–)* 72, no. 3, Ethnicity and International Relations (July 1996): 493–506.

Mazzoleni, Gianpietro, Julianne Stewart, and Bruce Horsfield, eds. *The Media and Neo-populism: A Contemporary Analysis*. Westport, CT.: Praeger, 2003.

McAlister, Melani. *Epic Encounters: Culture, Media, and U.S. Interests in the Middle East, 1945–2000*. Berkeley: University of California Press, 2001.

Michelmore, Christina. "Old Pictures in New Frames: Images of Islam and Muslims in Post–World War II American Political Cartoons." *Journal of American and Comparative Cultures* 23 (Winter 2000): 37–50.

Ministry of Justice, Immigration, and Naturalisation Service, IND Information and Analysis Centre (INDIAC). *A Review of Recent Literature on the Impact of Immigration on Dutch Society*, National Contact Point, the Netherlands. The Hague: European Migration Network (EMN), 2005.

Mirza, Munira, Abi Senthilkumaran, and Zein Ja'far. *Living Apart Together: British Muslims and the Paradox of Multiculturalism*. London: Policy Exchange, 2007.

Modood, Tariq. *Multicultural Politics: Racism, Ethnicity, and Muslims in Britain*. Edinburgh: Edinburgh University Press, 2005.

———. "The Place of Muslims in British Secular Multiculturalism." In *Muslim Europe or Euro-Islam: Politics, Culture, and Citizenship in the Age of Globalisation*, eds. N. Alsayyad and M. Castells, 113–30. New York: Lexington, 2002.

Muir, Hugh, and Laura Smith. *Islamophobia: Issues, Challenges, and Action: A Report by the Commission on British Muslims and Islamophobia*. Stoke on Trent: Trentham, 2004.

Naber, Nadine. "The Rules of Forced Engagement: Race, Gender, and the Culture of Fear among Arab Immigrants in San Francisco Post 9-11." *Cultural Dynamics* 18, no. 3 (2006): 235–67.

Ngai, Mai M. *Impossible Subjects: Illegal Aliens and the Making of Modern America*. Princeton: Princeton University Press, 2004.

Nguyen, Tram. *We Are All Suspects Now: Untold Stories from Immigrant Communities after 9/11*. Boston: Beacon, 2005.

Nielsen, Jorgen. *Muslims in Western Europe*. Edinburgh: Edinburgh University Press, 1992.

———, and S. Khasawnih. *Arabs and the West: Mutual Images*. Amman: Jordan University Press, 1998.

Nimer, Mohamed. *Islamophobia and Anti-Americanism: Causes and Remedies*. Beltsville: Amana, 2007.

Nomani, Asra Q. *Standing Alone: An American Woman's Struggle for the Soul of Islam*. San Francisco: Harper San Francisco, 2006.

Norris, Pippa, and Ronald Inglehart. *Sacred and Secular: Religion and Politics Worldwide*. New York: Cambridge University Press, 2004.

Open Society Institute. *British Muslims and Education*, 2005.

———. *Monitoring Minority Protection in the EU: The Situation of Muslims in the UK*, 2002.

Özyürek, Esra. "The Politics of Cultural Unification, Secularism, and the Place of Islam in the New Europe." *American Ethnologist*, 32, no. 4 (November 2005): 509–12.

Parekh, Bhikhu. "Integrating Minorities." In *Race Relations in Britain: A Developing Agenda*, eds. Tessa Blackstone, Bhikhu Parekh, and Peter Sanders, 19–21. London: Routledge, 1998.

Parliamentary Inquiry Committee (Tijdelijke Commissie Onderzoek Integratiebeleid), 5 vols. (2004).

Pease, Donald. "New Perspectives on U.S. Culture and Imperialism." In *Cultures of United States Imperialism*, ed. Amy Kaplan and Donald Pease, 22–37. Durham: Duke University Press, 1993.

Pew Research Center. *The Great Divide: How Westerners and Muslims View Each Other*. Washington, D.C., 2006. http://pewglobal.org/2006/06/22/the-great-divide-how-westerners-and-muslims-view-each-other/.

———. *Pew Global Attitudes Project 2008: Unfavorable Views of Jews and Muslims on the Increase in Europe*. Washington, D.C., 2008. http://pewglobal.org/reports/pdf/262.pdf.

Pick, Hella. *Guilty Victim*. New York: Tauris, 2000.

Poole, Elizabeth. *Reporting Islam: Media Representations of British Muslims*. New York: Tauris/Palgrave Macmillan, 2002.

Poole, Elizabeth., and J. E. Richardson, eds. *Muslims and the News Media*. New York: Tauris, 2006.

Prashad, Vijay. *The Karma of Brown Folk*. Minneapolis: University of Minnesota, 2000.

Prins, Baukje. "Effects of September 11 and the War in Iraq on British Newspaper Coverage." In *Muslims and the News Media*, ed. Elizabeth Poole and John E. Richardson, 89–102. New York: Tauris/Palgrave Macmillan, 2006.

———. *Voorbij de onschuld: Het debat over de multiculturele samenleving*. Amsterdam: Van Gennep, 2004.

———, and John E. Richardson, eds. *Muslims and the News Media*. New York: Tauris/Palgrave Macmillan, 2006.

Ramberg, Ingrid. *Islamophobia and Its Consequences on Young People*. Budapest: Council of Europe, 2006.

Razack, Sherene H. *Casting Out: The Eviction of Muslims from Western Law and Politics*. Toronto: University of Toronto Press, 2008.

Reeves, Minou. *Muhammad in Europe: A Thousand Years of Western Myth-making*. Reading: Garnet, 1999.

Reinharz, Jehuda, eds. *Living with Antisemitism: Modern Jewish Responses*. London: University Press of New England, 1987.

Rendall, Steve, Isabel Macdonald, Veronica Cassidy, and Dina Marguerite Jacir. *Smearcasting: How Islamophobes Spread Fear, Bigotry, and Misinformation*. New York: Fairness and Accuracy in Reporting (FAIR), 2008.

Robin, Corey. *Fear: The History of a Political Idea*. New York: Oxford University Press, 2004.

Rodinson, Maxime. *La fascination de l'Islam*. Paris: La Découverte, 1978.

Rohe, Matthias. *Muslim Minorities and the Law in Europe: Chances and Challenges*. New Delhi: Global Media, 2007.

Román, Ediberto. "Membership Denied: An Outsider's Story of Subordination and Subjugation under U.S. Colonialism." In *Moral Imperialism: A Critical Anthology*, ed. Berta E. Hernández-Truyol, 269–84. New York: New York University Press, 2002.

Rosaldo, Renato. "Cultural Citizenship, Inequality, and Multiculturalism." In *Latino Cultural Citizenship: Claiming Identity, Space, and Rights*, ed. William F. Flores and Rina Benmayor, 27–38. Boston: Beacon, 1997.

Runnymede Trust. *Islamophobia: A Challenge for Us All: Report of the Runnymede Trust Commission on British Muslims and Islamophobia*. London: Author, 1997.

Ruthven, Malise. *A Satanic Affair: Salman Rushdie and the Rage of Islam*. London: Hogarth, 1991.

———. "Islam in the Media." In *Interpreting Islam*, ed. Hastings Donnan, 51-75. London: Sage, 2002.

Said, Edward. *Covering Islam: How the Media and the Experts Determine How We See the Rest of the World*. New York: Pantheon, 1981.

———. *Orientalism*. New York: Pantheon, 1978.

Salaita, Steven. *Anti-Arab Racism in the United States: Where It Comes from and What It Means for Politics Today*. London: Pluto, 2006a.

———. *The Holy Land in Transit: Colonialism and the Quest for Canaan*. Syracuse: Syracuse University Press, 2006b.

Samad, Yunas, and Kasturi Sen. *Islam in the European Union: Transnationalism, Youth, and the War on Terror*. New York: Oxford University Press, 2006.

Sardar, Ziauddin. *Balti Britain: A Journey through the British Asian Experience*. London: Granta, 2008.

Sartre, Jean-Paul. *Anti-Semite and Jew*, trans. George J. Becker. New York: Schocken, 1948.

Savage, Timothy M. "Europe and Islam: Crescent Waxing, Cultures Clashing." *Washington Quarterly* 27, no. 3 (2004): 25–50.

Sayyid, Bobby. *A Fundamental Fear: Eurocentrism and the Emergence of Islamism*. New York: Zed, 1997.

Schatz, Roland, and Christian Klomer. *Muslim Organizations in German TV News—2007/2008: Topic Structure and Tone of Coverage*. Bonn: Media Tenor, 2008.

Scholten, Otto, Nel Ruigrok, Martijn Krijt, Joep Schaper, and Hester Paanakker. *Fitna and the Media: An Investigation of Attention and Role Patterns*. Netherlands: Netherlands News Monitor, 2008. www.nieuwsmonitor.net/d/4/wilders_report_en.pdf.

Schudson, Michael. *The Sociology of News*. New York: Norton, 2003.

Scott, John Wallach. *The Politics of the Veil*. Princeton: Princeton University Press, 2007.

Search for Common Ground. *Changing Course: A New Direction for U.S. Relations with the Muslim World*. Washington, D.C.: Leadership Group of the U.S.–Muslim Engagement Project, Search for Common Ground, 2008.

Sha'ban, Fuad. *Islam and Arabs in Early American Thought: The Roots of Orientalism in America*. Durham, N.C.: Acorn, 1991.

Shaheen, Jack. *Arab and Muslim Stereotyping*. Washington, D.C.: Center for Muslim-Christian Understanding, Georgetown University, 1997.

———. *Guilty: Hollywood's Verdict on Arabs after 9/11*. New York: Olive Branch, 2008.

———. *Reel Bad Arabs: How Hollywood Vilifies a People*. New York: Olive Branch, 2001.

Sibony, Daniel. *L'énigme antisémite*. Paris: Éditions du Seuil, 2004.

Slade, Shelly. "The Image of the Arab in America: Analysis of a Poll on American Attitudes." *Middle East Journal* 35 (Spring 1981): 143–62.

Sniderman, Paul M., Pierangelo Peri, Rui J. P. de Figueiredo Jr., and Thomas Piazza. *The Outsider: Prejudice and Politics in Italy*. Princeton: Princeton University Press, 2002.

Southern, R. W. *Western Views of Islam in the Middle Ages*. Cambridge: Harvard University Press, 1980. First published 1962.

Stockdale, Nancy. " 'Citizens of Heaven' versus 'The Islamic Peril': The Anti-Islamic Rhetoric of Orlando's Holy Land Experience since 9/11/01." *American Journal of Islamic Social Sciences* 21, no. 3 (Summer 2004): 89–109.

Stockton, Ronald. "Ethnic Archetypes and the Arab Image." In *The Development of Arab-American Identity*, ed. Ernest McCarus, 119–153. Ann Arbor: University of Michigan, 1994.

Stoler, Ann L. "Intimidations of Empire: Predicaments of the Tactile and Unseen." In *Haunted by Empire: Geographies of Intimacy in North American History*, ed. Ann L. Stoler, 1–22. Durham: Duke University Press, 2006.

Thaler, Peter. *The Ambivalence of Identity: The Austrian Experience of Nation-building in a Modern Society*. West Lafayette: Purdue University Press, 2001.

Tibi, Bassam. *Islam and the Cultural Accommodation of Social Change*, trans. Clare Krojzl. Boulder: Westview, 1990.

———. *The Challenge of Fundamentalism: Political Islam and the New World Disorder*. Berkeley: University of California Press, 1998.

Toynbee, P. "Last Chance to Speak Out." *Guardian* (October 5, 2001).

Turner, Bryan S. "Outline of a General Theory of Citizenship." In *Culture and Citizenship*, ed. Nick Stevenson, 11–32. London: Sage, 2001.

U.S. Census Bureau News. "High School Graduation Rates Reach All-time High; Non-Hispanic White and Black Graduates at Record Levels" (June 29, 2004), http://www.census.gov/PressRelease/www/releases/archives/education/001863.html.

U.S. Department of State. *Germany Country Report on Human Rights Practices 1998.*

U.S. Office of Immigration Statistics. *Yearbook of Immigration Statistics 2004.* January 2006.

van Dijk, T. A. *Elite Discourse and Racism.* New York: Sage, 1993.

van Donselaar, Jaap, and Peter R. Rodrigues, eds. *Racism and Extremism Monitor: Seventh Report.* Leiden: Department of Public Administration, Leiden University, 2006.

van Selm, Jonathan. "The Netherlands: Tolerance under Pressure." Migration Policy Institute (2003).

Verheyen, Dirk. *The German Question: A Cultural, Historical, and Geographical Exploration.* Boulder: Westview, 1991.

Vertovec, Steven. "Islamophobia and Muslim Recognition in Britain." In *Muslims in the West: From Sojourners to Citizens*, ed. Yvonne Yazbek Haddad, 19–35. New York: Oxford University Press, 2002.

Wagnleitner, Reinhold, ed. *Understanding Austria: The Political Reports and Analyses of Martin F. Herz, Political Officer of the US Legation in Vienna, 1945–1948.* Salzburg: Neugebauer, 1984.

Walgrave, Stefaan. "The Making of the (Issues of the) Vlaams Blok." Paper presented at the annual meeting of the American Political Science Association. August 28, 2002.

———, and Peter van Aelst. "The Contingent Nature of Agenda-setting: Different Agenda-setting Dynamics in Election and Non-election Times?" Paper presented at Third Annual Pre-APSA Conference on Political Communication: Faith, Fun, and Futuramas, September 1, 2004.

Werbner, Pnina. "Islamophobia: Incitement to Religious Hatred—Legislating for a New Fear?" *Anthropology Today* 21, no. 1 (2005): 5–9.

West, Diana. "West: The Politics of Intimidation." *Washington Times* (July 11, 2008). http://www.washingtontimes.com/news/2008/jul/11/the-politics-of-intimidation.

Williams, William A. *Empire as a Way of Life: An Essay on the Causes and Character of America's Present Predicament.* New York: Oxford University Press, 1980.

Yilmaz, Hakan, and Cagla Aykac, eds. *Perceptions of Islam in Europe: Culure, Identity, and the Muslim "Other."* London: Tauris, 2009.

Zawadil, Alexandra. *Austrian far-right leader Haider killed in crash.* October 11, 2008. http://www.reuters.com/article/idUSTRE49A2IM20081011.

Zine, Jasmin. "Muslim Youth in Canadian Schools: Education and the Politics of Religious Identity." *Anthropology and Education Quarterly* 32, no. 4 (December 2001): 399–423.

Zolberg, Aristide R., and Litt Woon Long. "Why Islam Is like Spanish: Cultural Incorporation in Europe and the United States." *Politics and Society* 27, no. 1 (1999): 5–38.

WEB SITES

http://www.enar-eu.org
http://www.islamophobia.org
http://www.islamophobia-watch.com

Index

Note: Page numbers followed by "*f*" and "*t*" denote figures and tables, respectively.